# 200 YEARS OF LOCOMOTIVE DEVELOPMENT

# 200 YEARS OF LOCOMOTIVE DEVELOPMENT

## AN ILLUSTRATED HISTORY

RICHARD MARKS

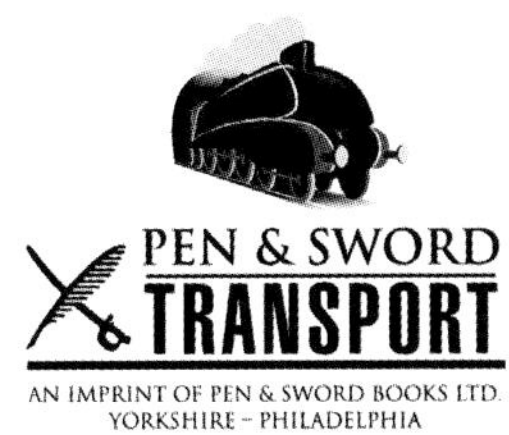

PEN & SWORD TRANSPORT

AN IMPRINT OF PEN & SWORD BOOKS LTD.
YORKSHIRE – PHILADELPHIA

First published in Great Britain in 2026 by
Pen and Sword Transport
An imprint of
Pen & Sword Books Ltd.
Yorkshire - Philadelphia



ISBN 978 1 03613 669 7



Typeset in 11/14 Palatino by SJmagic DESIGN SERVICES, India.

The Publisher's authorised representative in the EU for product safety is Authorised Rep Compliance Ltd., Ground Floor, 71 Lower Baggot Street, Dublin D02 P593, Ireland.
www.arccompliance.com

For a complete list of Pen & Sword titles please contact

PEN & SWORD BOOKS LIMITED
George House, Beevor Street, Off Pontefract Road, Hoyle Mill, Barnsley,
South Yorkshire, England, S71 1HN.
E-mail: enquiries@pen-and-sword.co.uk
Website: www.pen-and-sword.co.uk

or

PEN AND SWORD BOOKS
1950 Lawrence Rd, Havertown, PA 19083, USA
E-mail: uspen-and-sword@casematepublishers.com
Website: www.penandswordbooks.com

# CONTENTS

# ACKNOWLEDGEMENTS

I would like to thank John Scott-Morgan both for commissioning this book and for his invaluable assistance in its preparation. I would also like to thank Ros and Lexi for their help and patience during the preparation of this book.

I would also like to place on record my sincere appreciation for all those who make their images available under creative commons licences. It makes a book such as this viable and is much appreciated.

I have made every effort to find the copyright holders of every image in this book, if I have missed anyone, please contact me through the publisher.

# INTRODUCTION

The railway has been an important part of Britain's economy and society for over 200 years. The railway mania of the 1840s saw the start of what became a comprehensive network of railway lines. The new transport network spread across most of Britain, and by the 1870s it was possible to travel quickly between towns which had once been days apart by stagecoach. At the same time, and this was the main reason for constructing railways, freight began to transfer from the canals to rail. Faster and cheap freight services supported the growth of British manufacturing and allowed the Victorian retail revolution to occur.

National newspapers became possible. Someone in London could now read the *Scotsman*, which had been transported by rail overnight. The reverse was also true, *The Times* of London, and the *Guardian*, which was printed in Manchester, becoming available from Penzance to Inverness. National magazines became increasingly common, and the new media created the first theatre and music hall superstars. The railway was increasingly important to the arts, entire stage shows being transported by rail to theatres in every corner of Britain.

The railways, whilst an important part of the economic change occurring in nineteenth century Britain, did not cause economic growth, nor were they solely responsible for social change. They were however a key part in supporting the changes happening everywhere across Britain.

The railways were initially short lines designed purely to transport coal and ore from mines to rivers and ports. The Tanfield Railway (1725) in County Durham, Middleton Railway (1758) in Leeds, Lake Lock Railroad (1796) in Wakefield and the Stockton and Darlington Railway (1825) were among the first railways. All the earliest railways were animal drawn but used stationary steam engines to haul wagons up steep inclines, avoiding expensive viaducts across valleys. The haulage capacity of a draft animal was limited to a single wagon of coal or ore and they could only work for so long before needing a rest. A better solution was needed.

Steam engines became a key source of power for factories in the early nineteenth century. The stationary engines developed by Thomas Newcomen and James Watt had changed manufacturing by allowing mechanisation of manufacturing processes to develop further than horse or water power could have. The issue for the railways was that these engines were huge, of low power and required a building of their own. These engine houses could be seen across mining areas such as Cornwall and Yorkshire, and were often attached to the large factories which were built across the country. Whilst ideal for powering a mine or factory which did not need to move, the engines were completely unsuitable for use in transport.

An improvement was clearly needed before the steam engine could be of any use to the new railways. On to the scene came Cornish mining engineer Richard Trevithick who had been experimenting with designs to increase the power output of the steam engine. His experiments aimed to make them smaller and more portable so that they would be suitable as mobile power units in mines and factories, and as a means to power road and rail vehicles. At the same time, improvements in materials technology allowed higher pressure boilers to be constructed. The combination of new materials and Trevithick's engineering designs opened up new avenues for steam power.

The first mobile self-propelled vehicle powered by steam was a road vehicle. Richard Trevithick's machine, powered by his small high-pressure steam engine, was completed in 1801 and undertook trials on the streets of Camborne, in Cornwall. The steam carriage, named *Puffing Devil*, successfully carried passengers along Fore Street and Camborne Hill. The machine occasionally broke down, but this was only to be expected with such a groundbreaking piece of engineering. *Puffing Devil* was destroyed when the crew, retiring to a pub for refreshment, left the fire burning and the boiler ran dry. Trevithick was not dismayed by the destruction of his machine, correctly identifying the disaster as operator error.

*Puffing Devil* proved that Trevithick's designs had great potential and he continued to develop his ideas, patenting his high-pressure steam engine in 1802 with the help of his friend Humphrey Davey who was working in Penzance. The high-pressure engine design was used in a new design built by the Coalbrookdale Company in Shropshire for Trevithick. It consisted of a single horizontal cylinder inside the boiler which drove it through a flywheel connected to the driving wheels by gears. The flywheel was an innovative addition to Trevithick's design as it provided constant power to the wheels allowing for the smooth operation of the single cylinder machine. Little is known about the Coalbrookdale Locomotive, only a single drawing survives along with a descriptive letter which Trevithick wrote to his friend and colleague Davies Giddy. Nevertheless, the steam locomotive had been born.

Trevithick went on to design a locomotive for the Penydarren Ironworks in Merthyr Tydfil, South Glamorgan. The ironworks had purchased one of Trevithick's high pressure stationary engines which had proved very successful. Samuel Homfray, the owner of the works, approached Trevithick with a view to making the engine into a locomotive to haul trains of coal and ore on the ironworks' internal railway. Trevithick, with the assistance of the company engineer Rees Jones, converted the

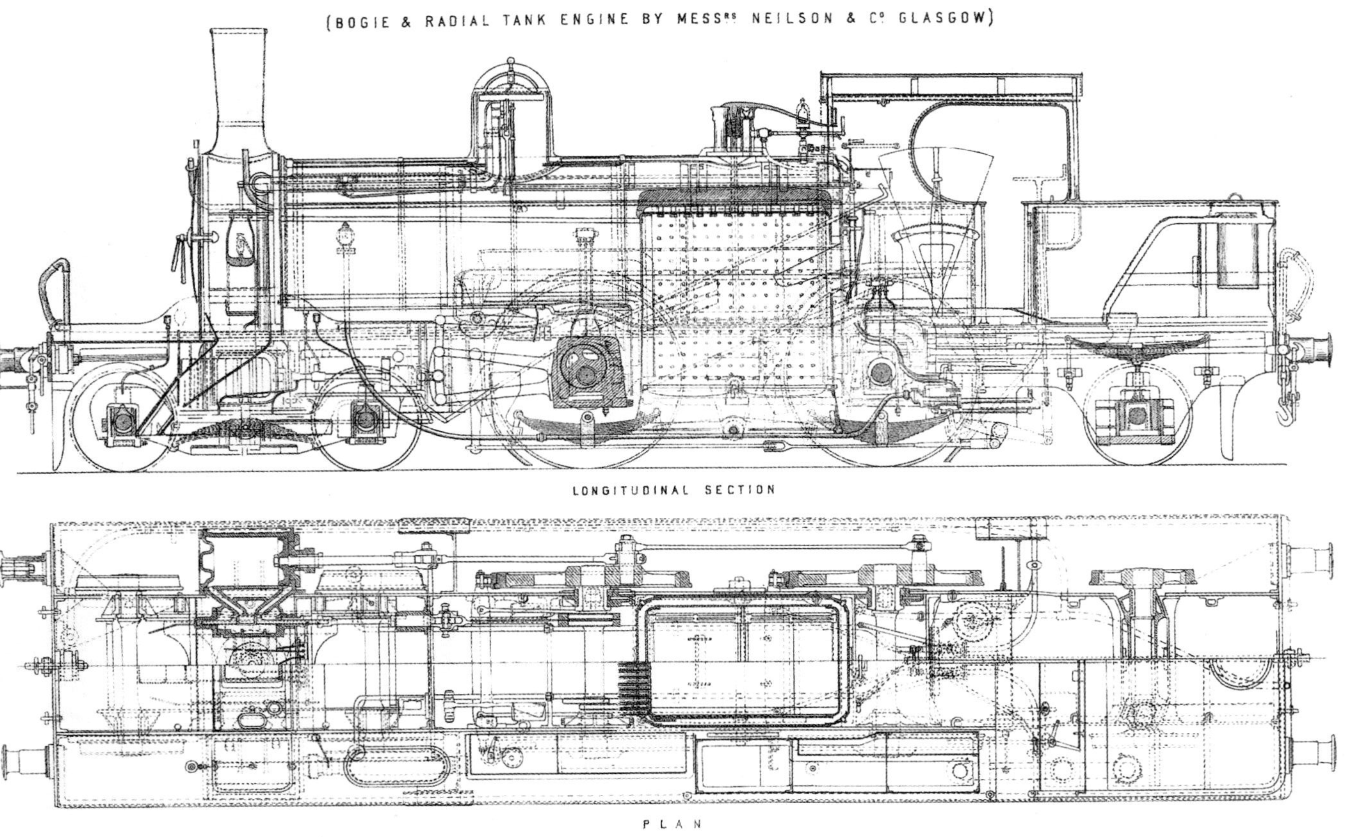


**Cutaway drawing** of William Adams' 415 Class of 1882. The sliding rear axle is of particular note. *Author's Collection*

engine as requested. The resulting *Penydarren Locomotive* successfully hauled a train of 10 tons of iron and 70 men the full 10 miles of the ironworks' railway.

Although slow, only capable of around 3 miles per hour, the locomotive was able to haul large loads, and more importantly, unlike a horse, it did not get tired. So long as there was a crew to operate the machine, it could continue to work long hours whenever needed, and maintenance could be undertaken when it was not working.

New engineers then took up the challenge of improving the steam locomotive. By the late nineteenth century advanced designs of engines could be found across Britain and their innovative approaches to engineering challenges created a locomotive building industry which would supply Europe and Scandinavia, the United States and Canada, as well as Africa and India, with their first railway engines.

The need to innovate to stay ahead of any competition and the engineer's desire to continually improve machinery led to steady advances in steam, and other forms of locomotive. Some were successful and resulted in forms of railway traction which are taken for granted in the twenty-first century, whilst others proved to be engineering dead-ends with little chance for improvement in the long term. There were however designs which, whilst failures then, proved to be ahead of their time. They were limited not by the design, but by a lack of suitable materials from which to construct them. Many concepts which were abandoned in the nineteenth century would be seen again later in the history of the railways.

As soon as other forms of energy were available, railway locomotive workshops and engineers began to experiment with them to prove their suitability for use in railway traction. The invention of the electric motor sparked the imagination of the railway engineers, and soon electric locomotives could be found at work on the railways in Britain. The earliest electric locomotives were adopted by London's new underground railways, on tramways and for shunting yards by the late nineteenth century. Meanwhile the invention of the internal combustion engine provided the railway engineers with another possible source of power.

The full history of locomotive design is a vast subject which cannot be fully covered in a book of this size and so it will concentrate purely upon locomotive designs used on Britain's railways. It is also not possible to provide a comprehensive account of every type and class of locomotive which was built or planned for Britain's railways, and so only those types which represented a notable advance in design have been selected. Detailed studies of every class of locomotive have been done elsewhere, in such publications as the Railway Correspondence and Travel Society's multiple volumes on the locomotives classes of the Great Western Railway (GWR), or in the Locomotive Portfolios from Pen and Sword.

It is also worth noting how railway companies evolved over time in Britain. Many started as small affairs which aimed to connect a few towns, ports or coalfields. As a company became more successful, they began to acquire their smaller neighbours to gain control of the traffic from an increasingly large area. The steady amalgamation of companies resulted in the creation of the Lancashire and Yorkshire (L&YR), London, Brighton and South Coast (LBSCR), London and North Western (LNWR), London and South Western (LSWR), North Eastern (NER), Great Western (GWR), Caledonian (CR) and North British (NBR) railways among others. They also all built new lines to reach previously untapped sources of profitable traffic.

Competition between companies could be fierce, that between the LNWR and L&YR being especially notable. Companies often built lines to stop other companies gaining footholds in their territory, even though many of these lines would be unprofitable. The competition between the London, Chatham and Dover (LC&DR) and South Eastern (SER) railways nearly bankrupted both companies. They finally agreed to form a joint company, the South Eastern and Chatham Railway (SECR) in 1899 to operate trains jointly.

The GWR did things differently. The company's first line was built to connect London to Bristol from which ships could be boarded for onward travel to New York. The company was successful and began to expand, but not always by directly building lines itself, nor by always buying out rival companies, although this did occur. The directors of the GWR set up companies, such as the Bristol and Exeter, and Oxford and Great Western Union railways to build new lines. This protected the GWR from any direct financial risk in the new project. Once the line was complete and open, the GWR purchased the shares of the company through a one-to-one share exchange whereby the shareholders received the same number of shares in the GWR.

After the First World War, Britain had 120 independent railway companies, many of which were worn out and needed investment following their exertions during the conflict. In order to address the situation and provide investment for the railways to modernise, the British government passed the Railways Act 1921, also known as the Grouping Act. The act amalgamated the majority of Britain's railways into four large companies, which was to take place by 1 January 1923. The result was the creation of the London Midland and Scottish (LMS), London and North Eastern (LNER), Southern (SR) and an expanded GWR. The LMS and LNER included the railways in Scotland, with the Irish railway companies previously owned by the pre-Grouping companies passing into the ownership of the new companies. The Southern Railway received all of the railway companies on the Isle of Wight, of which there were three by 1921.

After the Second World War, the railways were once again in need of reinvestment and modernisation, but this time the government favoured nationalisation so British Railways was created under the ownership of the British Transport Commission (BTC). British Rail was created when the BTC was closed down, with road transport reprivatized, but the railway remaining in state ownership until the 1990s when it was progressively privatised once more.

The railways developed a language of their own to describe locomotive wheel and power arrangements. In the case of steam locomotives, a common notation was used across the industry. Each locomotive class was defined by the layout of its axles and the wheels thereon, segregated by the number of leading wheels (two on each axle), the total powered or coupled driving wheels, and the arrangement of trailing wheels. A shunting locomotive with no leading wheels, six driving wheels (three axles) and no trailing wheels was identified as an 0-6-0. An express passenger engine with a leading bogie with four wheels, six coupled driving wheels and two trailing wheels was noted as a 4-6-2.

Diesel and electric locomotives were described differently. The number of powered axles on each bogie was used to denote the traction arrangement on each. This was because each axle was usually powered by a traction motor linked electrically or hydraulically to the main power supply, either a diesel engine and generator, or equipment fed from an electrical supply external to the locomotive. In each case, the same notation was used. Each bogie was categorised by the powered axles or in some cases the additional non-powered axles. A diesel or electric locomotive with two powered axles on each of its two bogies was referred to as a BO-BO. If it had three powered axles on each bogie it would be a CO-CO, although if the middle axle was unpowered it was an A1A-A1A. If the two bogies each with three powered axles and a leading or trailing unpowered axle depending on the direction of travel then the notation was 1-CO-CO-1. This standard steam and modern traction notation will be used throughout the book.

The only diesel locomotives which were not covered by the standard diesel and electric notation were the large number of shunting locomotives built for British Railways. These were more traditional in layout and did not have bogies, instead adopting the arrangement to be found on steam locomotives, thus all of British Railway's shunting engines were either 0-4-0 or 0-6-0s.

The aim of this book is to provide an introduction to 200 years of British locomotives as part of the Railway 200 celebrations taking place in 2025 to mark the opening of the S&DR on 27 September 1825. Whilst the S&DR was by no means the first railway in Britain, its opening marks an important point in the development of the railways and is justly celebrated as part of Britain's exceptional railway history.

# Chapter 1

# IN THE BEGINNING

When the first fire was lit in the firebox of Richard Trevithick's *Coalbrookdale Locomotive*, the world was changed forever. The engine not only changed railway traction but created a whole new branch of engineering from which some of the best known and most capable British engineers emerged. The development of the Penydarren Locomotive created a source of traction which allowed the railways to thrive. Penydarren also served as a public advertisement of the possibilities that steam traction offered.

One of the key moments in railway history, the demonstration of the capabilities of Trevithick's steam locomotive in Merthyr Tydfil, centred on a bet. The proprietor of the Penydarren Ironworks, Samuel Homfray, was so impressed with Trevithick's locomotive that he made a bet of 500 guineas (£220,000 in 2025) with Richard Crawshay, a rival ironmaster. Homfray bet that Trevithick's locomotive could haul the then unheard of load of 10 tons the full length of the Penydarren railway to Abercynon, a distance of 9.75 miles. The bet was accepted and on 21 February 1804, the demonstration took place. The steam engine hauled not only 10 tons of iron ore in wagons, but also others in which rode 70 men. The train successfully travelled the entire length of the line, at an average speed of just over 2 miles per hour. The bet was won and word soon spread.

The early railways had one other problem which needed to be addressed. The rails were often made of cast iron plates on wooden baulks which broke under the weight of the locomotive. A new development soon came about, the iron and then steel rail which was capable of supporting the weight of the locomotives. The plateway at Penydarren remained unsuitable for the heavy locomotive however, so it was placed back into the workshop, the wheels were removed and it returned to its original job of powering the hammers in the iron works. This was not the end for the design, though.

Hearing of the success of Trevithick's engine at Penydarren, Christopher Blackett, the owner of the Wylam Colliery near Newcastle upon Tyne, approached Trevithick to ask if he could have access to his locomotive designs. The colliery already had a wagonway which connected it to the coal staithes five miles away at Lemington on the River Tyne and Blackett saw a need to mechanise it to cope with increasing demand for coal.

Trevithick agreed and drawings were sent to his agent in the northeast, John Whitfield of Gateshead. Whitfield built a steam locomotive for Blackett in 1804 but made an important change to the design. The original design had plain wheels, relying on the flanged plates of the Penydarren tramway to keep the locomotive on the right track. The use of flanged plates originated in the way that the wagons had been used on the earliest railways. The wagons were basic road carts, which were placed on the flanged plates to make the route smoother, allowing horses to pull heavier loads. At the end of the journey the cart was often pulled off the end of the plateway and taken on to be unloaded onto a waiting ship or canal barge. This flexibility had proved useful, but as loads got heavier and more coal or ore was being extracted, a better solution was needed.

Whitfield was the first engineer to put flanges on the wheels of locomotives and wagons so they could run on rails. Whilst the wagons could no longer be taken off the rails for unloading, the simple expedient of extending rails right onto the wharves and the use of coal staithes from which wagon loads could be directly tipped into waiting vessels resolved the issue and made the unloading process easier. The flanged wheel locomotive proved a success, although the Wylam Colliery railway used wooden rails which broke under its weight. The wooden rails were replaced with iron plates in 1808, and in 1830 they were in turn replaced with stronger rails.

Elsewhere, other engineers were looking at other ways of improving haulage on industrial railways. In Leeds, industrialisation was taking hold and factories were growing rapidly. The need for coal for the engines which powered the mills in the city increased, and the owners of the Middleton Colliery saw an opportunity. The manager of the colliery and its railway, John Blenkinsop, had the cast iron plated wooden tracks on the colliery railway replaced with iron rails in 1799 in preparation for the replacement of horses by mechanical traction. The Napoleonic Wars had created a shortage of the animals, the army needing all the horses it could get as cavalry mounts and for hauling waggons and artillery. The shortages made steam traction increasingly attractive. The improvements made by Blenkinsop opened the way for steam traction at Middleton, but he needed assistance to achieve the changes he wanted to make.

A factory had opened in Leeds belonging to a new general engineering company. Fenton, Murray and Wood had opened in 1795, when the innovative engineer Matthew Murray started a partnership with David Wood, William Lister and James Fenton. Murray had been the mill engineer at Marshall's large textile mill in the city, whilst Fenton had been Marshall's partner and accountant. Lister and Wood had been factory engineers in Leeds. The four men opened a new engineering works in the Holbeck area of Leeds, close to the location of many textile mills to whom they provided machinery and steam engines. The company went from strength to strength with Murray becoming the technical director and sales manager, Wood took on the daily management of the works, with Fenton becoming the finance director.

Murray had begun to investigate how the steam engine could be made simpler, more compact, and in preconstructed parts which could be assembled on site for customers. Steam engines had often been made as one-off machines which frequently needed a lot of remedial work when installed, due to faulty manufacturing. Murray, Wood and Fenton believed that if they could improve the way in which steam engines were built, their engines would be more reliable and this would help sales. Murray was also interested in the possibilities offered by the manufacture of steam railway locomotives.

The company expected very high standards of workmanship from its employees and rewarded them accordingly, even going to the extent of providing central heating for the new works the company built. The result was that Fenton, Murray and Wood produced machinery and engines of high quality, and their reputation quickly spread.

As part of his investigations into improvements that could be made to steam engines, Murray modified existing parts to make them more efficient. One of the most important was a change to the valves which admitted steam into the cylinder which drove the engine. He added a mechanism which drove the sliding valve more accurately, inventing 'valve gear' which varied the admission of steam into the cylinder. This allowed the driver to select how the steam from the boiler was used. If the valve remained open for longer, the cylinder was pushed only by the pressure of the steam, which could be used to start the engine, whereas if the valve was closed for longer the expansive properties of high pressure steam would be used instead, making the engine more economic. Valve gear would be continually improved upon throughout the history of steam locomotives, but Murray led the way.

He created a second important improvement to steam engine design, which he patented, a mechanism which controlled the amount of air which entered the firebox depending upon the pressure of the boiler. This 'damper' altered the draft of the firebox making the fire burn more or less fiercely, creating the right amount of heat needed to keep the boiler at the correct working pressure. The damper became a common part of most steam locomotives from then on, although later dampers were manually operated by the fireman. Murray also invented the world's first mechanical stoker which automatically fed fuel into the firebox.

Murray's innovative approach and the high quality machines that the works produced came to the attention of Blenkinsop, who had also taken a novel approach for moving heavy loads by rail. Despite the belief promoted by engineers such as William Hedley that a heavy locomotive would have sufficient adhesion to be able to haul heavy loads of up to four times its own weight without any other assistance, Blenkinsop chose a different solution.

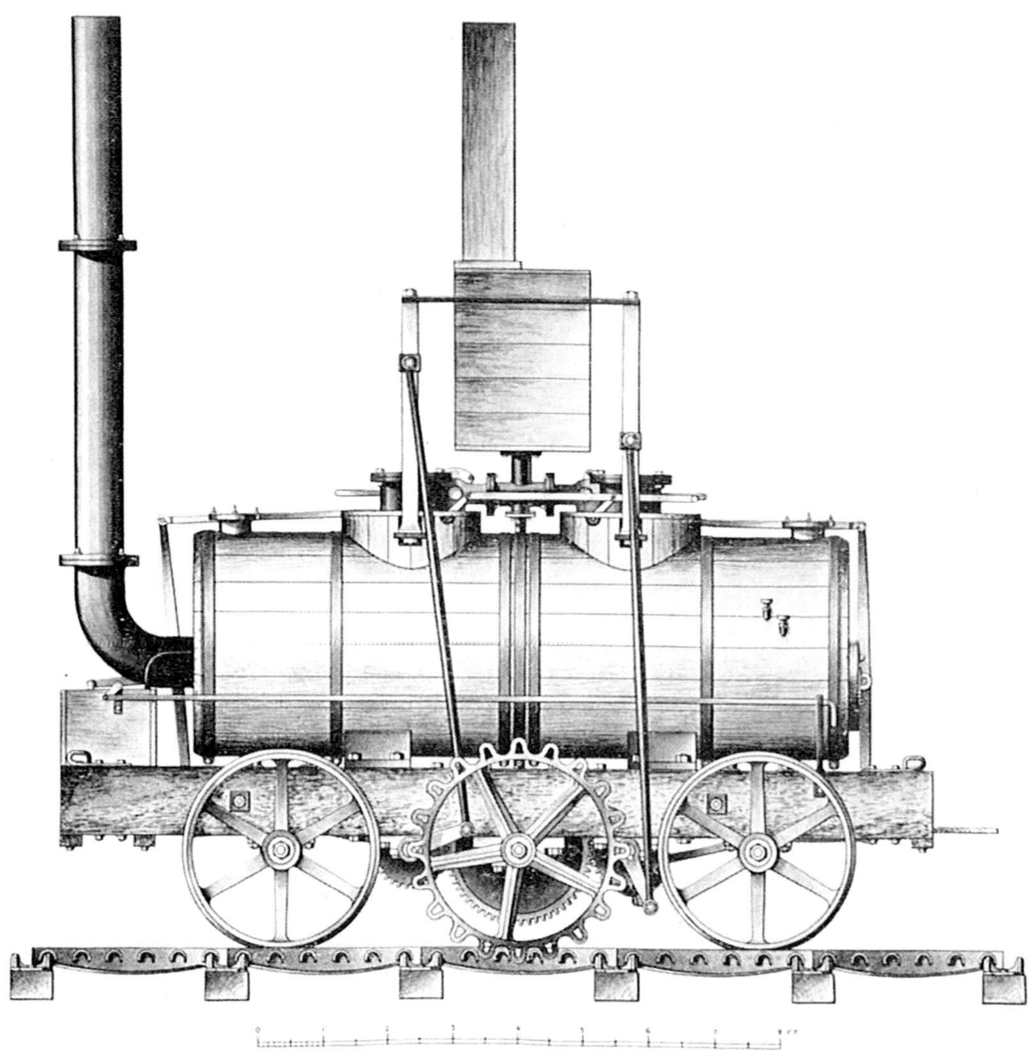

**Blenkinsop's rack** locomotive *Salamanca*, 1812. Engraving originally published in The Mechanic's Magazine 1829.

He designed a rack and pinion system for locomotives which consisted of a geared driving wheel on the locomotive which engaged with a toothed rack beside the rails and drove the locomotive along whatever the state of the rails. The system allowed lighter locomotives to haul heavy trains, making the continued use of cast iron plated wooden rails possible until the invention of malleable iron rails. The rack and pinion for locomotives was patented in 1811.

Blenkinsop approached Matthew Murray with a view to having a locomotive produced using his system. Murray designed a locomotive for the Middleton

Colliery Railway which combined Blenkinsop's invention with other new features, the most important of which was the adoption of a 2-cylinder arrangement to drive the wheels. All previous locomotives had a single cylinder which necessitated the use of a large flywheel to smooth out the tractive motion of the engine. Murray's twin cylinder arrangement balanced the forces produced by the engine, removed the need for the clumsy flywheel and produced a more powerful locomotive. The resulting Blenkinsop-Murray locomotive, delivered in 1812 and named *Salamanca*, proved to be a great success. The little 5 ton engine was able to pull loads of up to 90 tons with ease in all weather conditions. The success of *Salamanca* convinced the colliery to order three more to the same design; the second was named *Lord Wellington* and there are reports that the other two were also named although there is no evidence from contemporary sources to confirm the titles.

The type was probably the world's first commercially successful steam locomotive design that was mass produced. Fenton, Murray and Wood built other locomotives with one being sold to the Kenton and Coxlodge Collieries near Newcastle, at the request of Blenkinsop, which was named *Willington*. The Kenton locomotive was seen by George Stephenson, who modelled a design for a locomotive, named *Blücher*, on it but without the rack and pinion drive which made it less effective, although still relatively successful.

Further similar locomotives were produced under licence by Robert Dalgleish, the colliery manager and engineer at Orrell Colliery near Wigan. The first of the locomotives, named *Yorkshire Horse*, did good work for the colliery railway, which Dalgleish had already had relaid with stone sleepers and iron rails with the necessary racks alongside. A second locomotive similar to *Yorkshire Horse* was built a few years later. Dalgliesh had proved himself as a capable engineer and went on to be one of Britain's pioneering railway and civil engineers, being consulted during the construction of railroads in the United States of America.

The arrangement of the Blenkinsop-Murray locomotive limited its potential, the rack and pinion arrangement preventing higher speeds being reached. At the time this was not a problem, the main need was for a powerful locomotive to move large quantities of coal from the colliery. This it did extremely well. Developments in rail technology removed the need for Blenkinsop's system for most rail uses, better rails able to support heavier and faster locomotives provided a better solution to the evolving needs of the railways. His design does live on, however. Mountain railways still use a rack and pinion system, with the pinion wheel located on the driving axle between the locomotive's frames engaging with a rack located between the rails. The system allows mountain railway engines to ascend steeper gradients than would be possible using conventional traction.

The early locomotives had one important failing which took some time to resolve. There was no means by which to release the pressure in the boiler if it became too high. With careful management of the fire and water in the boiler most locomotives remained perfectly safe, but on some rare occasions a boiler might explode due to excessive stress over time. This fate befell two of the Blenkinsop-Murray locomotives. In time, the issue with controlling excess pressure in boilers would be addressed.

Elsewhere different directions to locomotive design and haulage on railways were being taken but not all were successful.

Some lines adopted the same system that was already being used on inclined slopes to haul wagons with a stationary engine located in an engine house pulling wagons using a cable. The system was limited by the need to connect the wagons to a different engine regularly. Whilst fine for short distances the stationary engine and cable was not a viable option for longer travel. Another attempt to address the problem of lack of adhesion with light locomotives was William Chapman's locomotive which hauled itself along a cable and had the same issues with flexibility and distance.

An even more bizarre attempt to provide a viable lightweight locomotive for heavy loads was William Brunton's *Mechanical Traveller* designed for the Butterley Company's railway between Crich Quarry and the Cromford Canal in Derbyshire. The design consisted of a conventional steam engine on a wheeled chassis, but the cylinders did not drive the wheels. Brunton's machine instead drove two mechanical legs at the rear which gripped the ground and pushed it along at up to three miles per hour. Brunton took out a patent on the design in 1813.

The ungainly looking contraption, named *Steam Horse*, which looked more science fiction than engineering fact, seems to have been relatively successful, although the historical records relating to the machine are limited. A second machine was built with a larger boiler for the Newbottle Colliery in County Durham, which suggests that the device might have actually worked. The second engine seems to have worked between 1814 and 1815 until the boiler exploded in July 1815 during a demonstration, killing thirteen spectators and injuring others. It was not a fault in the design which caused the first recorded railway accident.

The boiler had been fitted with a new invention, the safety valve. These valves were set to open when the boiler exceeded the working pressure that the barrel had been designed for, venting the excess steam and preventing the boiler from becoming overstressed. The accident was caused by the adjusting nut, which set the pressure at which the valve would open, having been screwed down too far, making the boiler dangerous. The adjustment had most likely been made by the locomotive crew which was not uncommon since many crews believed that if they allowed the boiler to work at higher pressure, the engine would be able to work harder with less effort on their part.

This dangerous practice was prevented later when a change was made to the design of safety valves. The nut was replaced with a specially shaped item which

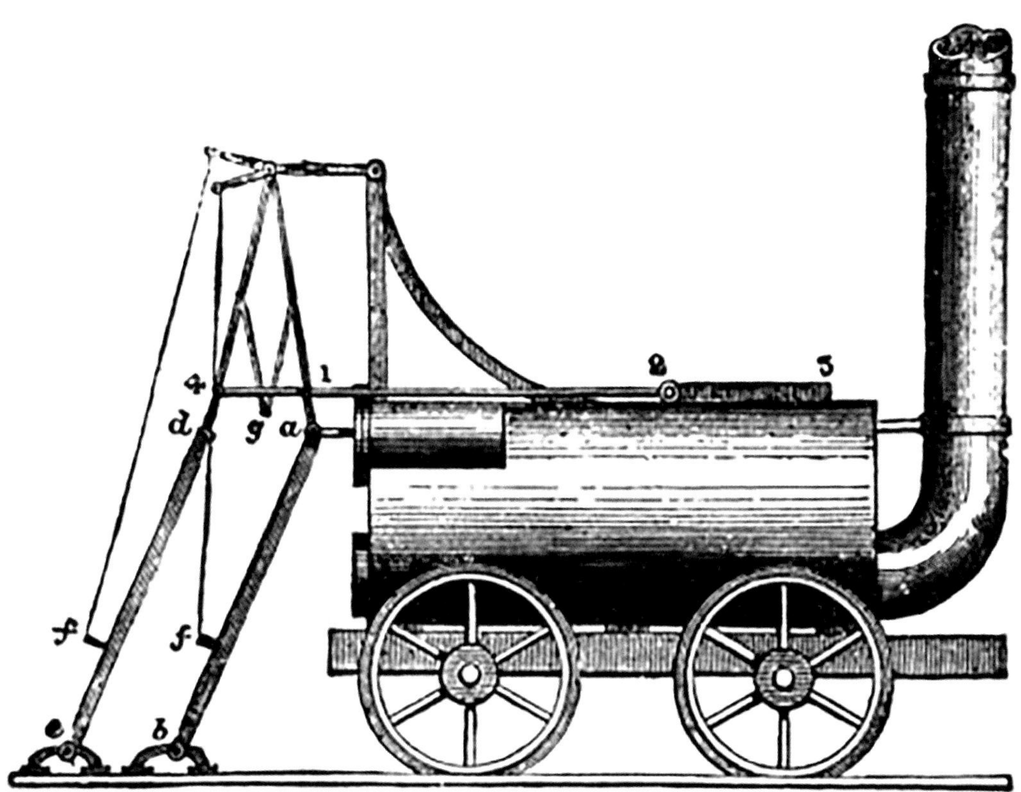

**Brunton's Mechanical** Traveller named *Steam Horse, 1813*. The legs at the rear are the means of propulsion.

a normal spanner could not adjust. At the same time, a spanner was invented that fitted the nut, only to be used by boilersmiths licensed to maintain boilers. It became a serious offence on the railways and in industry for anyone who was not a boilersmith to be found with such a tool in their possession and could result in instant dismissal from the company. This same mechanism is still used today to protect boilers and pressure vessels. As a result of the accident, no more of Brunton's strange engines were built. The fate of the other engine at Crich remains unknown.

Whilst Blenkinsop's rack and pinion system had proved successful, it was expensive to install and engineers had been working on a means to create a less expensive solution that removed the need for it. At this point Christopher Blackett returns to the story of locomotive development in Britain, alongside two new engineers who would become immensely important in the history of railways.

Blackett was still keen to mechanise his colliery railway and having ordered that the wooden rails on the colliery's railway be replaced with iron plates, approached Richard Trevithick for a second locomotive in 1808. Trevithick was no longer interested in building steam locomotives and refused. Not to be deterred, Blackett asked his mine manager William Hedley and the mine's foreman blacksmith, Timothy Hackworth to build a new steam locomotive.

Hedley and Hackworth built a manually operated test carriage to test adhesion under various loads on the new plateway at Wylam, before building the locomotive. The carriage was then used by the two men to build their first locomotive, which was built to Trevithick's design with a single cylinder and simple boiler. The locomotive proved to be a failure. The motion was erratic because of the single cylinder, something with Matthew Murray had already realised in his designs. The boiler was also not capable of producing enough steam. A new solution was needed.

Hedley and Hackworth, with the assistance of Jonathan Forster, the mine's engine wright, built a second engine. The three men based their locomotive upon Murray and Blenkinsop's twin cylinder design, but without the cogged drive wheel and an improved return flue boiler. The older single flue boiler consisted of a large tube passing from the firebox end of the boiler to the chimney, through which hot gases

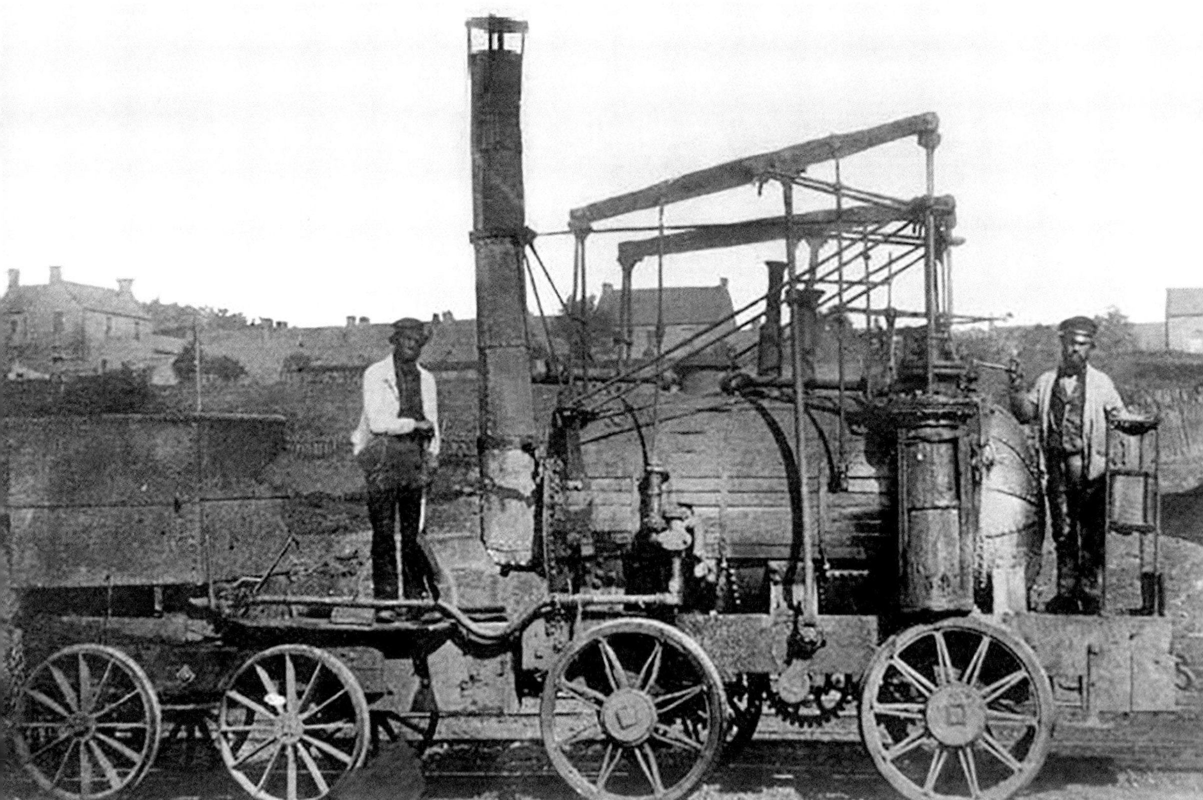

***Puffing Billy*** as rebuilt back to its original condition shortly before donation to the Patent Office Museum in 1862.

from the fire passed to heat the water. The new design used a tube which returned back on itself inside the boiler so that the hot gases passed through the boiler twice before being exhausted through the chimney which was now at the same end as the firebox. The improvement made better use of the hot gases to raise more steam making the engine more efficient.

The engine had another new feature, which Hedley had patented. The wheels were coupled together through a series of gears driven by a crank shaft which was in turn powered by the two cylinders either side of the boiler. The idea of coupling the driving wheels of a locomotive together would continue in later designs, but the gears were dispensed with by the engineers who followed in favour of a connecting rod on the outside of the driving wheels which allowed for greater speeds.

The engine, named *Puffing Billy*, first ran on the Wylam Colliery Railway in 1813. The new machine was a great success encouraging Hedley and Hackworth to build

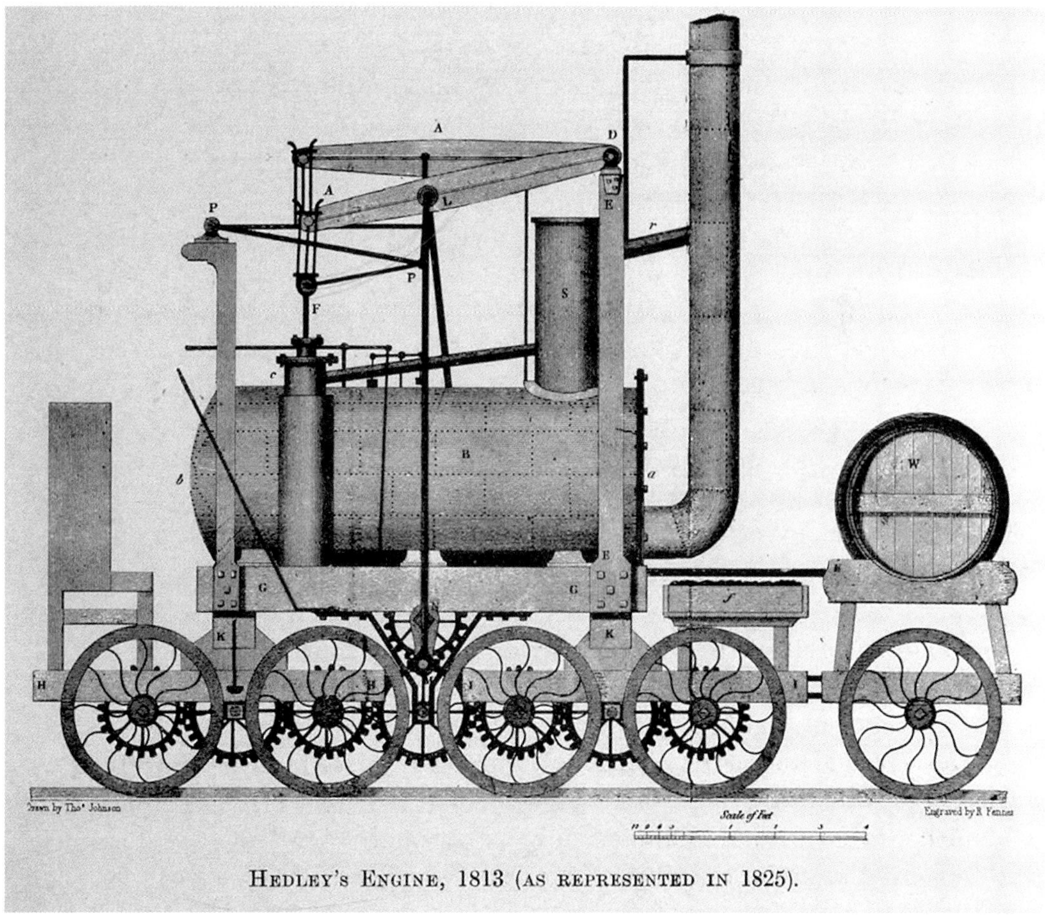



HEDLEY'S ENGINE, 1813 (AS REPRESENTED IN 1825).

**Puffing Billy** after rebuilding into an 8-wheel locomotive. *Thomas Johnson and R. Fenner.* 1825.

a second, named *Wylam Dilly*. A third locomotive appears to have been built later by Hedley and Hackworth but little is currently known about it, although it is likely to have been built to the same general layout.

The heavy locomotive kept breaking the iron plateway causing the three men to look to find a solution. They came up with a novel idea, which was later to be a key part of railway locomotive engineering. The problem could be addressed by spreading the weight of a locomotive, and so both *Puffing Billy* and *Wylam Dilly* were rebuilt with eight connected driving wheels and an additional wheel carrying the water cart in 1815. Whether the third engine was rebuilt is unknown but it seems likely. The modification worked, stopping the engine breaking the iron plates, although it created an ungainly machine. The engines ran in that form until the railway was re-laid in 1830 with stronger iron rails when they were rebuilt back to their original form.

*Puffing Billy* remained in service at Wylam until 1862 when it was sold by the owner of the mine, Edward Blackett, to the Patent Office Museum in Kensington which is now the Science Museum. *Wylam Dilly* is also preserved and can be found in the collection of the National Museum of Scotland.

Many are surprised by the professional backgrounds of the early locomotive engineers who had no formal engineering education and were often self-taught. Engineering was in its infancy and there were no textbooks or university courses to teach the principles to new students. Instead the pioneering engineers were experienced millwrights, mining engineers or blacksmiths.

Some of the most famous names in railway history started their working lives this way. Timothy Hackworth was a blacksmith; George Stephenson a brakesman controlling the pit winding gear at Water Row Colliery in Newburn, who educated himself at night school; Matthew Murray was a millwright. The late eighteenth and nineteenth centuries were an age of innovation which allowed the pioneers to express their ideas in metal and brass. Opportunity was everywhere and for those with a talent for innovation the possibilities were endless.

Timothy Hackworth was born in Wylam five years after George Stephenson who also grew up in the village. Hackworth's father was the colliery foreman blacksmith at Wylam and Timothy was apprenticed to him. Both men gained a reputation as mechanical engineers and boiler makers, and when Timothy succeeded his father as mine blacksmith it was unsurprising that William Hedley worked with him on the creation of the Wylam locomotives. Hackworth was a devout Methodist and refused to work on Sundays which led him into conflict with the mine's owners. Hackworth felt obliged to leave Wylam in 1816 but soon found work elsewhere.

In 1824, Hackworth went to Gateshead near Newcastle to work as relief manager in the workshops of the Forth Street factory of Robert Stephenson and Company who were making railway locomotives. Robert, a mechanical engineer, was the son of

George Stephenson who by now had become a civil engineer. Both men were much in demand. Hackworth was employed to manage the works as George Stephenson was busy elsewhere surveying routes for new railways, and Robert was in South America. Hackworth stayed for one year, before leaving to work as a contract engineer.

Meanwhile, the promoters of the S&DR were looking for someone to manage the proposed fleet of railway locomotives that the new railway would need. The directors of the railway approached George Stephenson who recommended Hackworth for the post, which was offered and accepted. Hackworth joined the railway on 13 May 1825 and became the S&DR's locomotive superintendent, the first person to hold such a post.

It seems that Hackworth was instrumental in the design for the first locomotive purchased for use on the new railway at Stockton whilst he was working for the Stephensons in Gateshead. The new railway had been proposed, as had many others, to initially transport coal and was to run from near Shildon to Darlington and on to Stockton although it differed in one important aspect. The previous

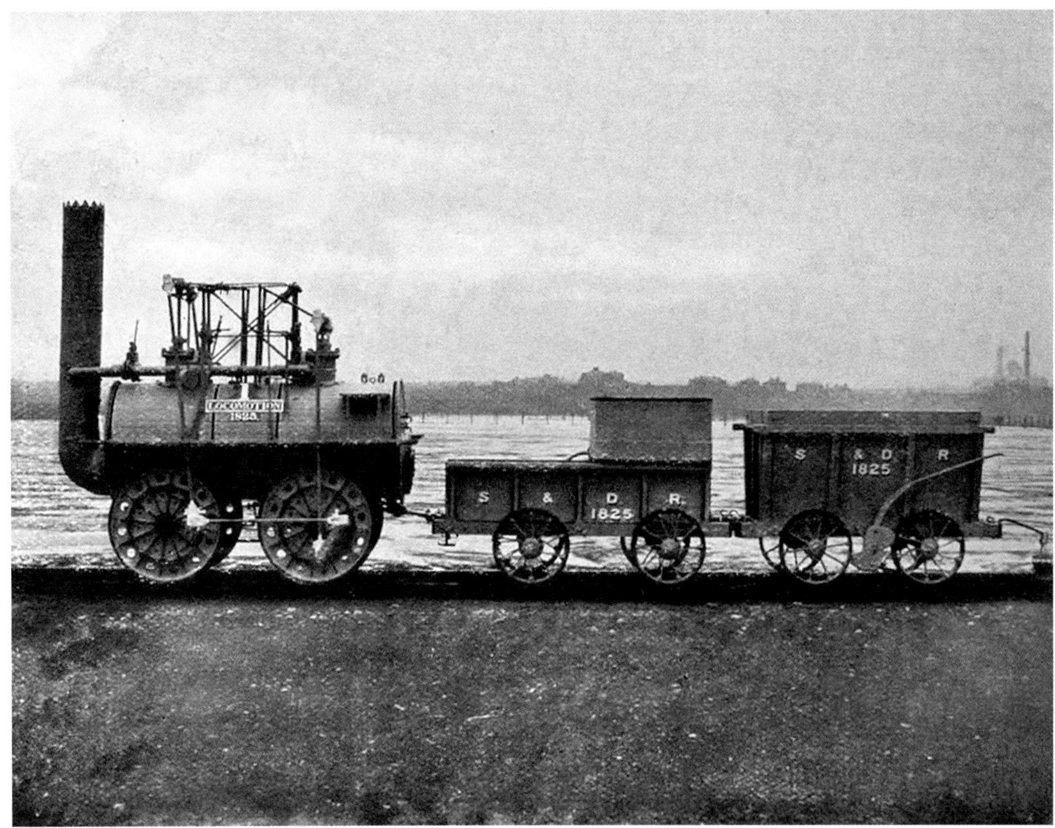

**Locomotion No. 1,** the steam locomotive that the Stockton and Darlington Railway opened with in 1825. Sometime before 1915. *William Weaver*

railways at Tanfield, Middleton and elsewhere had been private concerns only open to the colliery which owned the line. The Stockton and Darlington was to be a public railway, where the coal would be transported from many collieries by the railway company, or by trains run by the collieries themselves for a toll. The Stockton railway was the second such, the Surrey Iron Railway preceding it, although the new railway company was the first public railway to use steam traction. The new railway would be 25 miles long when it opened, a considerable distance at the time.

Hackworth's influence in Gateshead prior to joining the railway company may have guided the creation of the S&DR's first locomotive. The engine was named *Active* but is now known as *Locomotion No.1*. The design of the little engine was notable for the connecting rod which joined the two wheels on each side of the locomotive together, even though each axle was separately driven by its own vertical cylinder which was still contained within the boiler. Joining the wheels together meant that there was no need for a flywheel to smooth out the motion of the engine. The connecting rods performing that function as well as providing constant drive to each wheel set, making the engine more powerful.

A notable advance could be seen in the way the cylinder drive was arranged on the wheels. The cranks which the drive connected to were 'quartered', that is they were offset by a quarter turn of the wheel. This new development meant that the wheels could never become stationary with the cranks opposite each other which would have stopped the locomotive restarting. This arrangement became standard on all locomotives which followed, *Active* marking a jump forward in locomotive technology.

The engine was delivered just before the opening of the new railway in September 1825 and hauled the opening train. Three more of the same type followed named *Hope, Black Diamond* and *Diligence*. All four had engineering issues which needed to be overcome, a common problem with the earliest locomotives. Railway locomotive engineering at the time was in its infancy and the engineers were pushing the boundaries of what was possible and constantly innovating as they learned.

The S&DR had hired the right man. Hackworth's persistence and constant modification of the four engines made them more reliable even if not perfect. The four locomotives were constantly modified, so the preserved *Locomotion No.1* does not represent the machine that opened the S&DR, but it is nonetheless an important part of Britain's railway and engineering heritage. It certainly serves as a worthy memorial to Timothy Hackworth.

Hackworth's constant innovating led him to design a new locomotive for the railway, built at the Soho Works in Shildon which Hackworth had founded and owned, and in which the S&DR's locomotives were maintained. The new machine was the first locomotive designed to be capable of withstanding the rigours of everyday operation on what was a relatively long railway.

It departed from the traditional 0-4-0 arrangement, the additional set of driving wheels giving it an 0-6-0 arrangement. The locomotive, named *Royal George,* was delivered to the railway in 1827. The engine's design hid another important innovation among many other improvements. The base of the chimney contained a correctly aligned 'blastpipe' which took the exhaust steam from the cylinders and directed it, still at pressure, straight up the tall chimney. This created a lower pressure at the front of the boiler and drew air through the grate of the firebox making the fire burn hotter and more efficiently. Hackworth's attention to detail resulted in the identification of the precise size, position and alignment of the blast pipe and was a sea change in locomotive design, leading the way in precision engineering.

*Royal George* set the standard for British freight locomotives; the vast majority of later steam locomotives designed for purely freight work would be 0-6-0s. The initial steam hauled services on the S&DR were purely freight, which explains Hackworth's design for what was without doubt a purpose-built goods locomotive. Passenger

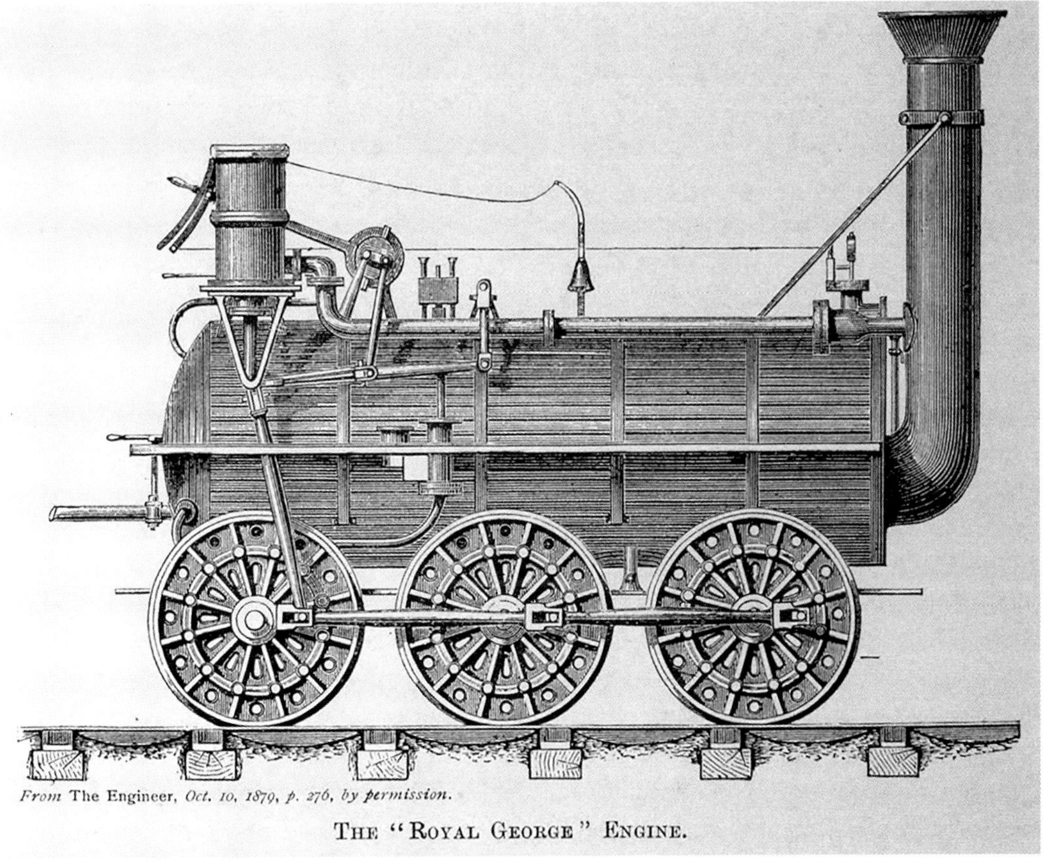



**The Royal George** steam locomotive, used on the Stockton and Darlington Railway. *The Engineer,* 10 October 1879.

services on the railway were hauled by horses using stagecoaches converted to run on rails, until the first steam passenger services started in 1833.

Shortly after the delivery of *Royal George*, Hackworth became involved in a new railway project which saw him competing with his erstwhile colleagues and mentors, George and Robert Stephenson. In 1829, the Liverpool and Manchester Railway (L&MR) was being constructed under the supervision of George Stephenson with considerable potential for both passenger and freight traffic between the port of Liverpool and Manchester, but there was a problem.

All of the locomotives which were in use at that time had been designed for slow and heavy freight traffic, with most only capable of modest speeds. Although these machines were ideal for hauling freight trains, they were unsuitable for faster passenger trains. A new type of engine was required, the passenger locomotive designed for lighter loads but higher speeds. A new era of British locomotive design was about to begin.

George Stephenson was an advocate for steam haulage and despite contrary arguments being advanced by others, his recommendations held sway with the railway's directors. Stephenson approached Hackworth for a report into the use of steam traction on the S&DR who responded with an honest assessment which stated that whilst there had been difficulties, he had overcome many of them and

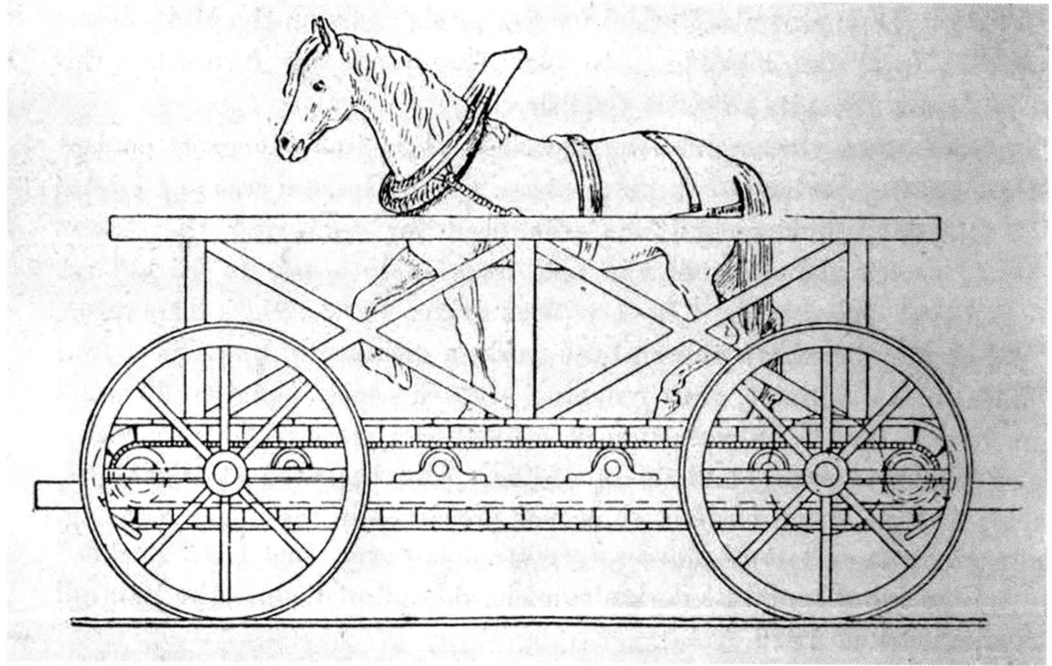

**Thomas Brandreth's** *Cycloped*. The horse is standing on the treadmill which drove the contraption. 1831. *Elijah Galloway*

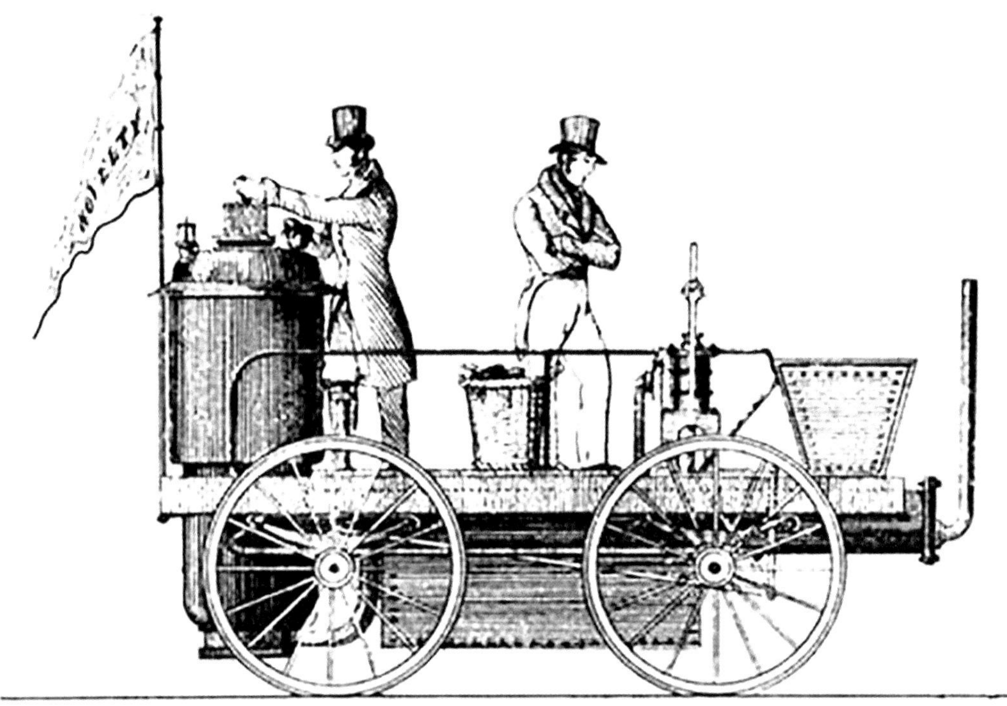

**John Braithwaite** and John Ericsson's *Novelty*. *The Mechanics Magazine*, 1829.

was confident that the remaining problems could be overcome. The L&MR directors were convinced and arranged a competition to assess what sort of locomotives would be best for their new railway.

The competition was the famous Rainhill Trials of October 1829, and its entrants were a motley collection of designs. One of the oddest, and most outdated designs was that tendered by Thomas Shaw Brandreth. His *Cycloped* consisted of a four wheeled platform which was driven by a treadmill on which a horse galloped. Brandreth does not seem to have considered how a horse was to gallop the entire 31 miles between Manchester and Liverpool. *Cycloped* appears to have proved unsuitable very early in the trials and serves to illustrate the dead ends that railway engineers occasionally ventured down.

The second design to compete in the trials was designed by John Ericsson and John Braithwaite. Braithwaite was a designer of steam powered fire engines, and the design for their locomotive, *Novelty*, shows its lineage. The engine had a small vertical boiler at one end and a cylinder which drove one pair of wheels. The water tank for the boiler was located under the floor of the locomotive between the wheels, referred as a well tank. The engine, of 0-2-2 configuration, is now recognised as the world's first tank engine, a locomotive which has no separate tender for coal and water. The design was quite advanced, with a new type of boiler and many other innovative features, justifying its name. It proved to be pushing the boundaries too far, design weaknesses causing the locomotive to fail and be withdrawn from the competition.

The first of the designs which were potential contenders was Timothy Burstall's *Perseverance*. The locomotive was a basic design consisting of a 4-wheel carriage with a vertical boiler and two cylinders driving the wheels. It arrived at Rainhill damaged and was unable to compete until the last two days of the trials where it only managed a top speed of 6 miles per hour. The engine had an innovative step forward in locomotive design however, it was the first to use roller bearings.

Timothy Hackworth entered the fray with a passenger locomotive of his own design, an 0-4-0 called *Sans Pareil*. It was extremely capable with two vertical cylinders at the opposite end to the chimney and firebox, driving one set of wheels directly, the others being joined by connecting rods. The boiler was similar to Hackworth's

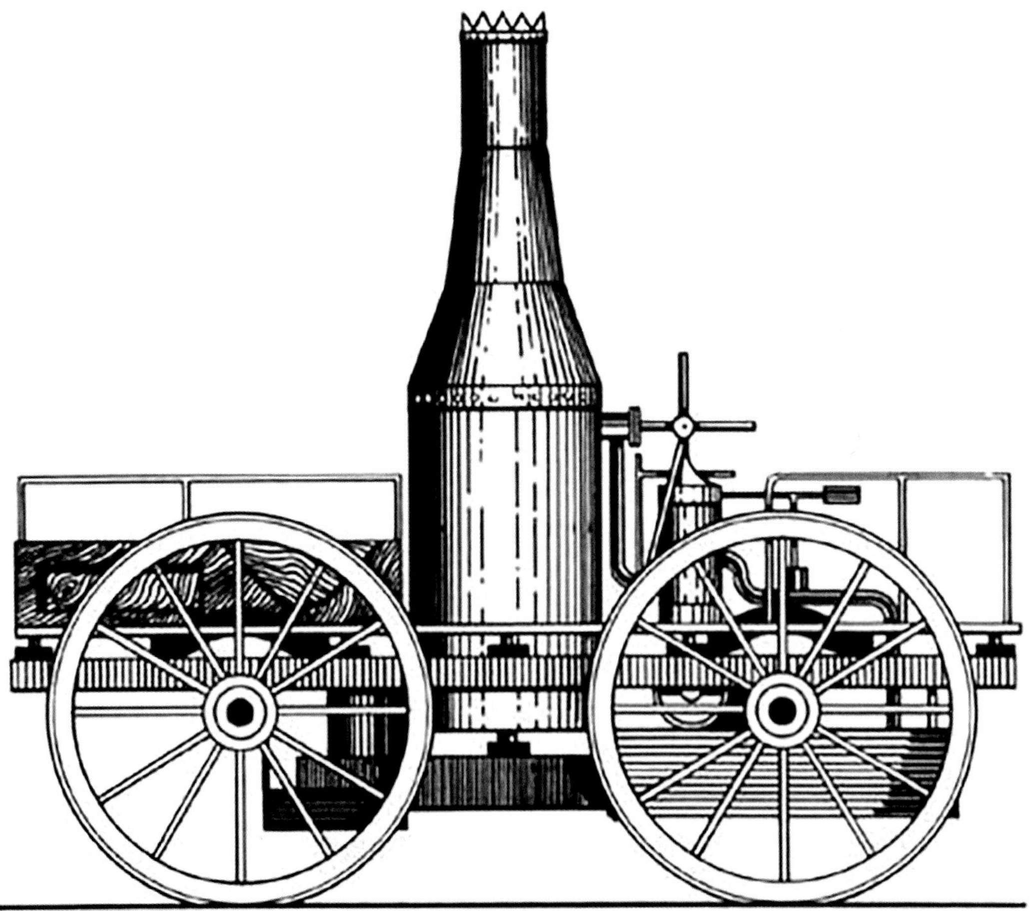

**Timothy Burstall's** *Perseverance. The Mechanics Magazine,* 1829.

designs for the S&DR, but with one innovation, a double return flue, joined with a U-shaped tube.

Hackworth's machine was slightly over the maximum weight specified by the L&MR for the trials and so was excluded from winning the prize. It performed well despite this, although at speed the engine tended to roll due to the vertical cylinders. The locomotive generally performed well until it had to be withdrawn from the trials due to a cracked cylinder. A myth has grown up around the failure of *Sans Pareil* because the engine was built for Hackworth by Robert Stephenson and Company, who were also competing in the trials. This appears to have no basis, since the company cast a large number of cylinders for Hackworth from which he chose the best two for his locomotive.

The locomotive was so capable that, despite not winning the trial, the L&MR purchased it and leased it to the Bolton and Leigh Railway (B&LR), opened in 1828, and in need of a freight locomotive. *Sans Pareil* ran on the B&LR until 1844 and was then used as a stationary boiler at Coppull Colliery until 1862. It was fortunately then restored to its original condition and presented to the Patent Office Museum.

The final locomotive and winner of the trial was Robert Stephenson's famous *Rocket*. The engine was a huge leap forward in railway locomotive technology. It consisted

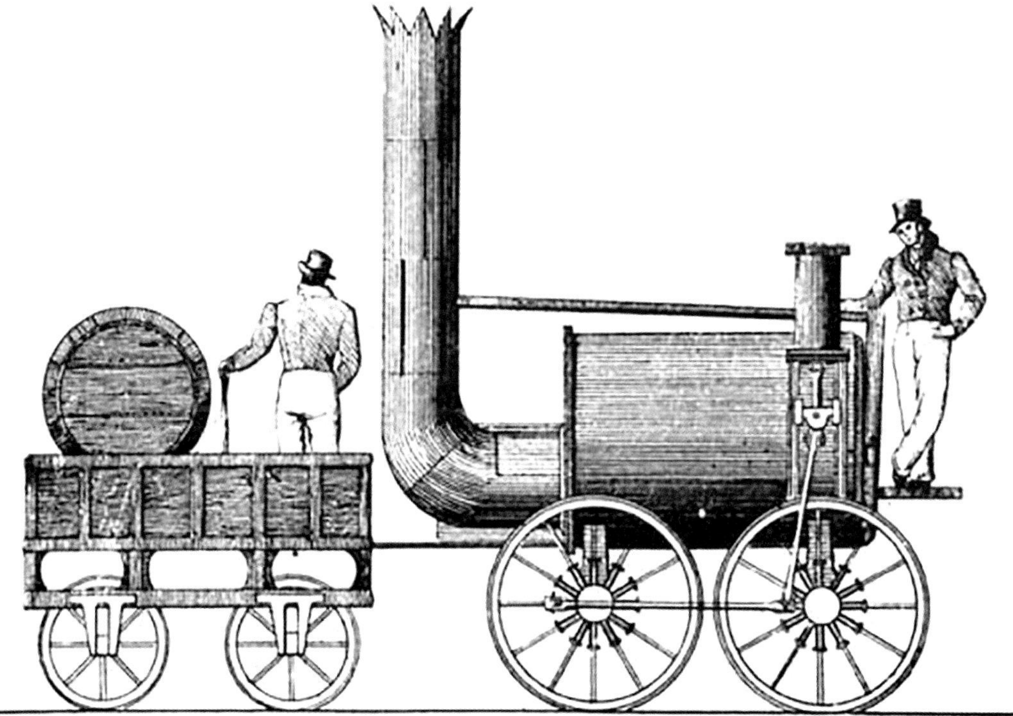

**Timothy Hackworth's** *Sans Pareil. The Mechanics Magazine*, 1829.

of a pair of large driving wheels, directly connected to a cylinder which sloped at 38 degrees towards the rear of the engine, on each side of the locomotive. One of the cylinders also drove a water feed pump, which had an innovation, a valve which could be used to control the amount of water being added into the boiler.

The locomotive had a small pair of trailing wheels which were not connected to the drivers, giving it an 0-2-2 arrangement. A small 4-wheel tender was provided with a large barrel to carry water and a space for coke. It was common for railway locomotives to use coke as fuel at the time rather than raw coal. The reason for choosing coke over coal was that the fuel produced a cleaner exhaust than coal, and local regulations had already been passed to prevent factories and railways belching out clouds of thick black smoke from coal fired stationary engines.

All railway locomotives would continue to burn coke in their fireboxes until the 1860s when the invention of the 'long firebox' and 'brick arch' allowed engines to burn coal. The 'brick arch' was placed over the fire in the firebox forcing gasses to pass back over the fire before travelling down the boiler tubes. The gasses were then burnt, any particles of soot being consumed, making the exhaust much cleaner.

*Rocket*'s boiler was of a completely new design, provided with 25 copper fire tubes which took the hot gases from the firebox through the boiler, heating the water before

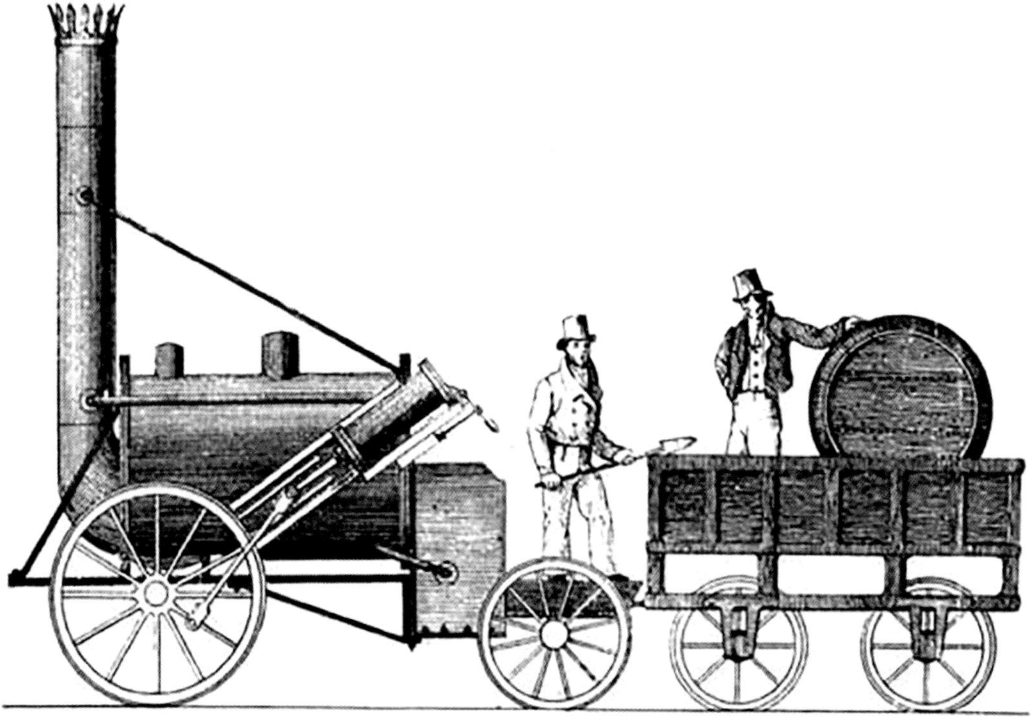

**Robert Stephenson's** *Rocket. The Mechanics Magazine*, 1829.

being expelled through the 16ft tall smokestack chimney. The multi-tube design increased the heating area in the boiler making it both more efficient and capable of raising more steam compared to the old flue designs.

The boiler was provided with a separate firebox which was double walled. The outer wall was separated from the inner wall by 'stays', the space between connected directly to the boiler water. The water in the jacket was heated directly by the latent heat from the fire, the hottest part of the boiler assembly. The water was boiled by both the heat from the fire, and the hot gasses passing through the boiler tubes. The new arrangement became the standard, albeit with gradual improvements over time, for locomotive boilers.

Stephenson's engine exceeded all of the requirements set by the directors of the L&MR and proved very reliable. No other entrant could match the speeds achieved by *Rocket*, which was able to travel at the then unheard-of speed of 30mph. The directors were impressed and awarded the prize to Robert Stephenson and the railway purchased the engine. The foundations for future locomotive design were now set.

*Rocket* was unfortunately involved in an accident. During the celebrations connected with the opening of the L&MR, the engine ran over the MP William Huskisson who was killed. He had crossed the line to great the Prime Minister, the Duke of Wellington, and *Rocket* was unable to stop in time. The accident was an indication of a flaw which no one had foreseen and which would not be addressed until the later nineteenth century. Most railway engines had a single handbrake, often on the tender which applied brake blocks when screwed down. The brakes were inefficient and slow to apply, and with the locomotive itself having no brakes it would need quite a distance to stop. Trains also had no continuous brakes, the only mechanism being a handbrake in the guard's compartment, or sometimes brakes on some coaches operated by a brakeman sitting on the roof.

When the railways had first been built, the lack of brakes was not a problem. A train travelling at just 5mph with a heavy load of coal or ore wagons would stop relatively quickly as soon as steam was shut off and a handbrake applied. With trains travelling at increasing speeds and with more powerful locomotives being developed, braking systems needed to be developed that could cope. The engineers cannot be blamed for this oversight, as many were trying to get their inventions just to move and pull loads, working out how to stop them when running at speed simply cannot have occurred to them until someone made the intellectual leap required to see the issue. There are comparisons throughout the development of engineering where the innovators simply could not have foreseen an issue until something occurred to make the problem obvious.

The L&MR ordered more locomotives of a similar design. *Arrow*, *Comet*, *Dart* and *Meteor* were delivered before the railway opened starting the concept of a 'class' of the same design and beginning the road to mass production of locomotives. A sixth locomotive, *Northumbrian*, was delivered to the railway, but with some major improvements, one of which was that the cylinders were horizontal. The new arrangement would become another feature of future steam locomotive design. It seems that *Rocket* and its sisters were rebuilt over time, which was not unusual, but were soon made obsolete by new designs such as Stephenson's 2-2-0 Planet and 2-2-2 Patentee classes of engines. Both these designs marked a new direction in locomotive design, where the cylinders were placed between the frames.

The railways settled down into a period of steady improvement, and the creation an increasing quantity of railway companies as the great time of railway building approached in Victorian Britain.

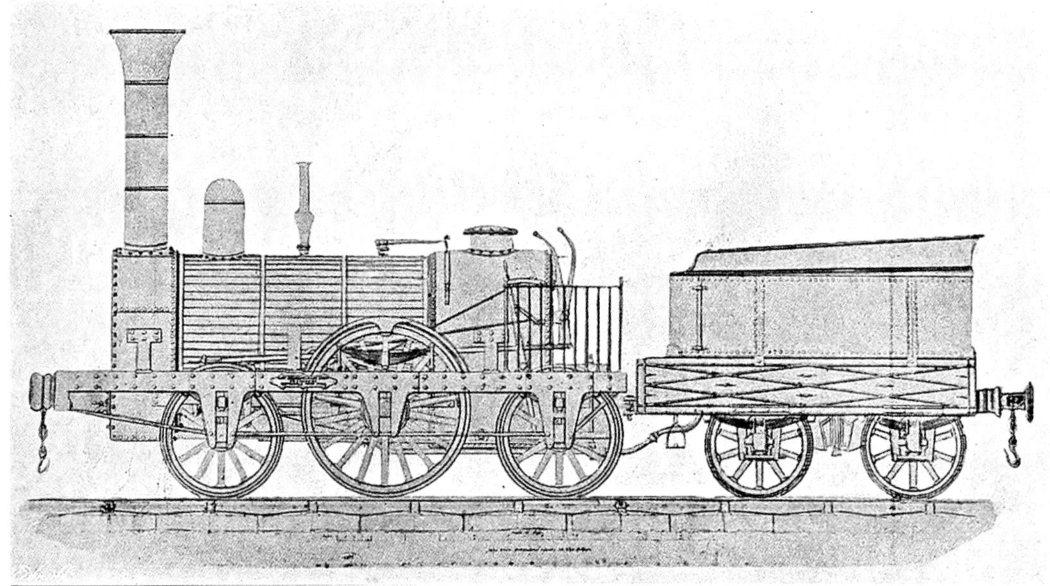

**Stephenson Patentee** type 2-2-2 locomotive number 123 *Harvey Combe* built 1835. *C.F. Cheffins*

# Chapter 2

# THE VICTORIANS

The Victorian period was a time of constant innovation in engineering and the railways were an important part of that constant evolution and change. As Britain's railway network grew, the railway companies began to be increasingly ambitious in their schemes. No longer was it acceptable just to link two relatively local cities together as the Liverpool and Manchester had, nor was it desirable just to build a railway for collieries. The directors and proposers of the new companies wanted more.

Railways were seen as the future of freight and public transport. With an ever increasing need to transport products from Britain's growing factories, not just in the industrial north but across all of Britain, and a population that was becoming better educated, more socially mobile and ambitious the traffic potential was there to promise good returns for investors. Although it has often been said by many historians and commentators that railways were a bad investment and never paid returns, this is not strictly true. Many Victorian railways were a success and paid good dividends to their shareholders. There were some companies that struggled and some schemes which were downright fraudulent, but the latter were in the minority. The process of getting a railway Act of Parliament, which was needed in order to build a railway, prevented many bad schemes being progressed.

New projects included longer distance railways such as the Great Western Railway from London to Bristol, the London and Birmingham, and the Leeds and Manchester railways. All these were successful schemes, the profits after opening allowing the companies to expand through the acquisition of smaller companies and construction of new lines.

This period of railway building, the Railway Mania, of the 1840s came to an abrupt end with the collapse of Gurney's Bank and the bursting of the railway stock market bubble. The drop in share prices as the stock market value collapsed allowed the larger more successful companies to buy up railways at a favourable price as well as investing in their own railway expansion plans. From this time emerged some of the largest companies Britain has ever seen.

The amalgamation of railways across Britain which created giants such as NER, GNR, LNWR, LSWR and GWR railways among others created a problem. These railways had increasingly wide networks on which were running a huge amount of trains. The GNR reached from London to York with lines radiating out from its main trunk route. The MR stretched from London to Leeds and later on to Carlisle, whilst the LSWR and GWR ran from the capital as far as Cornwall. The GWR and LNWR also controlled much of the traffic out of Wales, coal and steel being a major and highly profitable part of their operations. The situation in Wales was complicated by the existence of railway companies which had access to the collieries and steel mills and acted as feeder lines into the GWR and LNWR. Railway companies such as the Taff Vale (TVR), Rhymney and the Cambrian railways were profitable in their own right and avoided being swallowed up by their larger neighbours, although eventually they became part of the GWR.

Locomotives capable of longer distance journeys with increasingly heavy trains were needed to meet the requirements of these new networks. The competition between companies with similar routes created a need for faster express locomotives to win business. The race to get passengers the most quickly from Cornwall to London, and from London to Scotland, which became known as the 'railway race to the north' drove this innovation.

The large companies were able to create their own workshops to make everything they needed. Each had its own locomotive works, and although many continued to outsource to independent engine builders, the vast majority of their locomotives were built in-house. This resulted in the creation of 'centres of excellence' and the adoption of a house style in design aesthetics which became part of the railway's brand alongside liveries. The house style often reflected the designers' attitude to engineering, the Chief Mechanical Engineer or Locomotive Superintendent having free rein. One common theme can be seen on the vast majority of Victorian railway locomotives, a firm belief in the engineers' adage that 'if it looks right, it is right'. As a result, many Victorian locomotives were ornate in their design, creating an attractive series of engines many of which became design classics.

The railway workshops of Britain became synonymous with leading edge engineering, the workshops at Ashford (SER), Crewe (LNWR), Darlington (NER), Derby (MR), Doncaster (GNR), Eastleigh (LSWR), Horwich (L&YR) and Swindon (GWR) were all vast in scale and produced locomotives, as well as rolling stock and nearly everything else the companies needed. Many continued to produce locomotives for the companies which founded them, British Railways after nationalisation in 1948, and finally for British Rail Engineering Limited until the 1990s.

The workshops also reflected the company's belief in the way things should be done. Derby produced smaller locomotives, mainly to the 4-4-0 arrangement for passenger traffic as the Midland had a small engine policy, whereas Crewe, Doncaster, Darlington and Horwich very quickly moved on to 4-6-0 locomotives for express work.

One company's workshop stood alone, doing things very differently; Swindon. The majority of railways had been built to Stephenson's 'standard gauge' of 4ft 8½in (the gap between the rails), although there were exceptions where a different solution was needed due to the nature of the terrain that was being negotiated. These railways, built to gauges of around 2ft were referred to as narrow gauge. The GWR was built for fast running between London and Bristol, a philosophy which it kept as it expanded westwards. As a result Isambard Kingdom Brunel settled on a gauge of 7ft 0¼in which was referred to as broad gauge.

The wider gauge made for smoother running at speed, but as the railway network spread and interconnectivity was needed, the split in gauges became increasingly problematic. Through running was not possible, passengers and their luggage having to change trains at the interfaces between two companies. Worse still, freight would have to be transhipped from standard gauge to broad gauge wagon and vice versa delaying traffic and risking damage to goods from unnecessary handling. Eventually the standard gauge won out, simply because of the number of route miles which had been built to that size, and in 1892 the GWR was converted throughout to Stephenson's gauge.

Swindon works produced some incredible designs and would remain one of the true innovators in railway locomotive technology. The GWR's first locomotive superintendent, Daniel Gooch, completely reworked the existing fleet after his appointment in 1837 at the age of only 21. The GWR had been having issues with the fleet of disparate locomotives which Brunel had ordered from outside contractors to his own designs. Gooch had been hired, at the recommendation of Brunel, to remedy

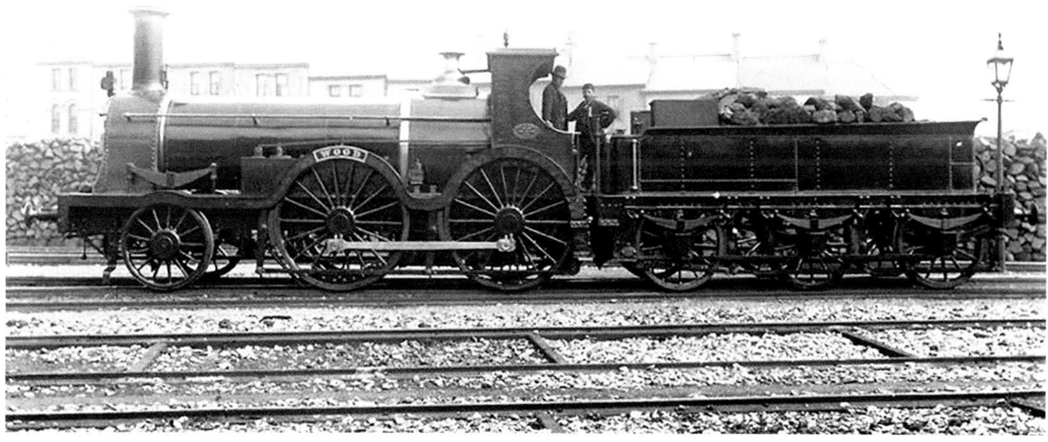

**Great Western** Railway broad gauge 2-4-0 *Wood*, a member of the Hawthorn class, outside the engine shed at Millbay station in Plymouth. c.1890. *Geof Sheppard Collection*

the problem and create the company's new workshops to design and build their own engines. Gooch convinced the GWR to purchase two engines being built by Stephenson's for the New Orleans Railway in the United States, which he had been partly responsible for designing. Once converted to broad gauge, the two engines, named *North Star* and *Morning Star* proved to be the most reliable the railway had.

Something better was required and so Gooch designed a new locomotive which became the basis of an entire class of engines built by a few contractors since the workshops at Swindon were not yet ready. The design for a 2-2-2 locomotive was innovative in many ways and became the basis for a class of sixty-two identical locomotives, possibly the first truly mass produced locomotive. The first locomotive was introduced into service in 1840, and was named *Fire Fly*. The class thus became known as 'fireflies'. It is claimed that *Fire Fly* set new records for sustained fast running, reaching an unprecedented average speed of 50mph between Paddington and Twyford in 1840.

As the nineteenth century progressed, a trend emerged among designs for high-speed passenger locomotives. Across Britain, locomotive engineers looked towards a

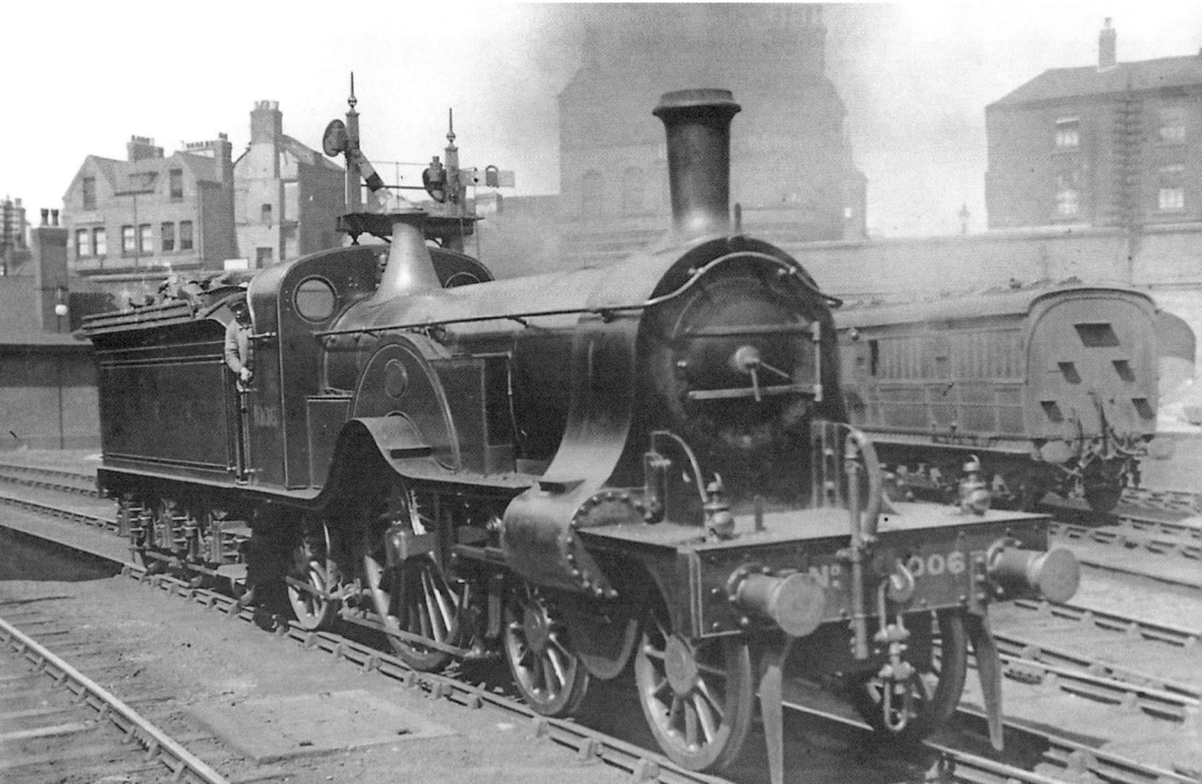

**Great Northern** Railway 'Stirling Single' 4-2-2 No.1006 at Nottingham Victoria, 13 January 1914. Patrick Stirling's class of express locomotive show how form and function can be combined to produce a very effective yet still elegant design. *F. Gillford*

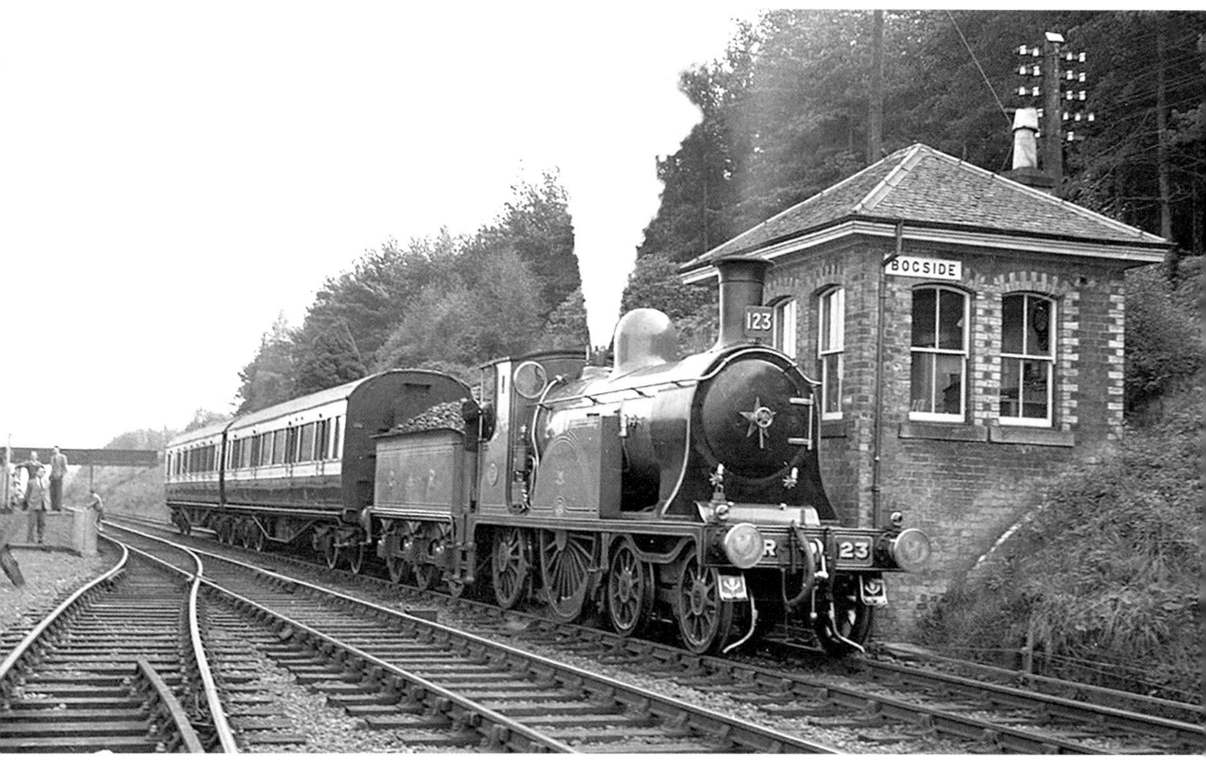

**Dugald Drummond's** 123 class No.123. The locomotive was restored by British Railways in 1958 and ran for a time on special trains, here passing Bogside Signal Box , Fife, in 1959 on one such train. *Stuart Sellar*

design with a single large driving wheel, often more than seven feet in diameter. The reason for this trend was a limitation in materials. In a design with smaller wheels, high speed can only be achieved by rotating the wheels faster. In order to do this, the cylinder pistons need to move more quickly as does the valve gear which may not be able to handle the forces involved with the materials available. If the engineer opts to use a larger driving wheel, then it needs to turn less quickly since the larger circumference of the wheel means it travels further for each revolution of the wheel.

The idea was adopted by almost all the railway companies' chief engineers and produced some attractive designs. The large splashers which surrounded the wheels lent themselves to the ornate finishes so beloved by Victorian engineers, and the longer boilers which were being developed dictated the use of a leading bogie and rear trailing wheel to support the firebox end of the locomotive. These factors combined to produce some of the most elegant railway locomotives ever designed.

William Dean's 3031, or Achilles Class for the GWR, Dugald Drummond's 123 Class for the Caledonian Railway in Scotland, and Patrick Stirling's 'Single' for the GNR with its 8ft 1in driving wheel, are prime examples of the Victorian engineers' ability to combine form and function into a single attractive yet capable design.

There was an issue that came with the decision to adopt this arrangement, however. The single wheel lacked adhesion. Since all of the power developed by the engine was being put through a single, small, point of contact with the rail, the locomotive was more prone to slip when starting with a heavy train. The problem was not of particular importance until the end of the nineteenth century, when increasingly longer and heavier trains became the norm. Eventually the single wheel engines were replaced, as the new century loomed and better materials became available, with locomotives of 4-4-0 arrangement, such as the GWR's City, LSWR T3, GER *Claud Hamilton* and NER 'R' Class.

Some single wheel designs such as the 115 Class designed by Samuel Johnson for the MR were introduced towards the end of the nineteenth century when steam sanding was introduced, which allowed a locomotive to blow dry sand onto the rails in front of the driving wheels to improve adhesion. These were short lived, the 4-4-0 and later 4-6-0 wheel arrangements making possible more capable locomotives.

Locomotive designs then began to segregate into distinct types based upon their intended use. Locomotives with larger wheels were primarily used for express passenger services. Those with smaller wheels which limited the speed they could run at, but provided more power, were used on freight. A gap developed which was

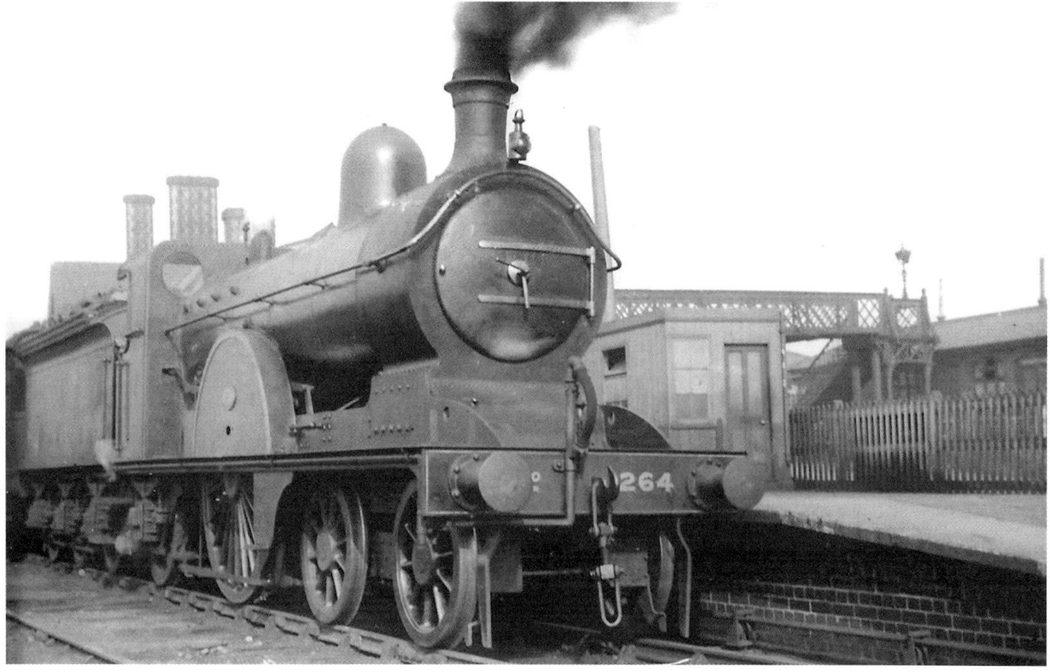

**GNR Ivatt** class A4/A5 4-2-2 No. 264 at Basford Station in 1912. *F. Gillford*

filled by locomotives with a medium sized set of driving wheels which gave a good balance of haulage power, whilst allowing for a good turn of speed for mixed use.

Freight was important to the Victorian railways as increasing industrialisation, the rise of retail outlets on the high streets which replaced local markets and increasing overseas trade demanded more frequent profitable goods services. Long distance transport of coal and iron ore, fish and vegetables and manufactured items created a need for vast numbers of freight locomotives to move the goods. Local short goods trains also became more common, delivering freight to local stations from larger yards. A variety of small and medium size goods engines were provided by the locomotive designers for all of the railways to meet the demand.

The NER was one of the earliest of the amalgamated railway companies to look to the provision of large classes of standard freight engines, mainly due to the amount of coal which was being transported from the Durham coalfields. The railway had thus built a large class of freight engines which had originally been designed for the S&DR by William Bouch, continuing to construct them until 1875, when a total of 192 had been built.

With a need to expand the freight fleet and to replace older engines the NER's locomotive engineer, Edward Fletcher responded by creating his '398' class of 0-6-0 goods engines in 1872, of which a total of 326 were built until 1883, 159 of them at

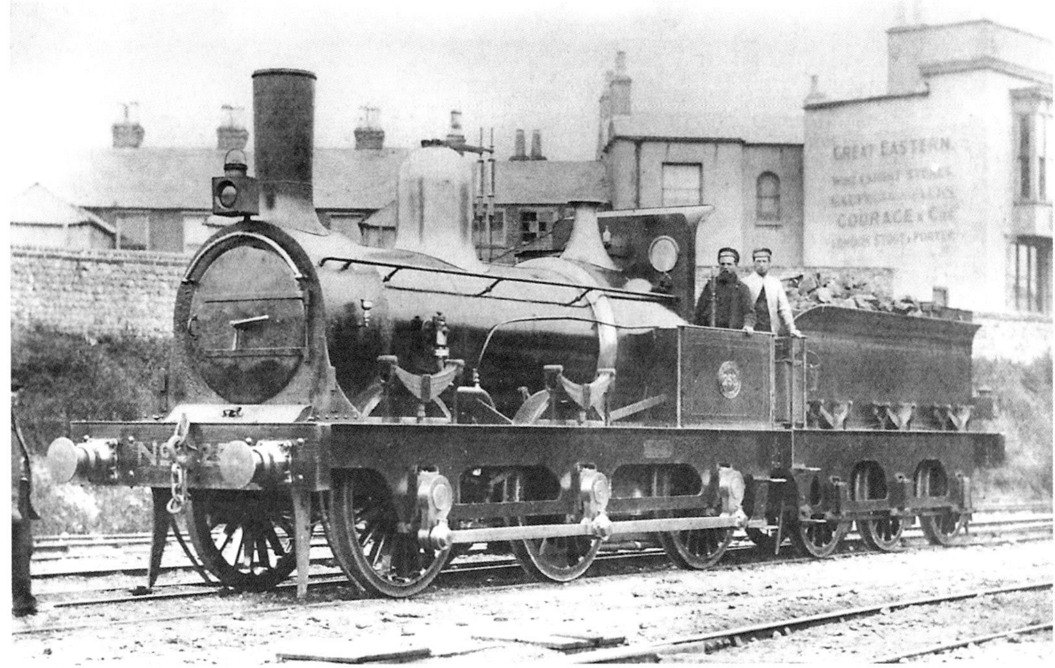

**LBSCR John Craven** (1813-1887) 'Standard Goods' 0-6-0 by Slaughter & Co. in 1868. New Cross, London 1869. *John Scott-Morgan Collection*

the company's Gateshead, Darlington and York works. The remainder were built by contractors such as Robert Stephenson, R and W Hawthorn (Newcastle upon Tyne), Sharp Stewart (Manchester) and Dübs and Company (Glasgow).

Elsewhere, increasing demands for freight led the designers of other railway companies to think along similar lines. The MR invested in a fleet of new freight locomotives, Matthew Kirtley's 480 Class, of which 237 were constructed between 1863 and 1869, 77 at Derby with the remainder built by subcontractors to speed up delivery. The L&YR had a similar need to the NER and Midland, since they also had heavy coal traffic from the collieries in Yorkshire as well as manufactured goods and agricultural produce. The solution to their problem came in the form of William Barton Wright's fine Class 25 locomotives of which 280 were built between 1876 and 1887, which were later supplanted by the excellent Class 27 designed by John Aspinall, of which 490 were built between 1889 and 1918.

Similarly the GWR required a fleet of improved freight locomotives, the demand for which was met by Joseph Armstrong and William Dean with their standard

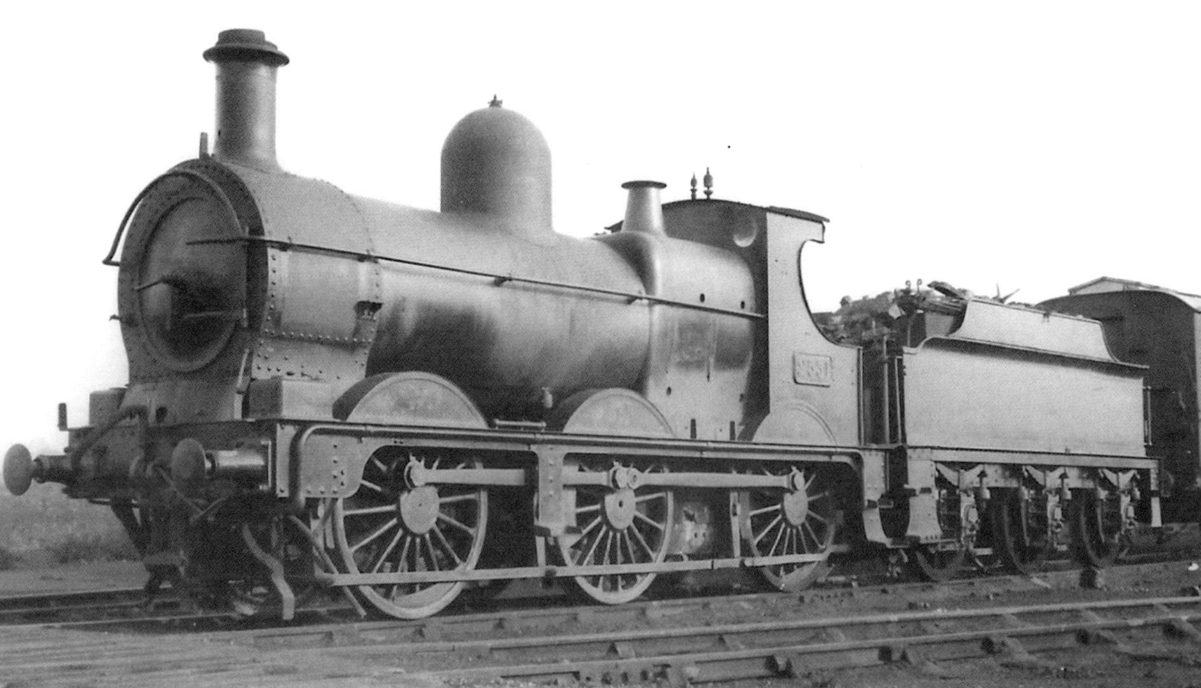

**Ex-GWR 'Dean** Goods 0-6-0 No. 2531. *Photomatic*

goods locomotives. Armstrong's 388 Class of 310 locomotives were all built at Swindon between 1866 and 1876. Dean's 2301 Class proved a capable and reliable class, of which 260 examples were built at Swindon between 1883 and 1899. The engines had long service lives, many surviving until 1959, which included sixty-two being requisitioned by the Railway Operating Department for service with the British Army in France during the First World War. With the outbreak of war in 1939 the engines were again requisitioned by the army.

Similar long-lived designs could be found in Dugald Drummond's 294 and 711 classes of which 244 were built for the Caledonian Railway between 1883 and 1897 and his 700 Class for the LSWR who built 30 in 1897.

A new provision on locomotives began to be seen as the nineteenth century progressed, the cab. The very earliest locomotives made little provision for the comfort of the crew, at best a simple plate being provided for the crew to stand upon. Later designs began to provide a spectacle plate designed to provide some protection from sparks and the worst of the wind. It consisted of only a sheet of metal into which two glass windows, the spectacles, had been placed. As time passed the locomotive engineers started to design engines with a small cab, eventually a large cab with side windows was provided for the crew.

The nineteenth century was a time of experimentation, and the railways were no different. Many railway companies experimented with a system referred to as

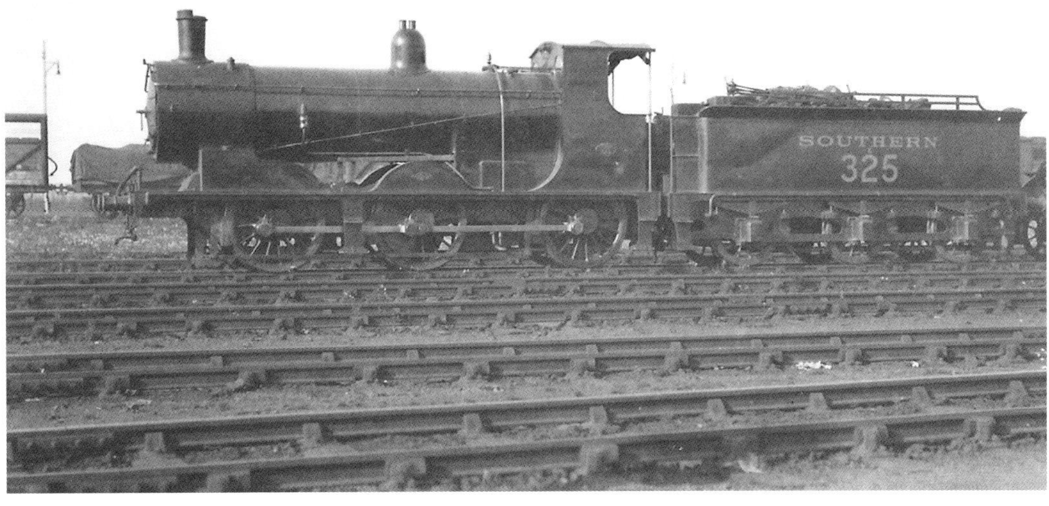
**Ex LSWR 700** Class 0-6-0 No.325 in Southern Railway ownership. September 1925. *Author's Collection*

compounding. This involved using the energy in the steam twice before exhausting it. The steam was first passed into small high pressure cylinders, which drove the wheels and then into larger low pressure cylinders where more of the expansive properties of the steam could be used to also drive the wheels. The system made better use of the energy in the steam making the engine more efficient and reducing fuel consumption. It was more complex and made the locomotives harder to drive than a 'simple'. Some overly complex designs were created for compound locomotives, one of the most notable, the 2-2-2-2 arrangement *Greater Britain* Class designed by Francis Webb for the LNWR in 1892 of which ten were built.

The design was overly complex with the outside pair of high pressure cylinders driving the trailing driving wheels, whilst the low pressure inside cylinder (between the frames) drove the leading drivers. The driving wheels were not connected. Webb's successor George Whale had the class scrapped, preferring more conventional locomotives.

Webb continued to create compound locomotives culminating in the handsome Jubilee Class of 1897, most of which were named after Royal Navy battleships. These were Britain's first 4-cylinder compounds with two outside high pressure and two inside low pressure cylinders but this time Webb had coupled the driving wheels. Unfortunately, like many of Webb's compound designs the class was unreliable in

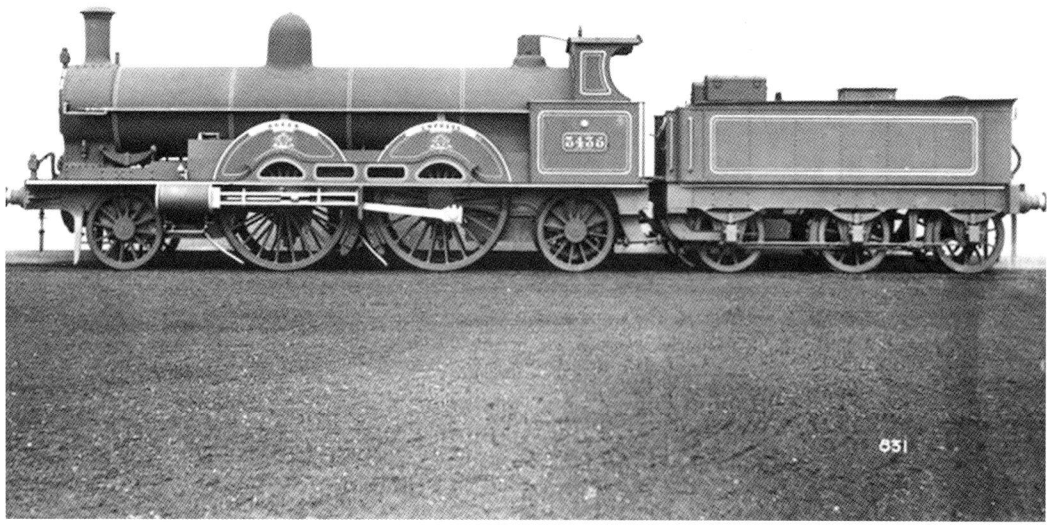

**LNWR Greater Britain** Class 2-2-2-2 Compound No. 3436 *Queen Empress*. Note the unconnected driving wheels.

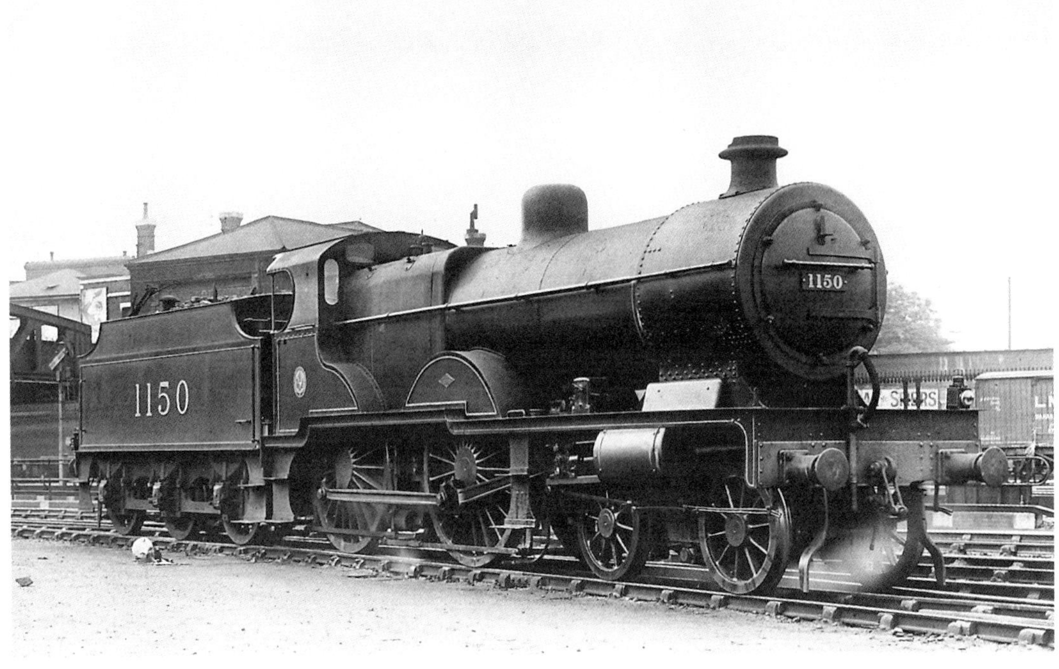

**Fowler 4P** Compound No.1150. *John Scott-Morgan Collection*

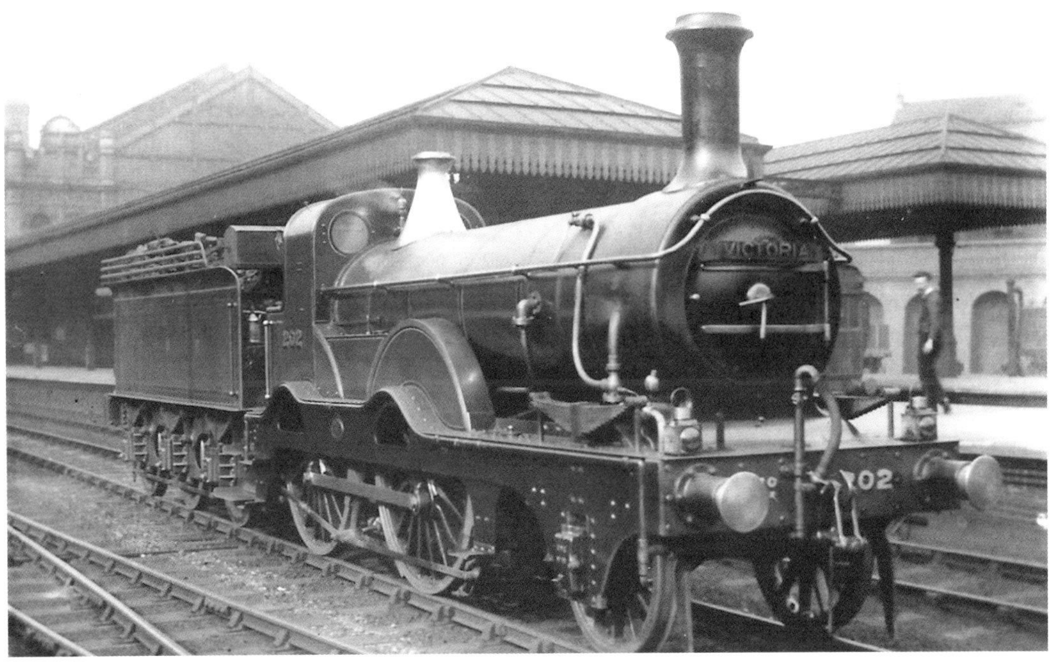

**GNR Stirling** rebuild of a Sturrock 2-4-0. Some passenger locomotives were built to the 2-4-0 arrangement. No.202 is at Nottingham Victoria in 1909. *F. Gilford*

service and all forty were rebuilt as two cylinder 'simple' locomotives by Whale to become his *Renown* class.

The North Eastern and Midland railways were also experimenting with compounding. The NER built just a single example to a design by Wilson Worsdell in 1893. The 3CC class was a 4-4-0 of conventional appearance with two inside cylinders, one high and one low pressure. It was rebuilt in 1898 as a 3-cylinder compound, with only a single inside low pressure and two outside high pressure cylinders. The locomotive was built as a test bed to assess the ideas of Walter Mackersie Smith and seems to have performed better than Webb's designs, remaining in service until 1930.

The only other railway company to experiment with compound locomotives was the Midland. Samuel Johnson's 1000 class was a three cylinder 4-4-0 designed for high speed passenger work in 1902. Johnson's successor Richard Deeley designed an enlarged and simplified version with a new innovation, the superheater. All of Johnson's original locomotives were rebuilt to Deeley's plans. The design proved a success and forty-five were built in total.

With the end of the century drawing near, the foundations of locomotive design had been laid. The basic principles of engine building had been mastered and the railway workshops were well equipped and skilled ready for the new century. The growth in railway travel and freight traffic that would be seen in the future would drive incredible changes and some world class locomotives would be produced.

# Chapter 3

# THE NEED FOR SPEED

The nineteenth century ended with the 4-4-0 locomotive as the dominant design for fast passenger engines. To a degree this continued across Britain, especially on the MR which preferred small engines which were of use everywhere due to the light axle loadings which allowed them to work on every route. On heavier trains, the company resorted to double-heading with two locomotives. This was more expensive since two crews would be needed and the consumption of coal was greater than it would have been with a single larger engine.

The rest of the railway world disagreed, and whilst still designing and building smaller passenger engines began design larger locomotives. There was only so far that the 4-4-0 steam engine could be pushed, and most of the locomotive engineers believed that six coupled designs with an extra pair of driving wheels would be the way forward.

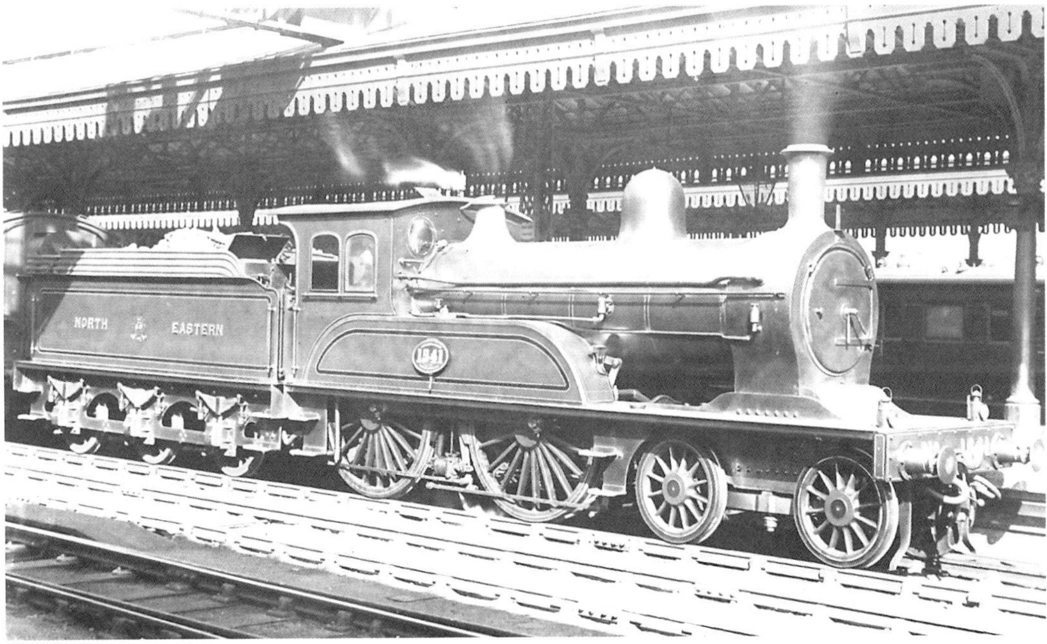

**NER F1** Class 4-4-0. July 1910. Of note is the large cab provided on North Eastern Railway locomotives. *John Scott-Morgan Collection*

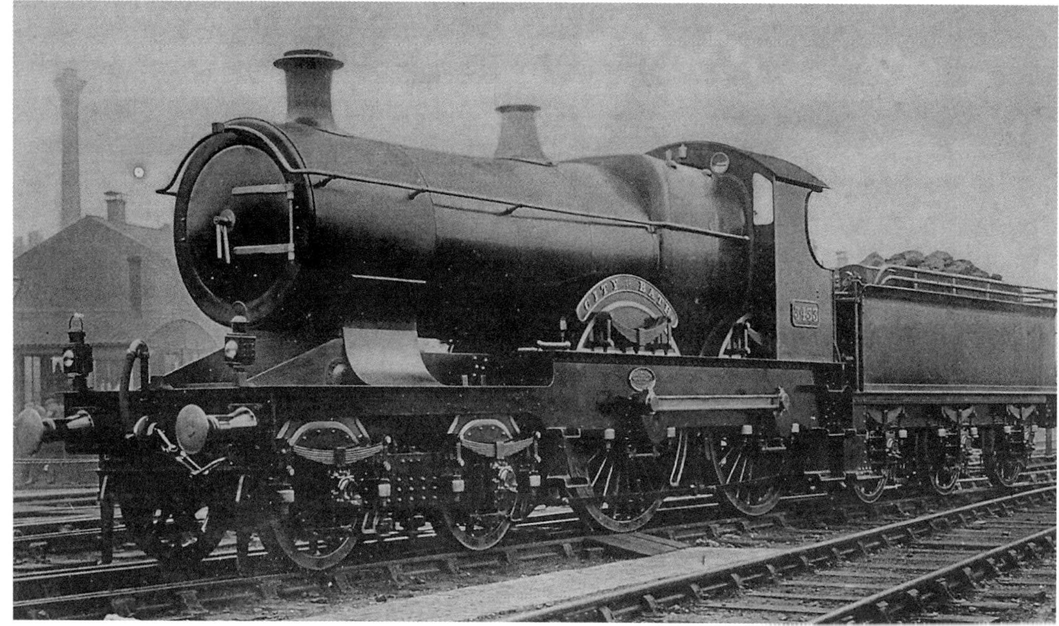

**The first** of Churchward's City Class 4-4-0s for the GWR No.3433 *City of Bath*. Of note are the outside frames of the locomotive. Commercial Postcard, *John Scott-Morgan Collection*

The Highland Railway in Scotland had need of a strong freight engine, and their solution was the fifteen members of the 'Big Goods' or 'Jones Goods' class of 1894, the first 4-6-0 locomotives designed in Britain. The machines, designed by the railway's chief engineer David Jones, were elegant and capable locomotives ideally suited to the needs of the railway, remaining in service until 1940. The engines were replaced by more modern locomotives but fortunately the first member of the class, No.103, survives in preservation.

Wilson Worsdell on the NER led the way in 4-6-0 passenger locomotive designs, with his S and S1 Classes of 1899 of which forty were built up to 1909. The GWR was thinking in a similar vein, and in 1902 George Jackson Churchward, who had succeeded William Armstrong as the company's chief mechanical engineer, designed the company's first 4-6-0 starting a long tradition of GWR passenger engines of the same arrangement. The new engines were the 2900 or Saint class. The saints were very capable engines and a total of seventy-six were built, the last being completed at Swindon in 1913. In the same year John Robinson, the chief engineer on the GCR, designed a class of 4-6-0 engines, not for fast passenger trains but to meet the growing need for fast goods trains, especially those carrying fish from the sea fishing ports such as Grimsby. The Class 8, commonly known as Fish Engines, were

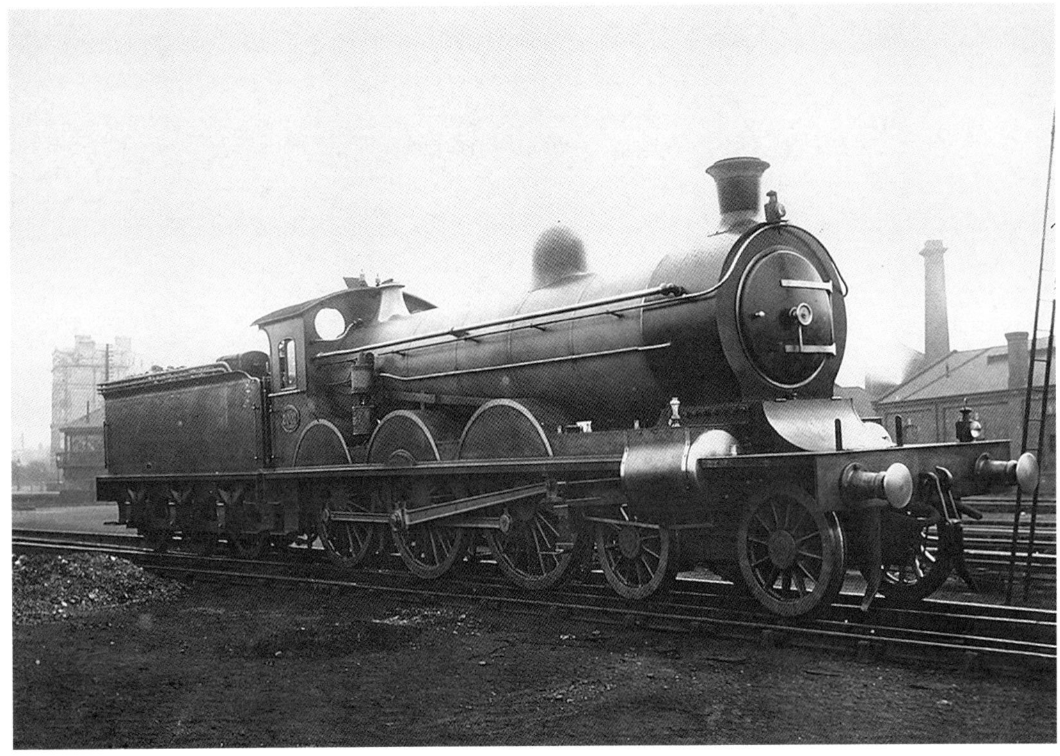

**Wilson Worsdell's** North Eastern Railway 'S' Class 4-6-0 No. 2002. C.1900.

huge, very much an exemplar of Robinson's design style, and very suited to the jobs for which they had been designed.

In 1906, two notable designs of 4-6-0 passenger locomotive entered service. On the Caledonian Railway, John McIntosh's Cardean Class, at the time the most powerful locomotive in Britain entered service, whilst on the GWR the first of Churchward's 4000 or 'Star' class entered service. The Stars were a novel 4-cylinder design, with two external and two internal cylinders which resulted in a fast and very powerful locomotive of which 73 examples were built by 1923.

Whilst the Stars were being built at Swindon, Robert Urie, who was the chief mechanical engineer of the GWR's great rivals the LSWR, was not idle. In 1914 the first of his mixed traffic 4-6-0s the H15 class entered traffic followed in 1919 by the railway's new express passenger locomotive, the superb N15 or King Arthur class. The N15s were all named after characters from the King Arthur legend and were fast runners, meeting the LSWR's needs on expresses to Exeter from Waterloo. Seventy-four of the class were built serving the LSWR and the Southern Railway, into which the LSWR was grouped in 1923, well.

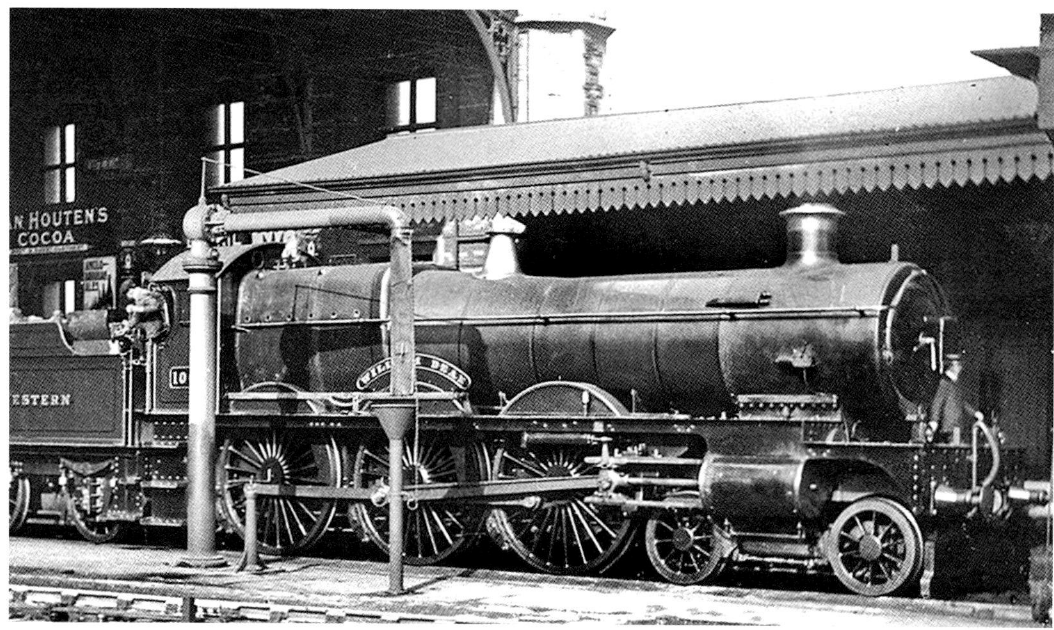

**Prototype Saint** 4-6-0 No. 100 *William Dean*. after fitting of a short cone taper boiler, at Bristol c.1920. *Trainiac*

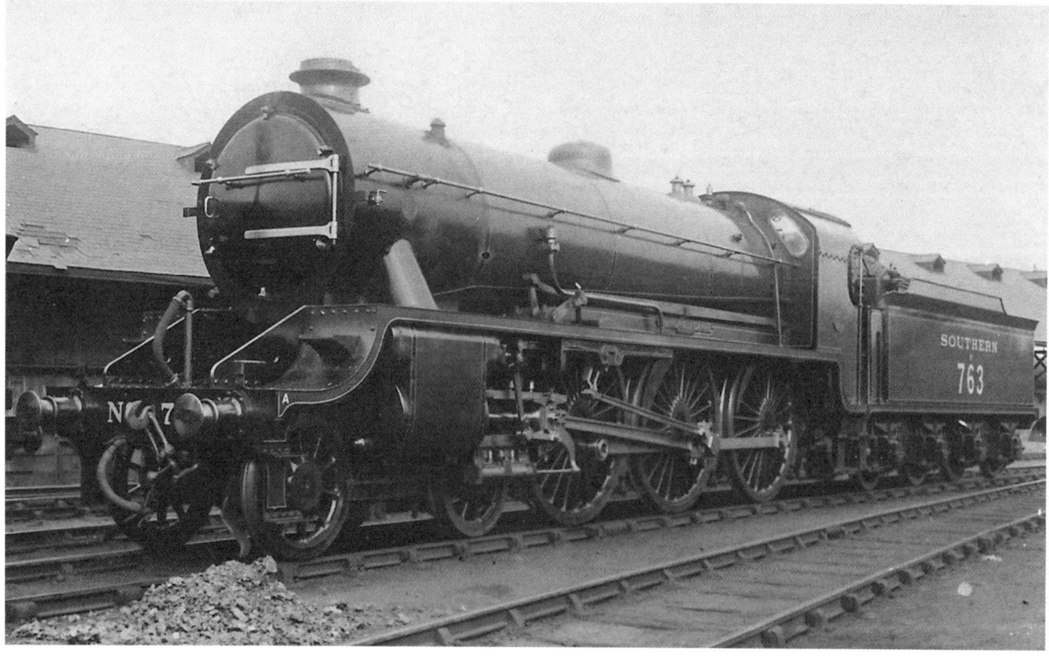

**N15 King Arthur** Class No. 763 in original form c.1925 before the addition of smoke deflectors and naming. The locomotive was named *Sir Bors de Ganis* one of the knights of Arthurian legend. Commercial Postcard. *John Scott-Morgan Collection*

The LNWR also began, like most of the other railway companies, to build 4-6-0 arrangement locomotives. Charles Bowen Cooke, Chief Mechanical Engineer of the LNWR, introduced some new designs to meet the demand for locomotives capable of hauling the increasingly heavy trains which the railway was running. His first two classes of 4-6-0 passenger engines were both superheated, which involved passing the steam from the regulator valve, which allowed steam into the cylinders from the boiler to pass back through the boiler tubes where it was heated again, drying it out and increasing the available energy in the steam before it passed into the cylinders. Superheating became increasingly common on British locomotive designs as the twentieth century progressed, although not all designs were fitted with the device.

The first of Bowen Cooke's new passenger engines entered service in 1911 and was of a 2-cylinder design with cylinders located between the frames. The initial engine was named *Prince of Wales*, the class being referred to by that name as was traditional on the LNWR. Two hundred and forty six of the class were built between 1911 and 1924, with 110 contracted out to William Beardmore & Co (90) and North British Locomotive Company (20) both of which were located in Glasgow. The remainder were all built by the LNWR at their Crewe works. One additional engine was built by Beardmore in 1924 and displayed at the British Empire Exhibition at Wembley the same year.

Bowen Cooke's second new type was introduced in 1913 and was a much larger 4-cylinder design, with two inside and two outside cylinders. The first of the class was named *Sir Gilbert Claughton* in honour of the chairman of the LNWR at the time, thus the locomotives which followed were referred to as Claughtons. One hundred and thirty of the class were built between 1913 and 1921, all of which were constructed at Crewe. Both the Prince of Wales and Claughtons were displaced later as new, more advanced, designs were built.

The 4-6-0 wheel arrangement, which become synonymous with the GWR, was not favoured by all designers. The layout of the locomotives restricted them to having to be provided with a long, thin firebox as it had to fit between the frames. The firebox also had to be designed to fit around the trailing driving axle which could result in overheating due to the heat of the fire. Some favoured a different approach to the design of fast passenger locomotives, the 4-4-2 or 'Atlantic'.

The 4-4-2 consisted of a leading bogie to guide the locomotives into curves and points, the same as could be found in the 4-6-0 arrangement, but with only two pairs of coupled driving wheels. At the rear of the locomotive could be found a single axle in a pony truck (a single axle bogie). The difference in design allowed for a wider firebox to be provided as it could sit above the frames. A wider firebox allowed for a bigger grate on which to build the fire and thus a larger heating area.

The design was introduced to the United Kingdom by William Adams, the locomotive superintendent of the North London Railway (1858-73), GER (1873-78)

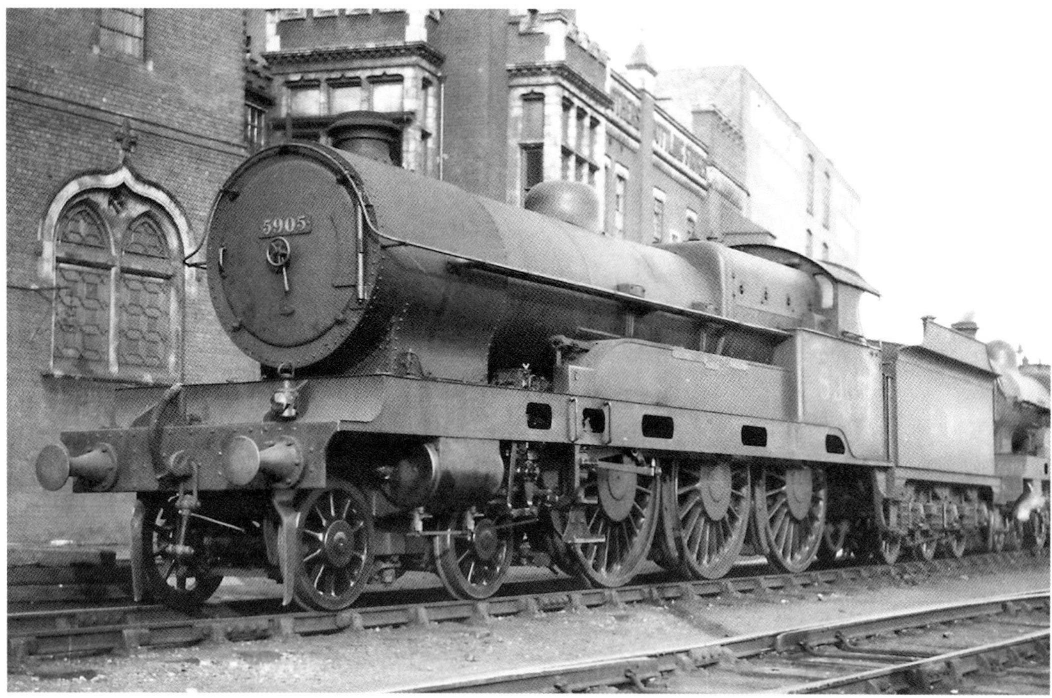

**Bowen Cooke Claughton** class 4-6-0 No. 5905 *Lord Rathmore* at Kentish Town, 1930.
*John Scott-Morgan Collection*

and LSWR (1878-95), with the creation of the 1 Class for the London, Tilbury and Southend Railway (LT&SR) in 1880. The design was the first time the 4-4-2 arrangement had been used anywhere in the world. It was developed further to create Adams' superb 415 Class of 1882, which like the LT&SR design was designed for commuter services. Whilst the earliest designs were for tank engines where the firebox was still restricted in width, the rear wheels supporting the weight of the coal bunker rather than the firebox, many engineers saw the potential in using the arrangement. Large numbers were built by the LT&SR, the Great Central Railway (GCR), and LBSCR, whilst Churchward designed the 2221 Class for the GWR, later superseded by his 2-6-2 tank engine designs. On the LNWR the arrangement was adopted with fifty of Whale's Precursor tank class built at Crewe.

The 4-4-2 arrangement was much favoured by some locomotive designers for express passenger tender locomotives. The first to appear on Britain's railways were the C1 class of 1898 designed for the GNR by Henry Ivatt, and the L&YR's Class 7 of 1899 designed by John Aspinall. The success of Ivatt and Aspinall's designs inspired other engineers to build locomotive of the same arrangement. Churchward experimented with the type on the GWR, the company purchasing three De Glehn compound locomotives in 1903 and 1905 for testing. Churchward built, or rebuilt,

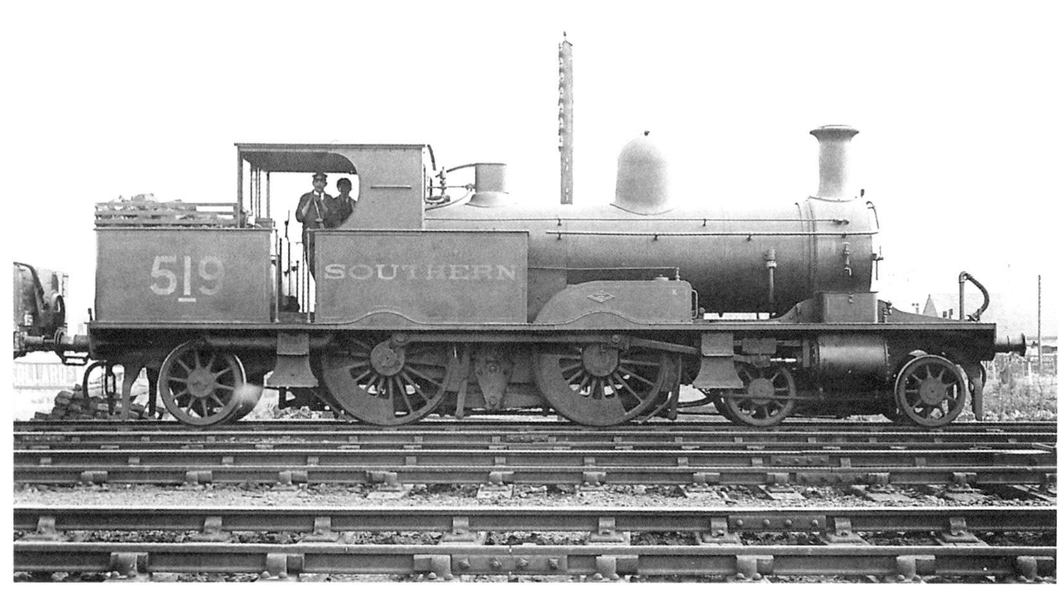

**Adams 415** Class No. 519 in Southern Railway ownership. *Author's Collection*

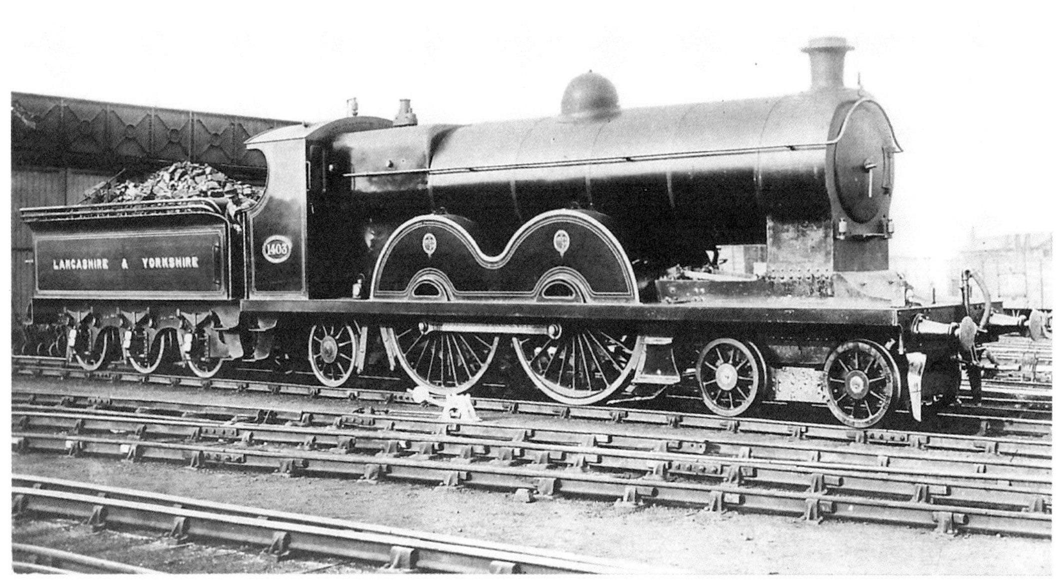

**Lancashire and Yorkshire** Railway Aspinall Class 7 4-4-2 No. 1403. Commercial Postcard, *John Scott-Morgan Collection*

fourteen of his 2900 Class to the arrangement but these were later rebuilt to the 4-6-0 arrangement as they had proved unsatisfactory.

Wilson Worsdell designed two classes of Atlantics for the NER between 1903 and 1906, with two more classes built to Vincent Raven's V/09 and Z designs between 1910 and 1917. The LBSCR adopted the design for its needs but only built a handful of Douglas Marsh's H1 design (five) and Lawson Billinton's H2 class (six). The NBR also saw promise in the arrangement, building twenty to the design of William Reid, whilst the GCR built just four to the design of John Robinson.

Despite the promises that the arrangement had and the elegance it provided to so many designs, it was superseded by the 4-6-0 type by 1918, since the Atlantics proved to be liable to slipping and less powerful than the six coupled types. They were not quite a dead end in engine design though, the wider firebox able to be placed on a locomotive with a trailing truck had sparked the imagination of many railway engineers. What if a wide firebox could be combined with power of a six coupled design? The result was the 4-6-2 or 'pacific' wheel arrangement, of which just five were built before the Grouping in 1923, although the arrangement became common thereafter.

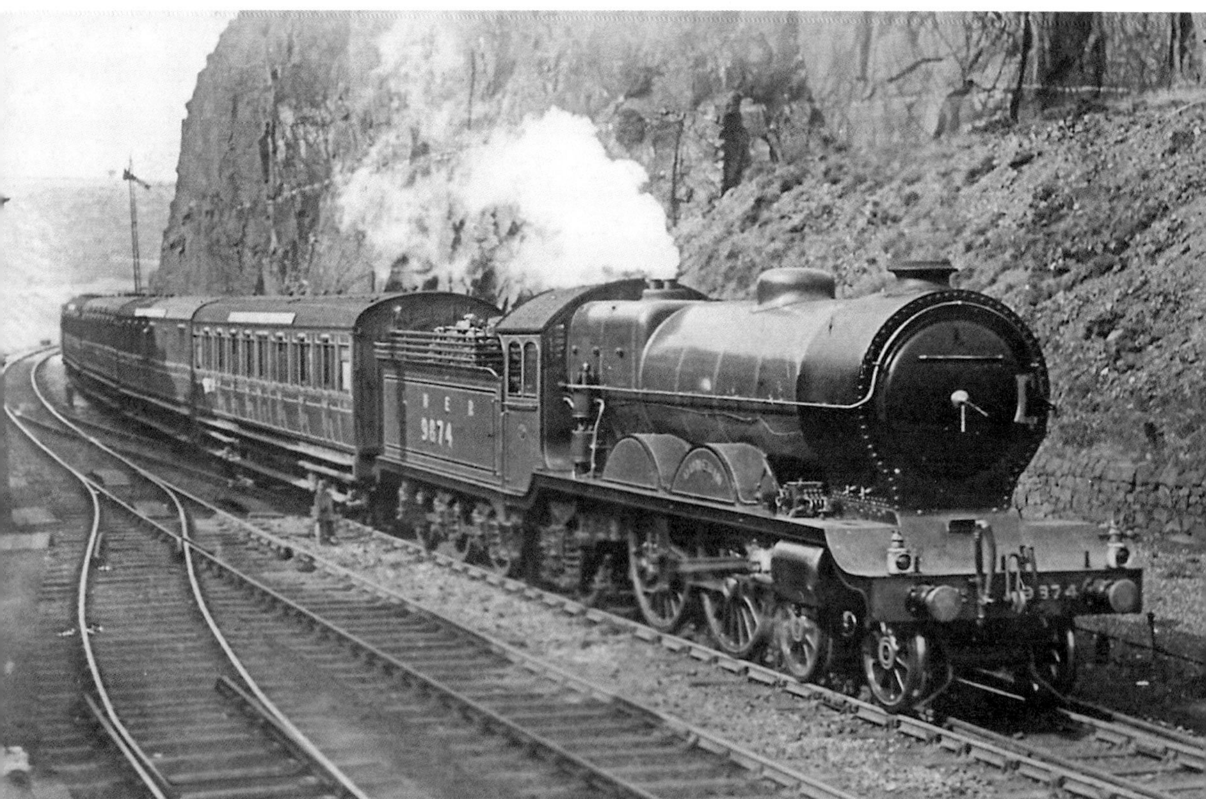

**Ex-North British** Railway H Class 4-4-2 No. 9872 *Dunedin* in LNER days. *John Scott-Morgan Collection*

The first of the type to see the light of day was the GWR's single pacific *The Great Bear*. The engine was built in 1908. There is some disagreement as to the reason for the locomotive's construction, O.S. Nock stating that the design was driven by Churchward as an experiment, whilst others say that it was a result of the GWR director's demand for the largest locomotive in Britain. Either way it was built and entered service, despite the GWR standardising on the 4-6-0 arrangement for its passenger locomotives. The engine was not a success, proving no more capable than other designs and it was rebuilt in 1924 as a Castle Class.

Other railways found the pacific design more successful. The GNR and NER built a pair of pacifics to the designs of Nigel Gresley, who had succeeded Ivatt as the company's chief mechanical engineer, and Raven respectively. Raven's locomotives were huge with one of the largest boilers seen at the time, but seem to have been effective, but only five were built (two by the NER in 1922 and three by the LNER in 1924). Raven's design may well have become more numerous but for the Grouping and the arrival of the Gresley pacifics. The GNR pacifics of A1 class were fine machines, proving to be strong and capable of hauling heavy loads at

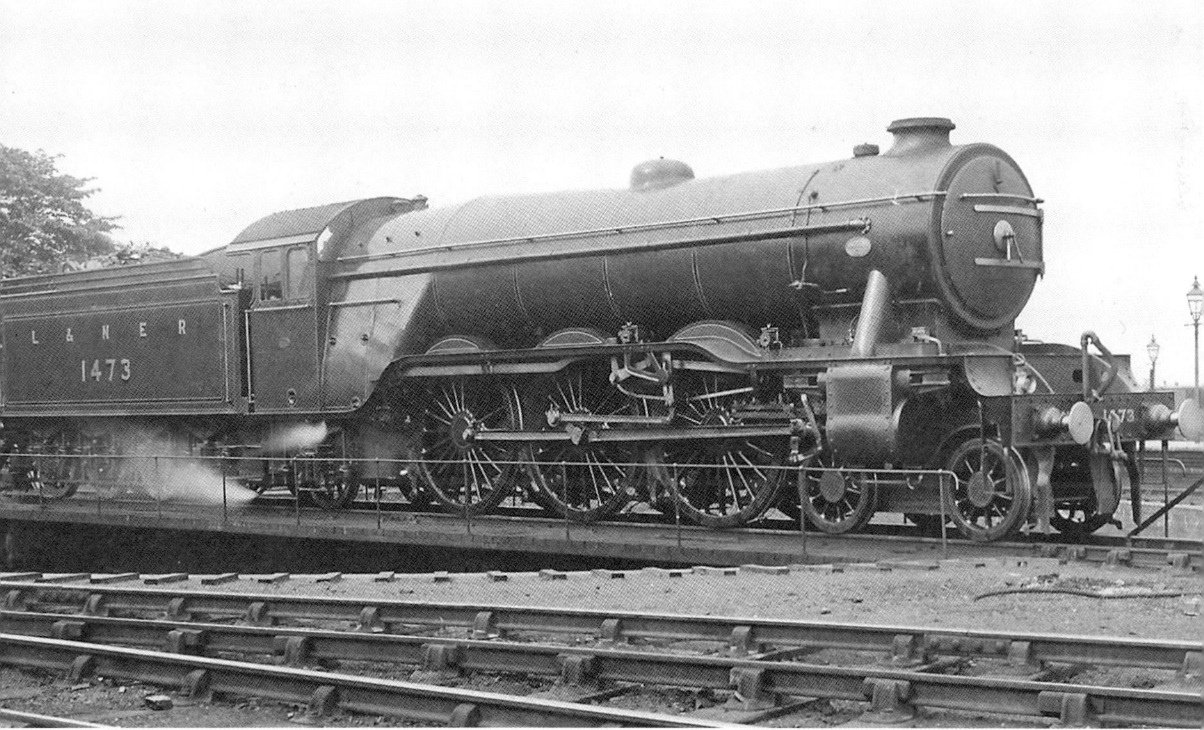

**Gresley A1** Class 4-6-2 No. 1473 before naming. The new pacific was named *Solario* after a racehorse, many of the class were named after famous racehorses. Commercial postcard. *John Scott-Morgan Collection*

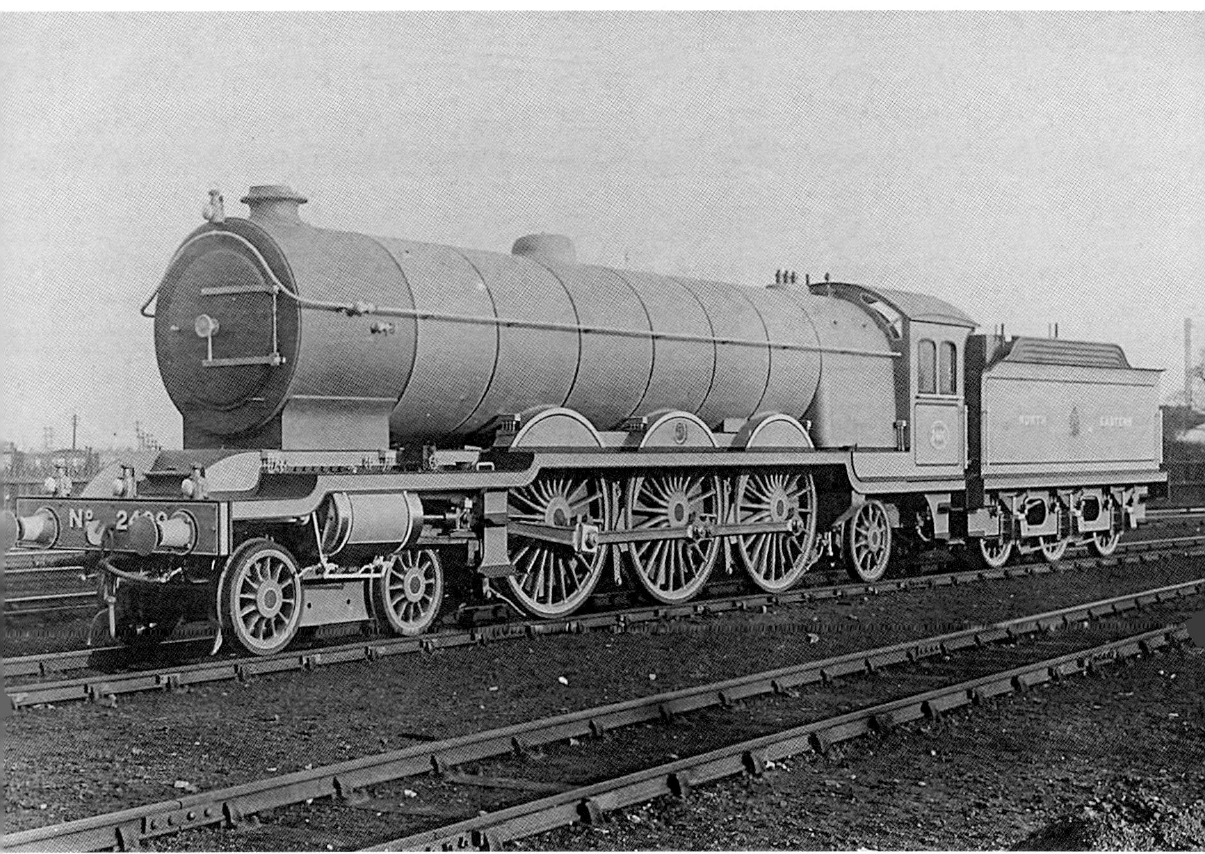

**A portrait** of the first of Vincent Raven's pacifics designed for the NER, No.2400 *City of Newcastle* at Darlington in 1922 when new. The locomotive is in photographic works grey, a colour used for official portraits of locomotives. *John Scott-Morgan Collection*

sustained high speeds. The first arrived, like Raven's machines, in 1922, and were named *Great Northern* and *Sir Frederick Banbury* after the last chairman of the GNR. The engines were to a 3-cylinder layout, with one inside and two outside cylinders, an arrangement that Gresley would favour throughout his career.

The A1s were later rebuilt into the A3 class, of which the world-famous *Flying Scotsman* was one of seventy-one engines. The locomotives were coupled to large 8-wheel tenders which allowed them greater range due to the increased water and coal capacity available. In 1928, Gresley introduced a new feature to the design of the tenders, a corridor connection. The new tenders had a narrow passage running down one side which led to a corridor connection at the rear. The connection could be linked to the gangway at the leading end of the first coach in a train, which allowed a replacement crew carried on the train to be exchanged with the crew who started the journey without stopping. It had been common to change locomotives or crews at a convenient midway point on a long-distance journey, and whilst the new A3s were more than capable of travelling very long distances, especially with the use of water troughs to replenish the tanks on the move, the crew were not. The corridor connection to the train allowed for the non-stop running between London and Edinburgh which the new 'Flying Scotsman' train required. The LNER had taken the lead in services between London and Scotland over its rival, the LMS.

Elsewhere, other railway companies continued to persevere with the 4-6-0 designs, although some extremely capable locomotives resulted. On the GWR, Charles Collett had taken over from Churchward as the railway's chief mechanical engineer in 1922. Churchward had left the railway with arguably the most capable fleet of locomotives inherited by the four post Grouping companies (known as The Big Four), but Collett saw the need for continual improvement as trains became heavier and needed to be faster to compete with other company's services.

The GWR had been improving its infrastructure after its experience with *The Great Bear*, which was too heavy to work on many parts of the network. As a result the lines from Paddington to Plymouth and Wolverhampton were upgraded to allow higher loadings. The line into Cornwall was restricted by the maximum weight of a locomotive that could be allowed to cross Brunel's Albert Bridge over the River Tamar. Collett began to look to an improved express engine, since by 1926 the other companies had begun to catch up, and pass, the GWR.

Collett's first express passenger design was created to replace the aging Star class which was becoming less able to handle heavy trains at speed. The new engines were partly based upon the Star but with larger cylinders, of which there were to be four (two inside and two outside), a larger boiler, and a more comfortable cab. The resulting design was the superlative Castle class, the first of which, *Caerphilly Castle*, emerged from Swindon in 1923. One hundred and seventy-one were built, including a number constructed by British Railways after the nationalisation of Britain's railways. The engines would become familiar sights across the entire GWR network hauling express trains from London to Penzance, Swansea and Birmingham until they were withdrawn by British Rail in the 1960s.

With a need to increase the GWR's motive power further, Collett and his assistant Frederick Hawksworth designed the 6000 or King class. Entering service in 1927, the first of thirty-one Kings were the ultimate in GWR express passenger traction.

At the same time, the SR's Chief Mechanical Engineer Richard Maunsell, who had previously held the same role at the SECR, was designing a new express locomotive. Maunsell was an experienced engineer and recognised the quality of the designs which he had inherited from the LSWR, created by Robert Urie. Urie's N15 King Arthur class were still being built for the SR's express passenger services and were still very fine engines, but by the middle of the 1920s it was becoming clear that the railway needed a more powerful engine for its long-distance expresses. To meet this

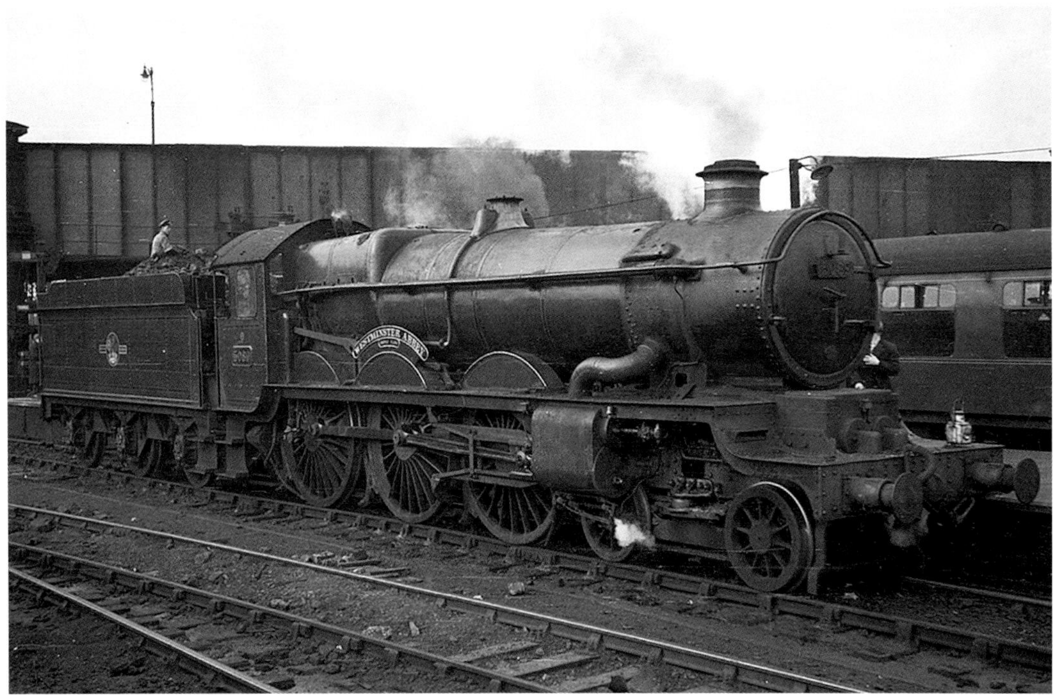

**Ex-GWR Castle** Class 4-6-0 No. 5089 *Westminster Abbey* at Chester in 1961. The locomotive is a 1939 rebuild of a Churchward Star Class. *Alan Murray-Rust*

need, Maunsell designed the Lord Nelson class of 4-6-0s. The engines were solid and powerful engines, which, like the GWR Castles, had a much improved cab for the crew, with half being given large, 8-wheel bogie tenders to allow then greater range since there were no water troughs on the SR. The locomotive's 4-cylinder layout made them the most powerful 4-6-0s built for the SR. The engines had an innovative feature which offered a huge step forward in British locomotive design.

The new engine had a split drive, the inside cylinders drove the front coupled axle, whilst the outside ones drove the middle coupled axle, which gave better weight distribution across the wheels of the engine and reduced hammer blow on the rails caused by the forces being transmitted through the cranks. The engines were also novel in two other ways. The crank axles were set at 135 degrees rather than the traditional 90 which required four sets of valve gear which was unusual at the time. The second difference from traditional designs was that the fire grate was in two sections, flat at the rear and then sloped towards the front to clear the rear axle, rather than the single sloped grate to be found on most other designs of 4-6-0.

The class were named after British admirals, the first emerging from Eastleigh works in 1926 was named *Lord Nelson* and they were thus referred to as Lord

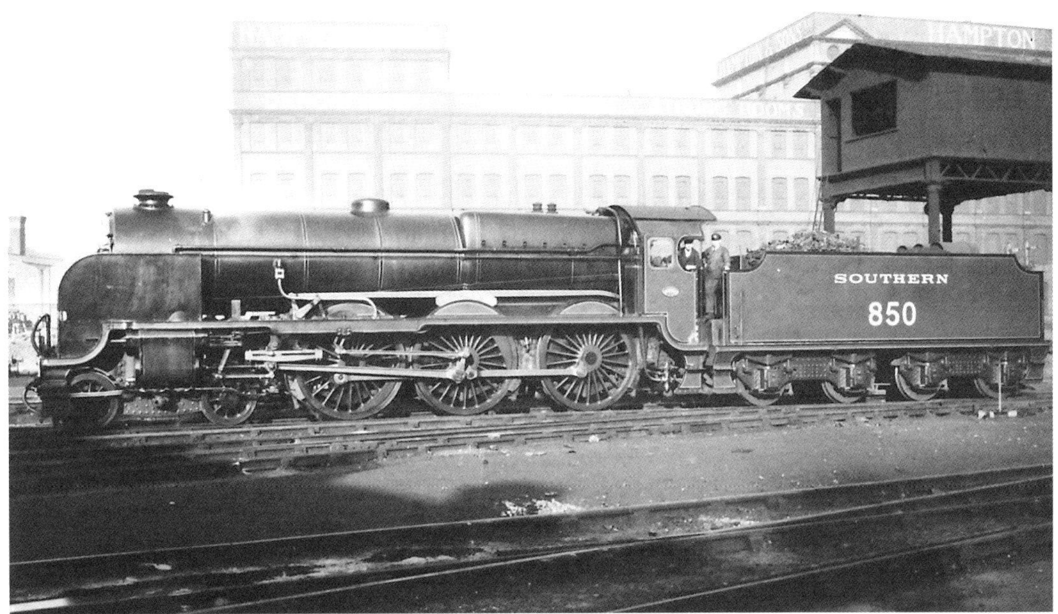


**The first** of Richard Maunsell's Lord Nelson Class 4-6-0, No. 850 *Lord Nelson*. The large bogie tender was to allow the locomotives to carry large amounts of water as the SR had no water troughs to replenish from. *John Scott-Morgan Collection*

Nelsons. A total of sixteen were built. The locomotives proved very successful, but they could not go everywhere and another solution was needed for expresses on secondary routes where the older classes of 4-4-0s were coming to the end of their useful working lives.

Maunsell's solution was a cut-down development of his Lord Nelsons with a 4-4-0 wheel arrangement. The need to produce a lighter locomotive to operate on the SR's secondary routes meant that a boiler similar to that used on the King Arthur's was needed. In order to provide the power needed for fast, heavy expresses, Maunsell opted for a 3-cylinder design, the resulting engines being the most powerful 4-4-0 designed for Britain's railways. The adoption of the smaller boiler design to save weight also allowed the engines to be designed with an unusual curved cab shape which allowed them to fit in the restricted width of the Hastings line caused by narrow tunnels. The engines were still overweight for the Hastings route and the line needed to be upgraded in order to accept them, but when it was the locomotives proved to be ideal.

The class, officially referred to as Class V, were all named after British public schools, and so the locomotives became known as the Schools Class. The first left Eastleigh Works in 1930 with another thirty-nine following it.

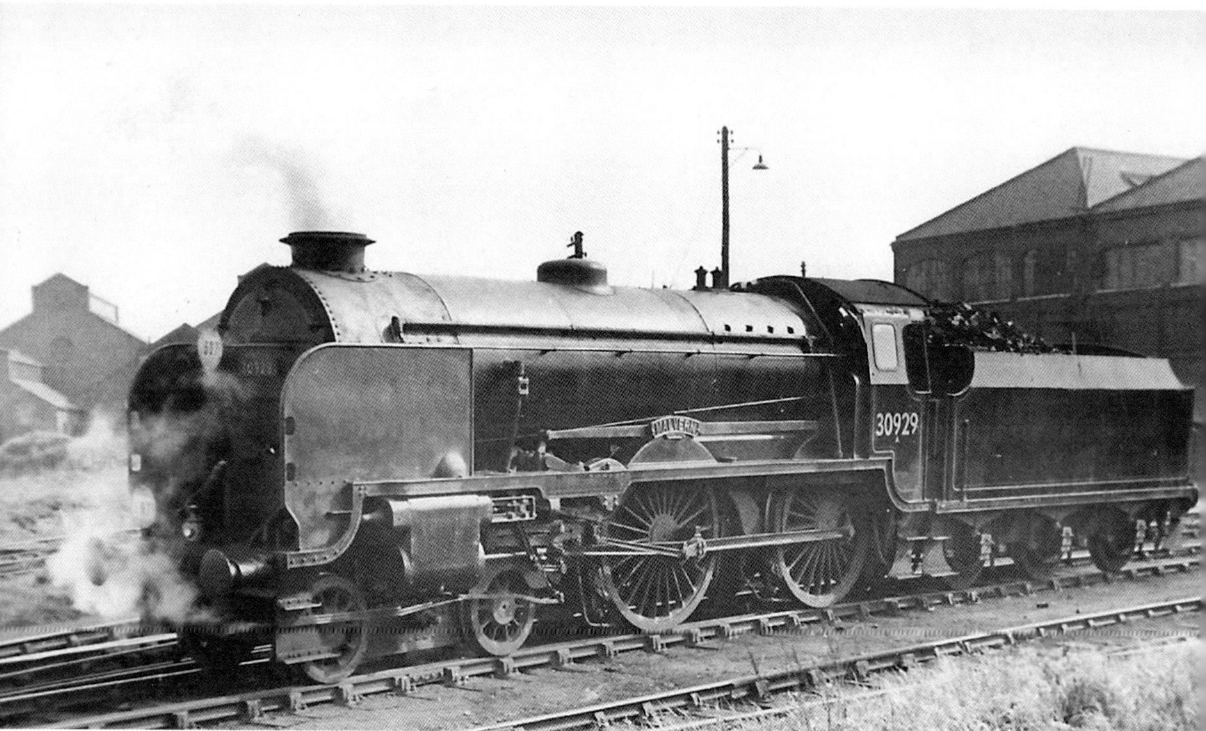

**Maunsell V** Class (Schools) 4-4-0 No.30929 *Malvern* at Newhaven Town Shed on 14 May 1949. *Author's Collection*

Meanwhile the LMS were having issues with their motive power and were looking for a solution. The elderly 4-4-0 and 4-6-0 classes were beginning to struggle with the heavier loads on the main routes from London to Carlisle via Preston and Leeds, and something better was becoming urgently needed. The LMS had followed the old MR small engine policy which meant frequent double heading of trains. The chief mechanical engineer of the LMS, Henry Fowler, was dissatisfied with the situation and began designs for a pacific locomotive to fill the gap. Disagreement between the chief engineer and the operating department of the LMS resulted in the directors arranging a loan of a GWR Castle class engine, *Launceston Castle*, for one month.

The GWR engine was a success and the planned pacific was abandoned in favour of a large and powerful 4-6-0 design. The LMS approached the GWR for a set of design drawings for the Castle upon which it was planned to base the new locomotive but this was denied. The SR was more cooperative and a set of drawings for the Lord Nelsons were sent to Derby. The resulting engine was a combination of best practice from Derby and Eastleigh with influence from the North British Locomotive Company to whom the construction had been subcontracted due to the urgency of providing the new engines.

The new machines, of which fifty were built by North British and a further twenty by the LMS works at Derby between 1927 and 1930, proved to be a great success. The entire class were named initially after regiments of the British army, with some locomotives named after withdrawn LNWR engines, although these were later renamed with regimental titles. The first was named *Royal Scot*, the class becoming known by that name. The engines were improved and then later rebuilt by the LMS and British Railways with new boilers and cylinders.

The LMS would build a further series of 4-6-0 express engines after William Stanier joined the company to succeed Henry Fowler upon his retirement. Stanier had worked at Swindon and was a very capable and experienced engineer, with his own ideas. Initially he seemed to be continuing along the lines of his erstwhile employer, creating two classes of 4-6-0 one for express passenger and the other for mixed use. The first was the Jubilee class, the first of which entered service in 1934. The engines were actually a modification of Fowler's Patriot class of express locomotive which

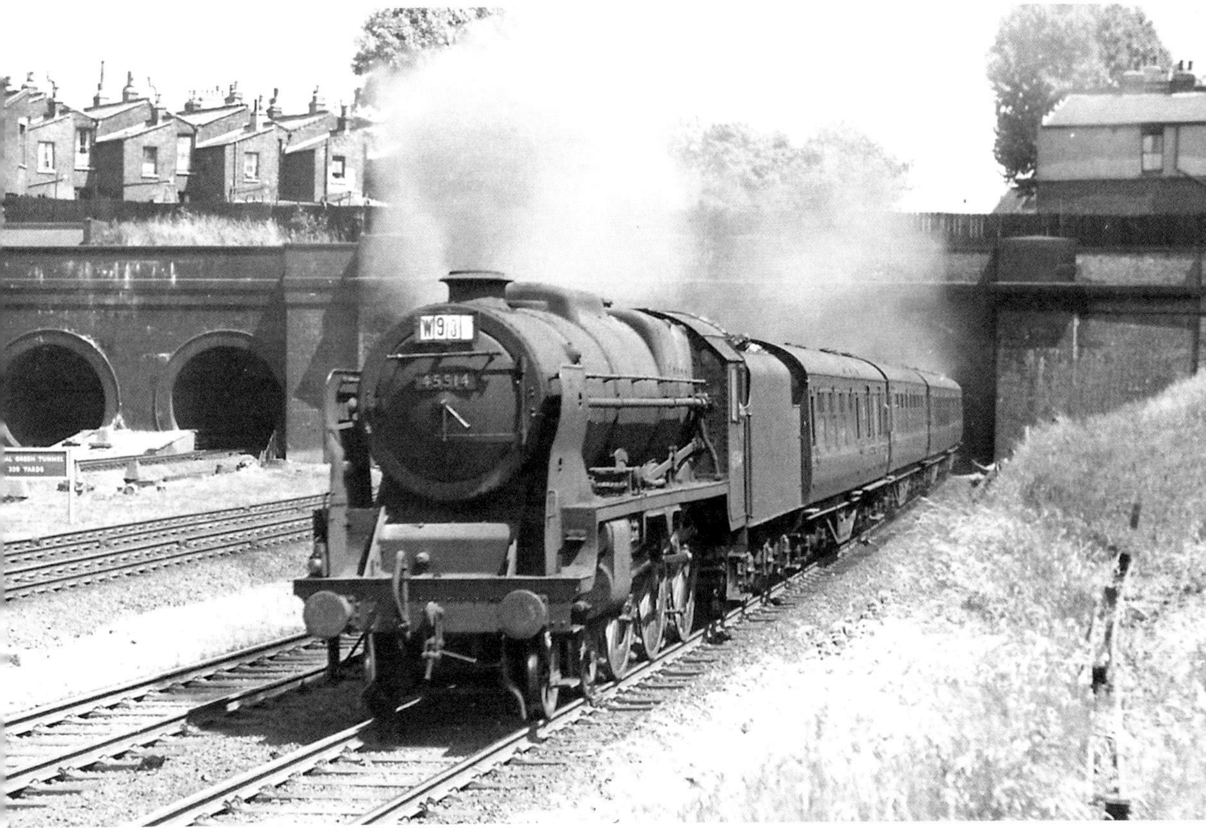

**Rebuilt Patriot** Class 4-6-0 No. 45514 *Holyhead* on a Euston to Blackpool train leaving Kensall Green Tunnel in June 1959. The original Fowler locomotives were rebuilt by H.A. Ivatt in 1946. *Author's Collection*

had begun to enter service in 1934, the last five of which were built with Stanier's new design of boiler to create the Jubilees. The engines were not initially successful, but modifications made them into excellent machines.

In 1935, one of the class had been named *Silver Jubilee* in honour of the silver jubilee of George VI, giving the name to the class. One hundred and ninety one of the engines were built at Crewe (131), Derby (10) and by North British (50), and they could be found working express services on most of the main lines of the LMS network. Some of the class, like a number of locomotives on other railways, were fitted with a double chimney and blastpipe, an innovation that allowed more powerful boilers to be used without the need to have a very tall and wide chimney to provide the drafting that they needed to raise steam properly. The device had a downside in that it sometimes softened the blast of steam leaving the chimney which could cause it to drift along the boiler blocking the view of the driver. In order

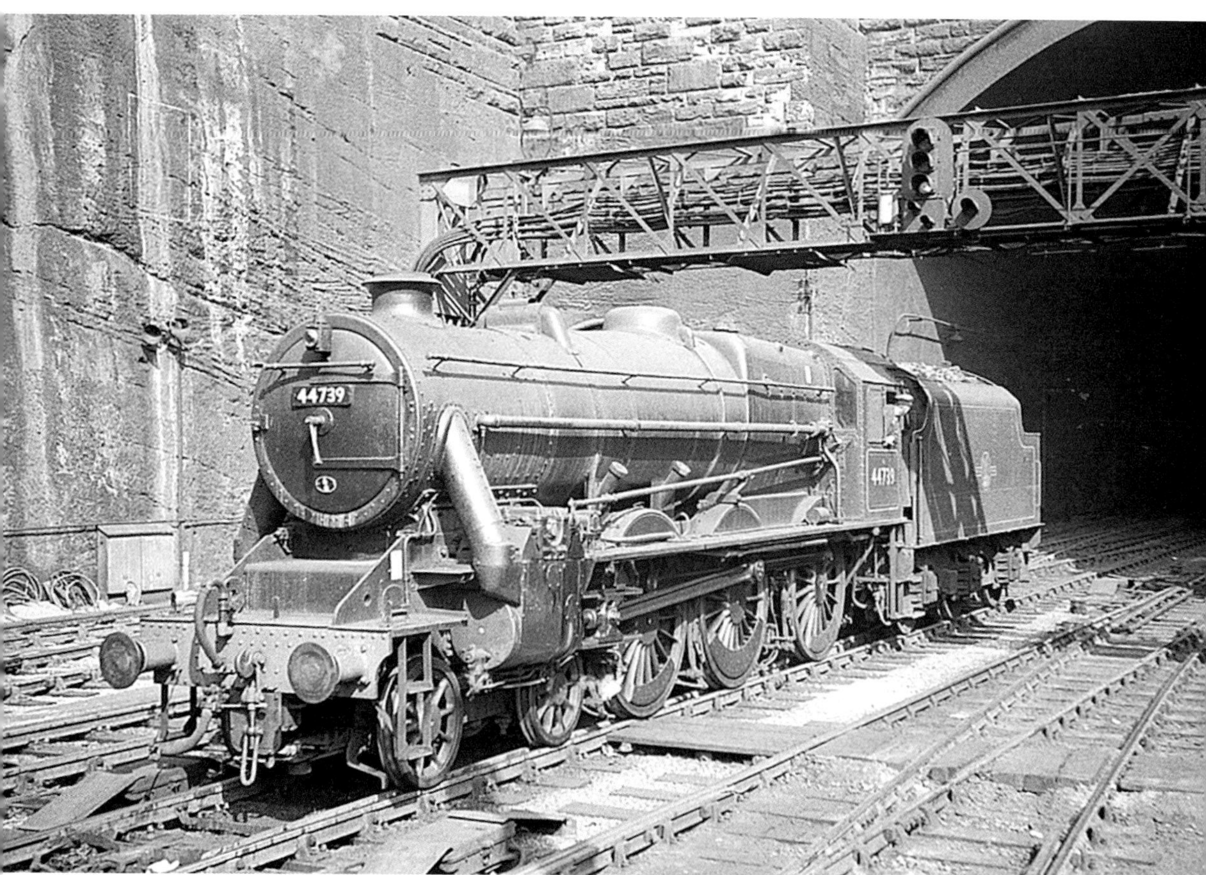

**Stanier 5MT** 'Black 5' 4-6-0 No. 44739. Liverpool Lime Street August 1960. The locomotive, built in 1948, is fitted with Caprotti valve gear, notable by the cutaway footplate to make way for the cam box on the top of the cylinders, and different steam pipes from the smokebox. *Alan Murray-Rust*

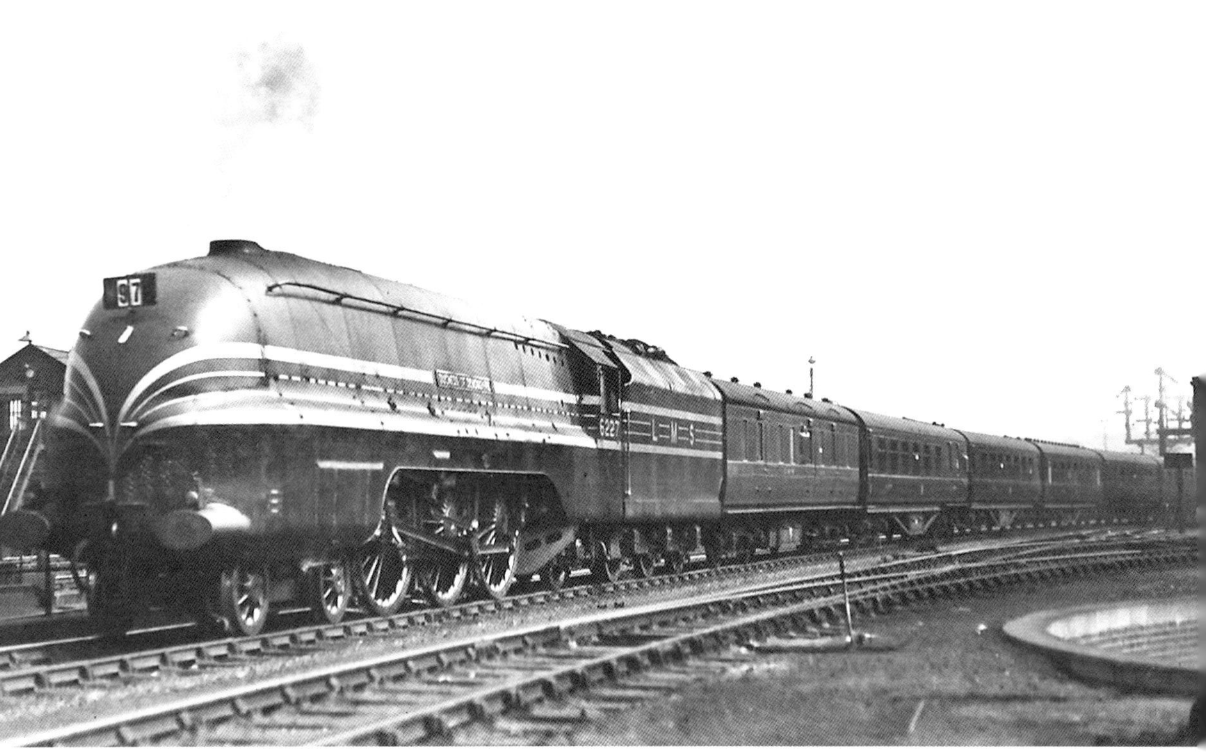

**Streamlined Coronation** Class 4-6-2 No. 6227 *Duchess of Devonshire*, passing Camden Shed with a Glasgow express. The Locomotive is wearing the livery used on the Coronation Scot train which matched the coaches. *John Scott-Morgan Collection*

to resolve this, some classes, but not the Jubilees, were fitted with smoke deflectors, two large plates either side of the smokebox at the front of the boiler which trapped air and forced it upwards taking the smoke and steam with it.

The second of Stanier's new types was a mixed traffic 4-6-0, which could often be found working fast and intermediate services all over the LMS. The class became known as Black 5s due to them usually carrying a lined black livery in both LMS and BR days. The engines were well laid out, with ergonomically designed cabs for the crew which made them popular. A total of 842 were built between 1934 and 1951 at Crewe (241), Derby (54), Horwich (120), Vulcan Foundry (100) and Armstrong Whitworth (327).

The new 4-6-0s were very capable but something larger was needed and so Stanier returned to the idea of a large pacific to cover the long-distance expresses to Scotland from London. The result was the Princess Royal Class, a large 4-cylinder 4-6-2. The first of these impressive and capable machines left Crewe in 1933 followed by one other, a further ten were built in 1935. The influence upon Stanier from his time at

Swindon can be seen in the some of the features of the engines, although the design was also clearly very much his work. The class were all named after princesses, the first, named *The Princess Royal* after Mary, the only daughter of George V, gave the name to the whole class. Whilst successful, Stanier embarked on a set of improvements and modifications which resulted in a new design which began to enter service on the LMS in 1937.

The Coronation class were much larger engines than the Princesses, and like their earlier sisters they were 4-cylinder pacifics. A total of thirty-eight of the machines were built by Crewe Works between 1937 and 1948, with most built in a streamlined form, with a casing around the boiler until 1944 when all further new engines were built in conventional form, whilst the older engines had the casings removed. The streamlined locomotives were provided, to a degree, as a response to Gresley's new engines for the LNER although there was a fascination with the possibilities that the new scientific understanding of air flows offered and all of the Big Four experimented with it to some degree.

On the LNER, a new train was being planned in the early 1930s which was to be both fast and luxurious. The new Silver Jubilee trains which were to be introduced in 1935 needed a new locomotive to haul them, and Nigel Gresley responded with his world famous A4 class of streamlined pacifics. The stock for the train was also to be streamlined. The LNER's aim was to steal the lead from the LMS on the expresses to Scotland, which the A4s promised to achieve. The locomotive was encased in a streamlined casing which featured a curved sloping front end which not only improved the aerodynamics of the engine, but also served to create an airflow over the top which blew the steam and smoke away from the large cab. The engines were a new step forward in locomotive design, with streamlining not only applied to the exterior.

All of the steam pipes were very carefully designed to aid gas flow to reduce loss of energy in the steam. Gresley and his team at Doncaster had created a locomotive which was not only capable of high-speed running, but was much more economic, consuming less coal and water than the A3s which came before. The class proved themselves to be extraordinary machines, with 35 built at Doncaster works, all of which retained their streamlined casings until withdrawn by British Rail in the 1960s when they were replaced by Deltic diesel locomotives. One member of the class, *Mallard*, holds the world record for steam traction, achieving 126mph in 1938.

The GWR dabbled with streamlining as a response to the introduction of the A4s on the LNER. Seeing the opportunities for publicity, the railway's board of directors tasked Swindon with providing a streamlined engine. Swindon allocated a castle class, *Manorbier Castle*, for the experiment and a somewhat half-hearted attempt at streamlining was fitted to it. A bulbous nose cone was fitted to the smokebox front with shaped steel sheets fitted elsewhere on the locomotive. The end result

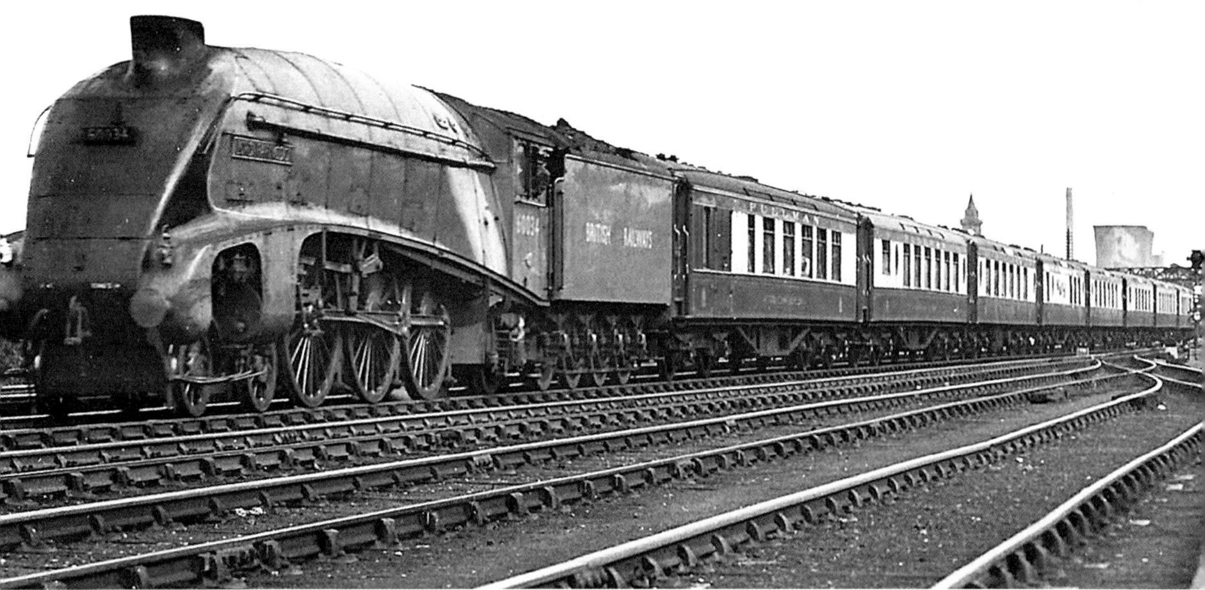

**Gresley A4** 4-6-2 No. 60034 *Lord Faringdon* on a train of Pullman cars. The photograph must have been taken very early in the British Railways period as the tender has 'British Railways' which was only applied very briefly. *Author's Collection*

was a mishmash which neither provided the elegance of Gresley's A4s nor the impression of power given by Stanier's Coronations. The experiment was ended and the sheeting removed from *Manorbier Castle* since it made little difference to the performance of the engine. Strangely, the GWR had successfully introduced trains with streamlining with the introduction in 1933 of their diesel railcars but failed to do so on a steam locomotive.

The Southern Railway entered the streamlined era in 1941. The company had required a new CME as Richard Maunsell was due to retire, and in 1937 the post was offered to Oliver Bulleid, who was working at Doncaster as Gresley's assistant. Bulleid accepted the post. His first steam locomotives for the SR were the ground breaking Merchant Navy class pacifics, although the first new engines produced under his reign were three diesel shunting locomotives which had been designed by Maunsell.

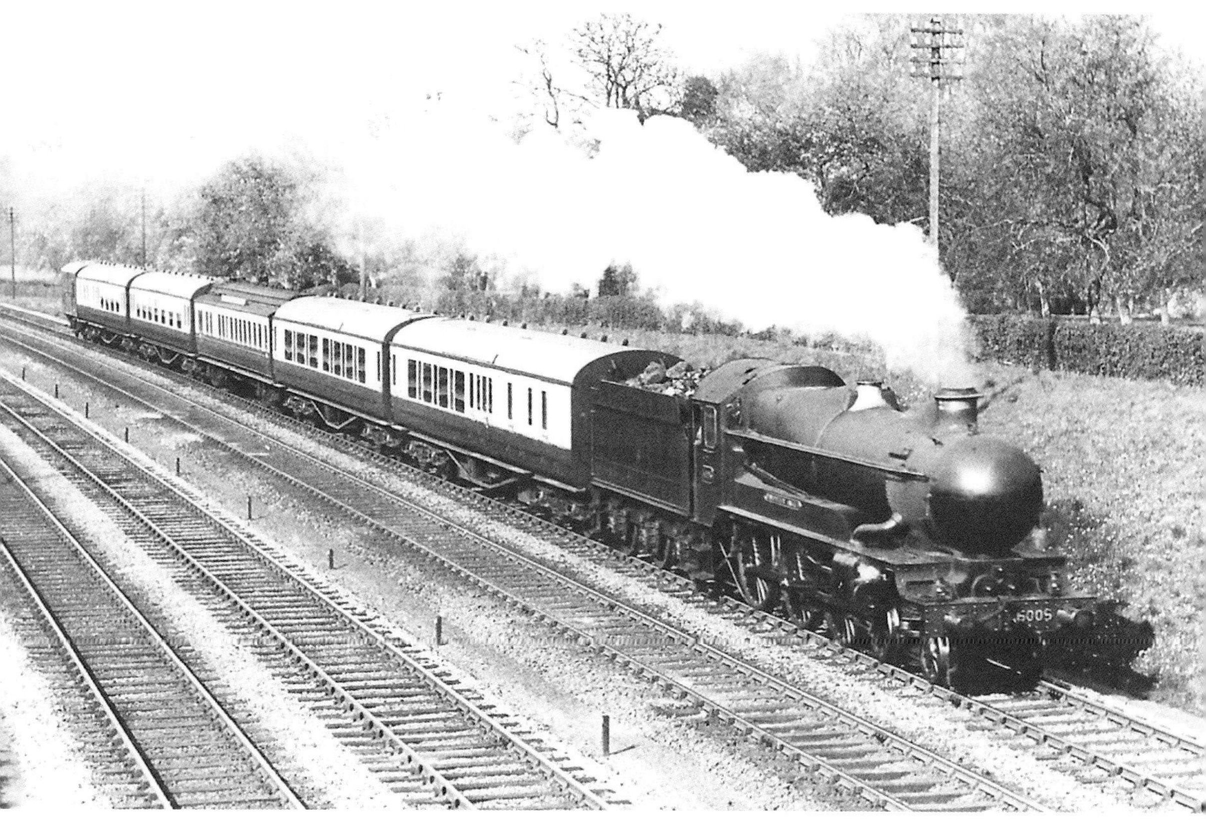

**GWR Castle** Class 4-6-0 No. 5005 *Manorbier Castle* in 'streamlined form c.1935. The bulbous dome over the smokebox, plated in wheel splashers and fairing directly in front of the cab seem to be the only attempts to streamline the locomotive. *John Scott-Morgan Collection*

The new steam class were promoted as mixed traffic engines to get around wartime restrictions on locomotive construction, the first entering service in 1941. They were in fact high powered express passenger engines, although they were definitely not of conventional design.

Bulleid's new design differed from everything that had come before. Conventional locomotives had valve gear which consisted of mechanical linkages which adjusted how long the cylinder valves were open for and when they opened. Bulleid's design dispensed with this, instead operating the valves for the three cylinders through a chain driven system located between the locomotive's frames. In order to keep the system lubricated, it was placed in a large oil bath.

The engines were 'air-smoothed', having a casing around the boiler and a wedge-shaped cab front, all designed to improve the flow of air along the locomotive. The front end was different from that of the A4s and Coronations. Unlike the aerodynamic fronts on Stanier's and Gresley's designs, the front of the merchant

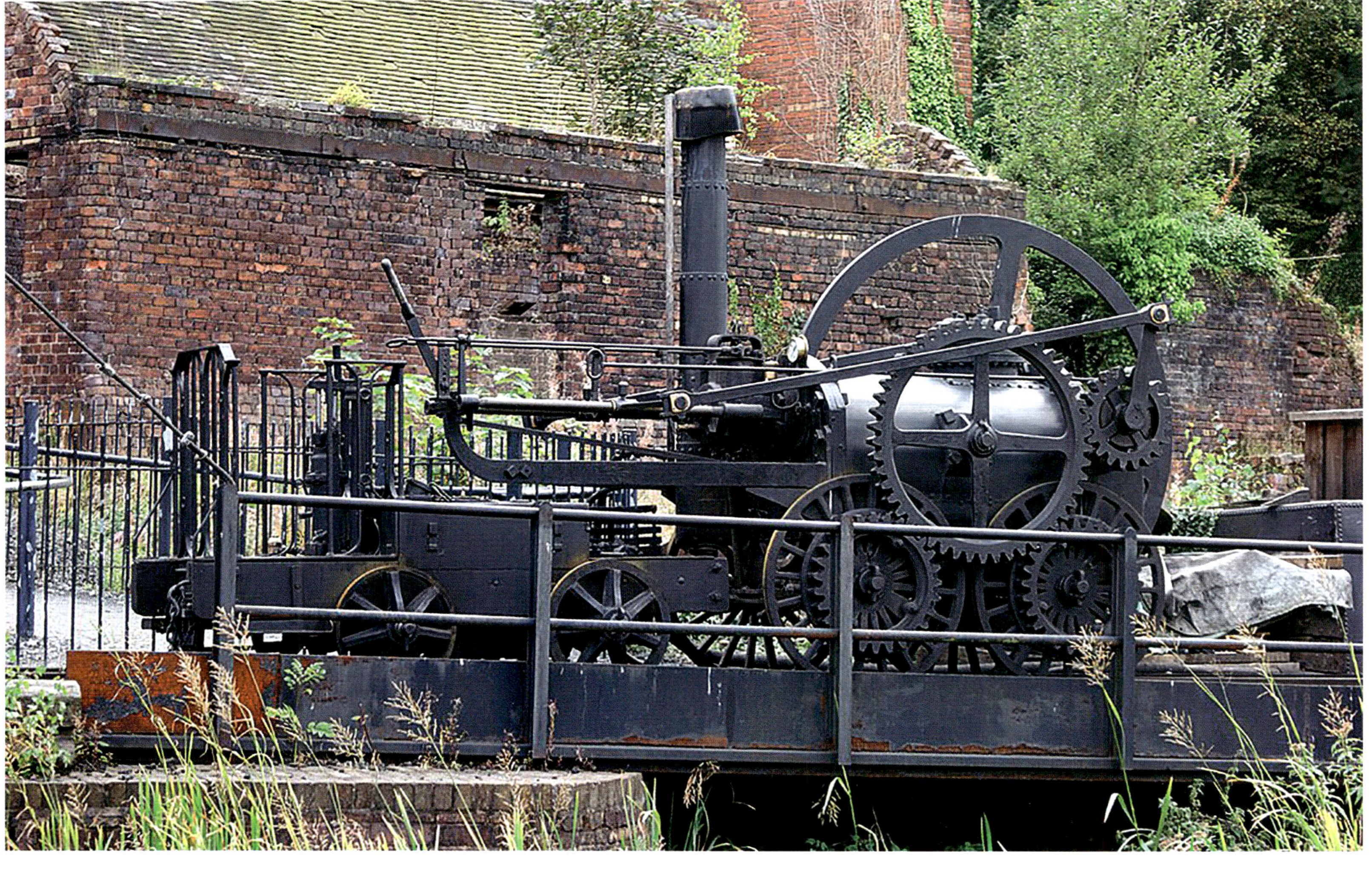

**Working replica** of Richard Trevithick's locomotive of 1803 at Blists Hill Museum in 2009. *Hugh Llewelyn*

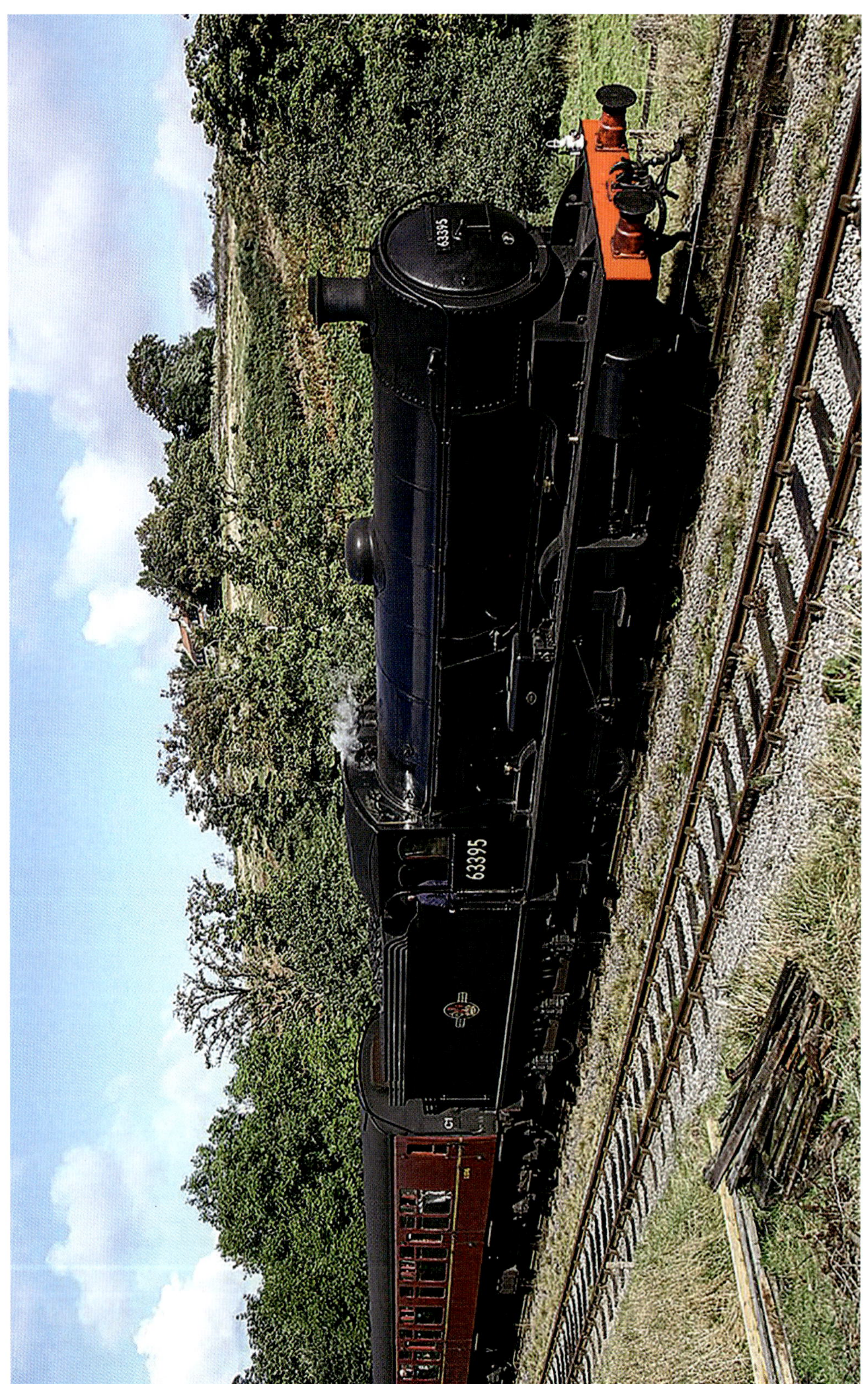

Preserved **NER** T2 Class 0-8-0 No. 63395 on the North Yorkshire Moors Railway, 1 October 2016. *Charlie Jackson*

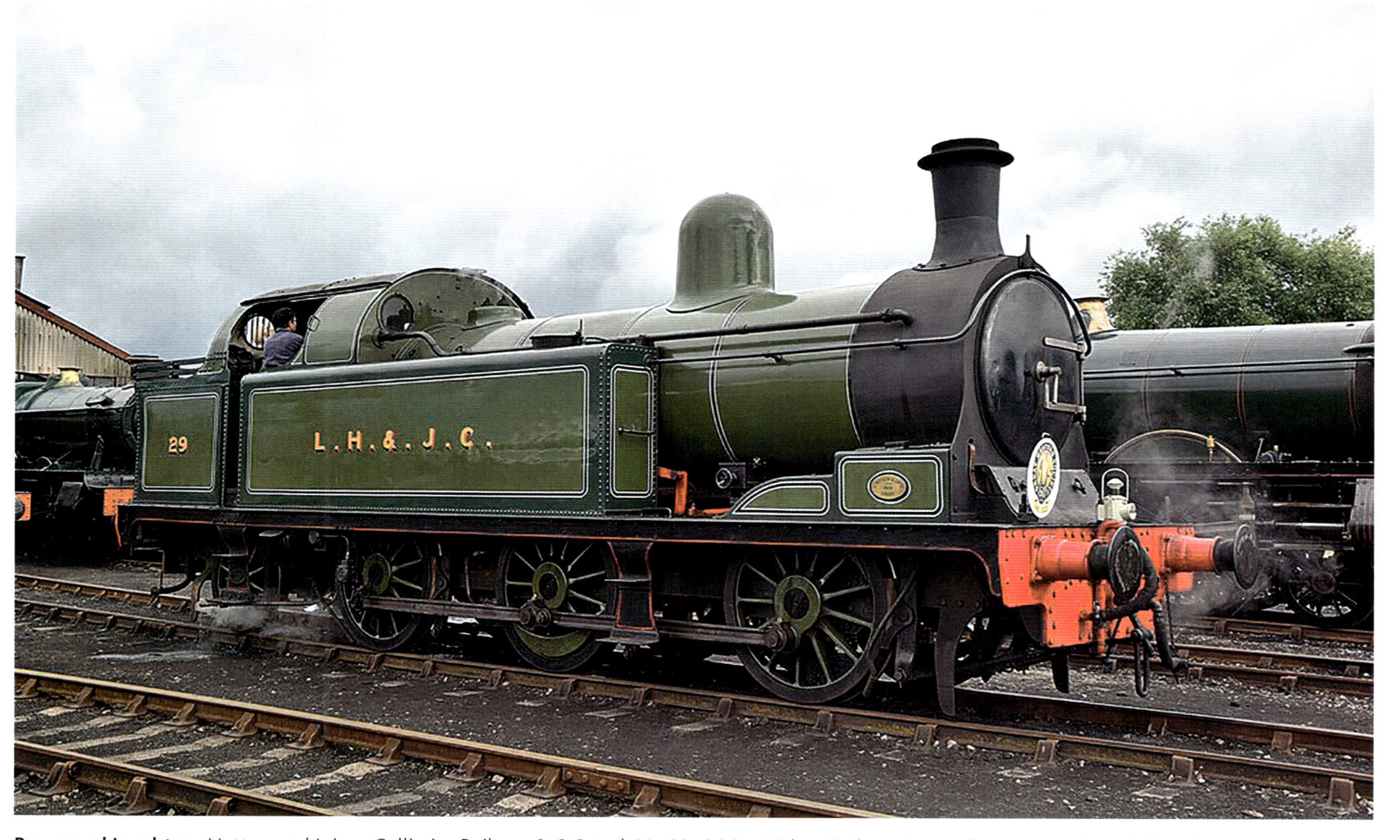

**Preserved Lambton,** Hetton and Joicey Collieries Railway 0-6-2 tank No.29 visiting Didcot Railway Centre from its North Yorkshire Moors Railway home on 31 July 2021. *Hugh Llewellyn*

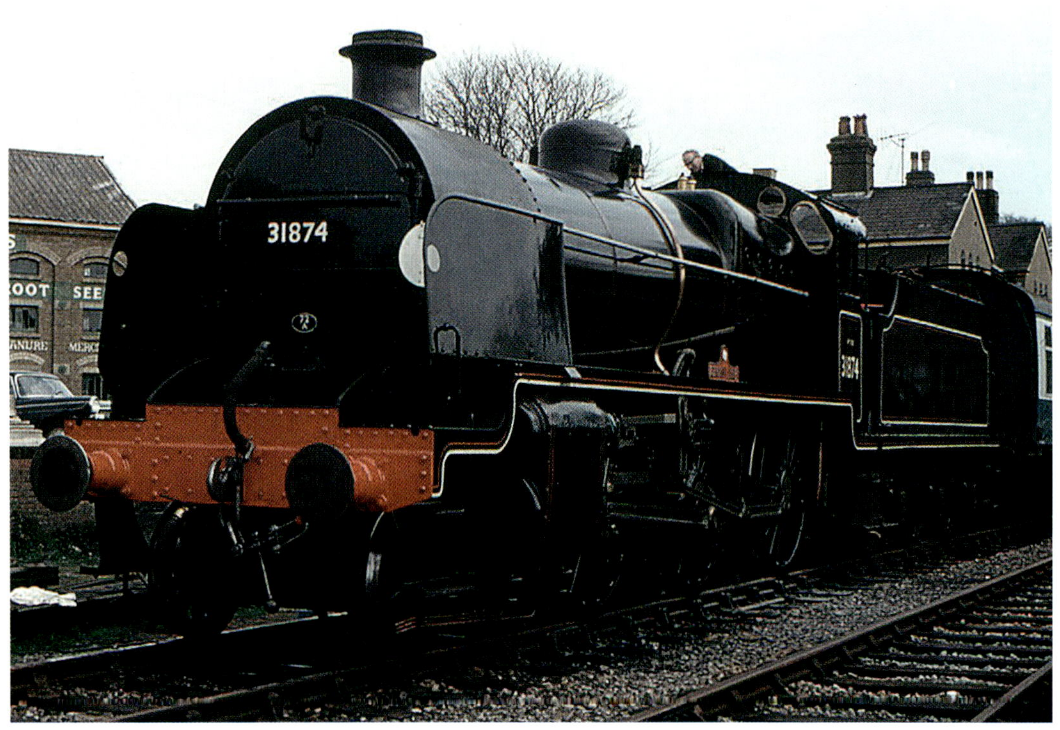

**Ex Southern** Railway N Class 2-6-0 No. 31874 on the Mid-Hants Railway early in preservation.
*Barry Lewis*

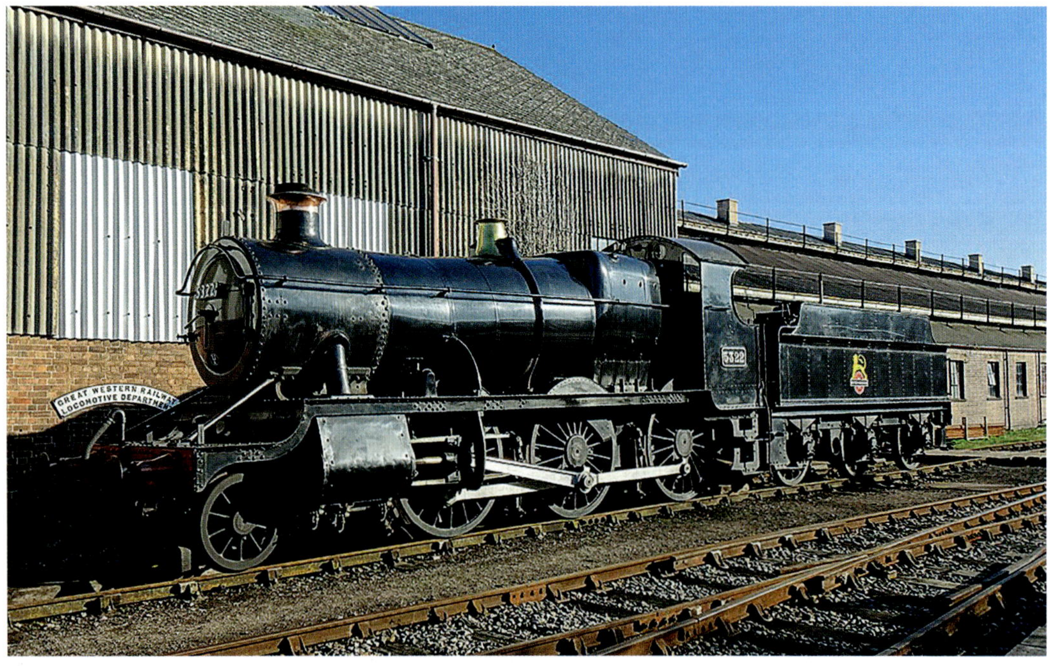

**GWR Churchward** 4300 Class 2-6-0 No.5322 at Didcot Railway Centre, 18 November 2018.
*Hugh Llewelyn*

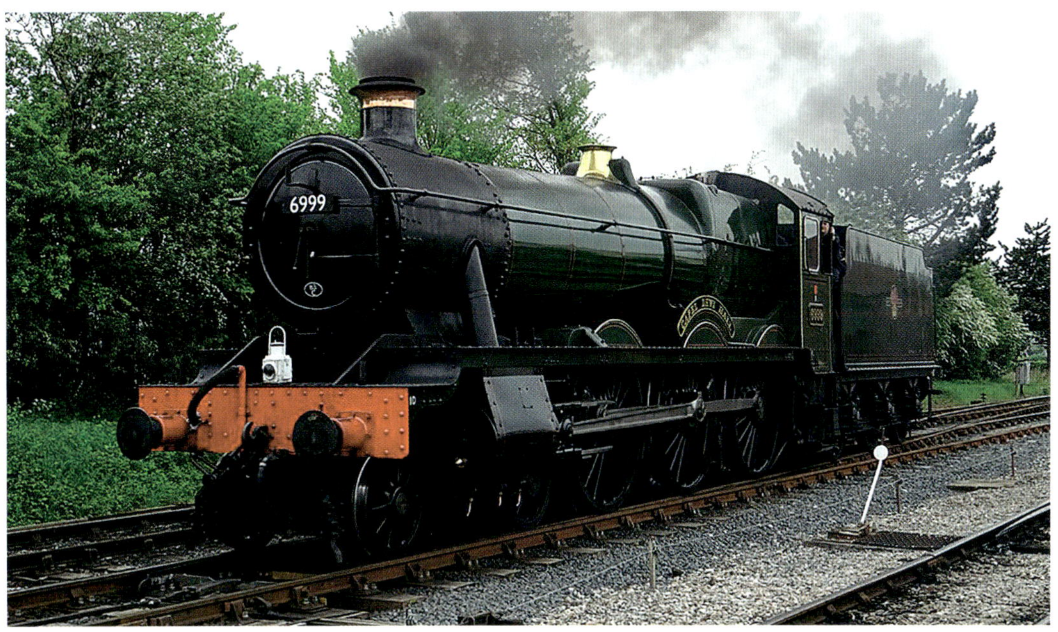

**Preserved Hall** Class 4-6-0 No. 7903 *Foremarke Hall* masquerading as scrapped classmate No. 6999 *Capel Dewi Hall* at the Cotswold Festival of Steam on the Gloucestershire Warwickshire Steam Railway, 13 May 2023. *B. Ward*

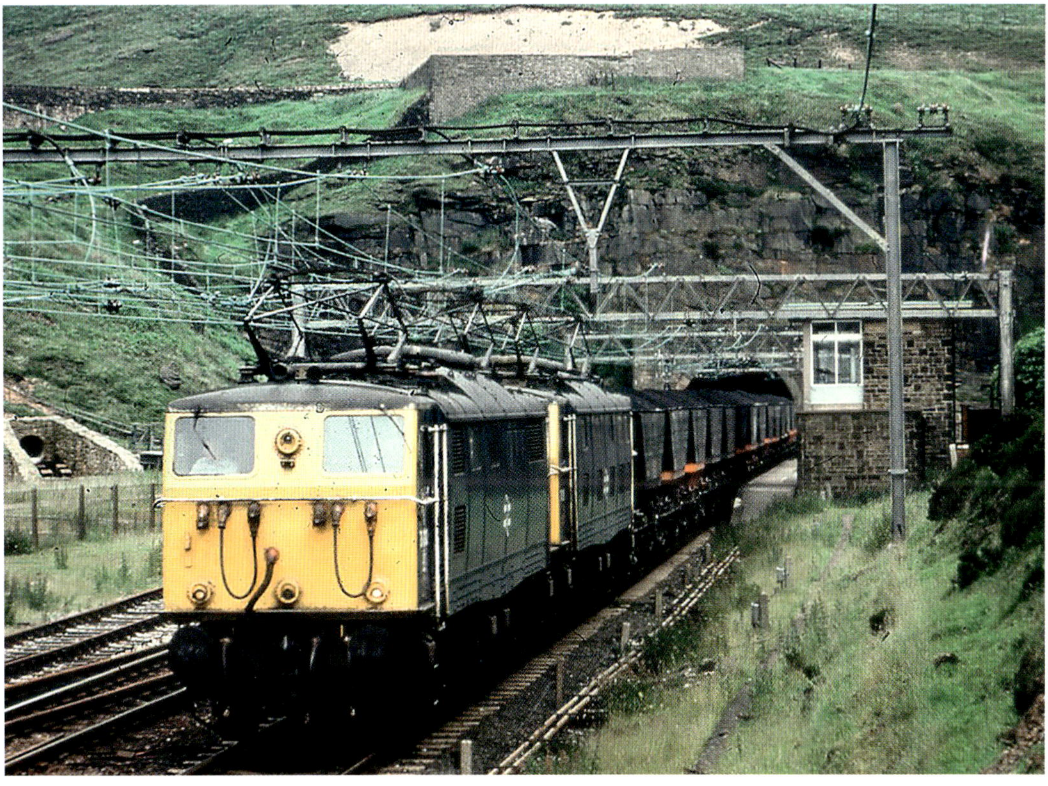

**A pair** of Class 76 (EM1) BO-BOs leaving Woodhead tunnel on a train of coal hoppers. The locomotives often worked in pairs on heavy trains such as this. *Gordon Pitway via Steve Knight*

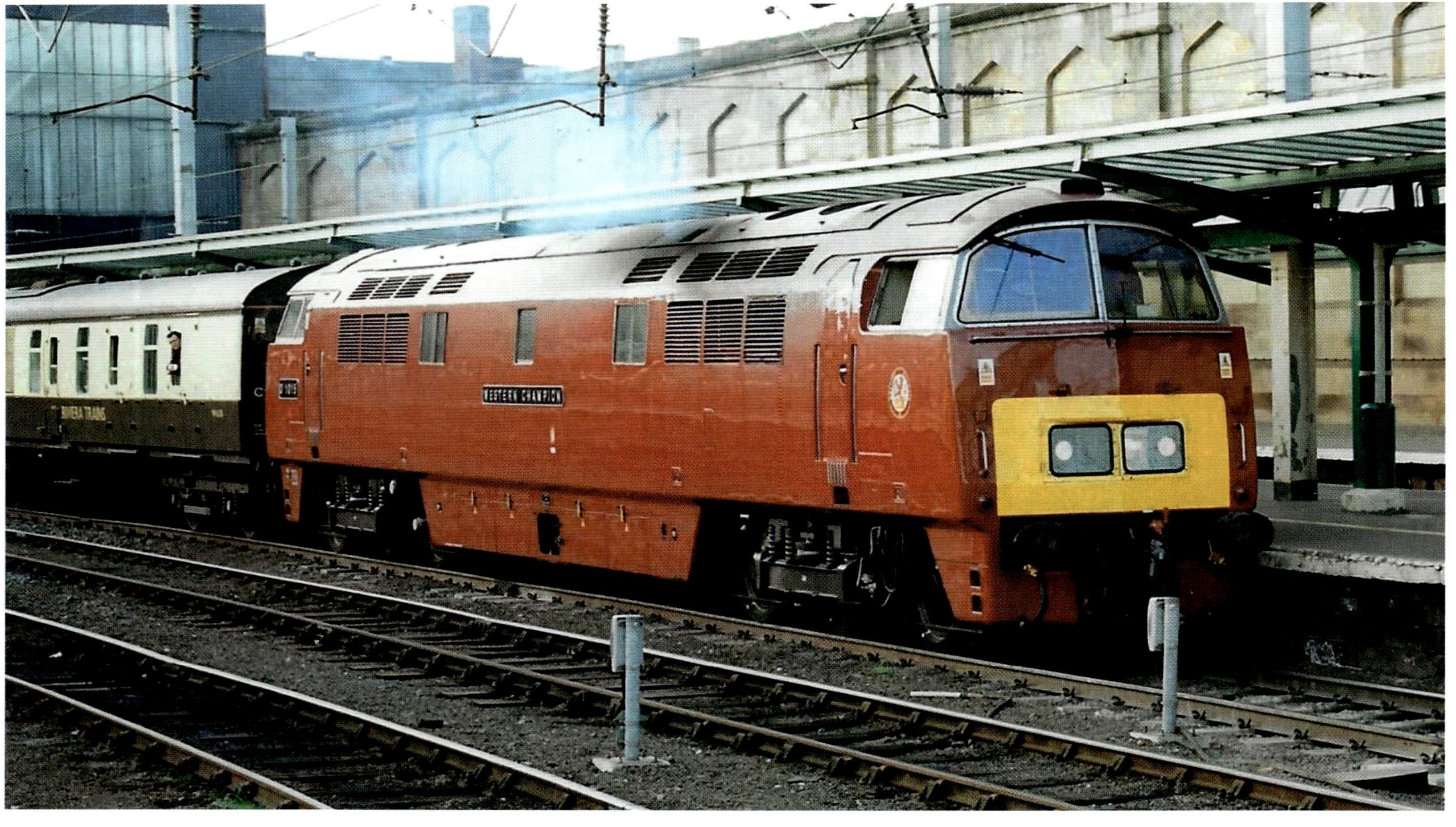

**On 3** May 2008, preserved Class 52 'Western' No. D1015 *Western Champion* waits at Carlisle with a special train. The locomotive is painted in the maroon livery applied to most members of the class, although when new D1015 was painted in an experimental golden ochre colour. Other members of the class were painted 'desert sand (D1000)' or green (D1035-D1038). They were repainted into the 'rail blue' corporate livery after 1966. *Robert Carrington – Author's Collection*

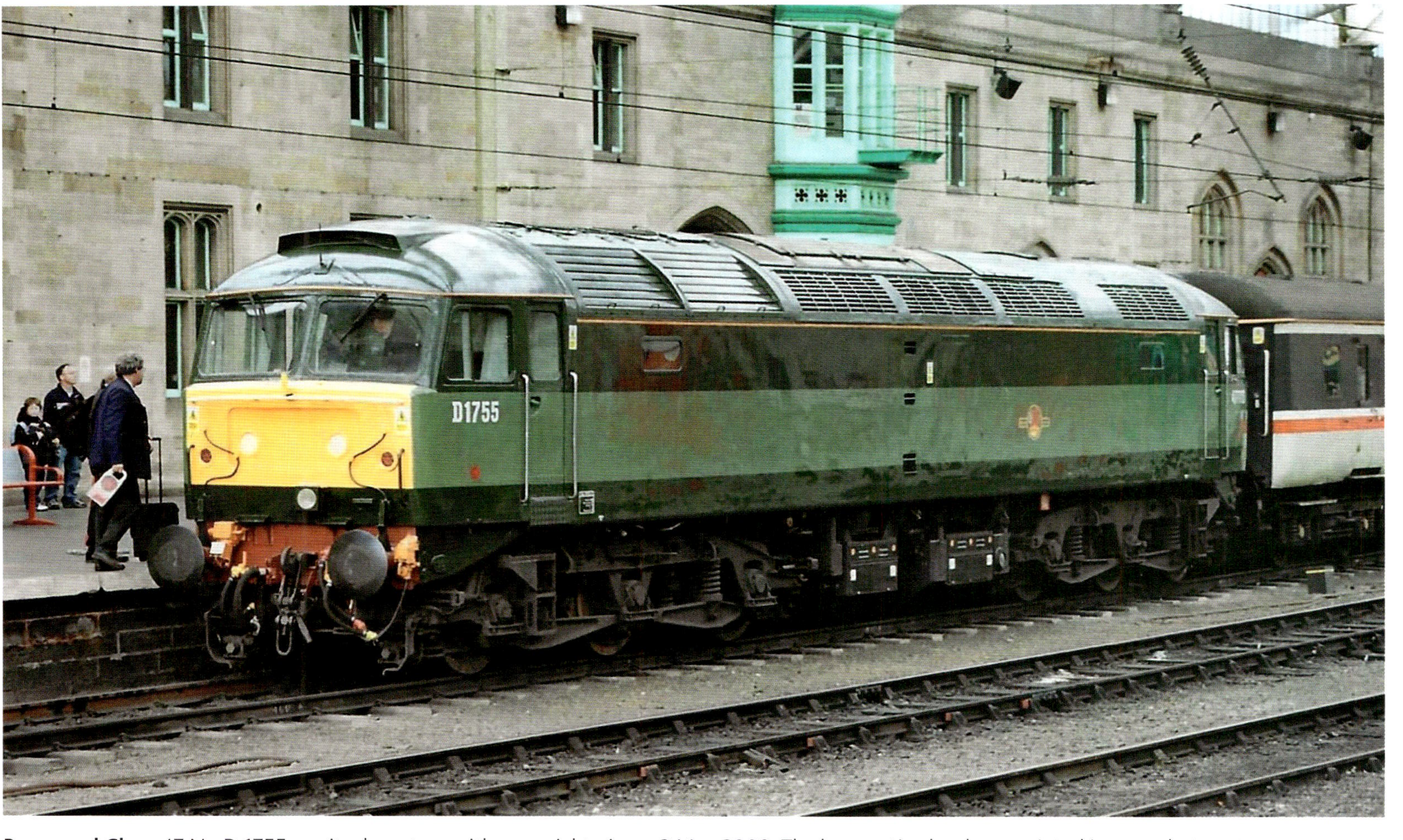

**Preserved Class** 47 No D.1755 awaits departure with a special train on 3 May 2008. The locomotive has been painted in an early two-tone green livery with British Railways' second crest, which was often referred to as the 'ferret and dartboard' due to the use of a lion holding a locomotive wheel in the centre of the crest. *Robert Carrington – Author's Collection*

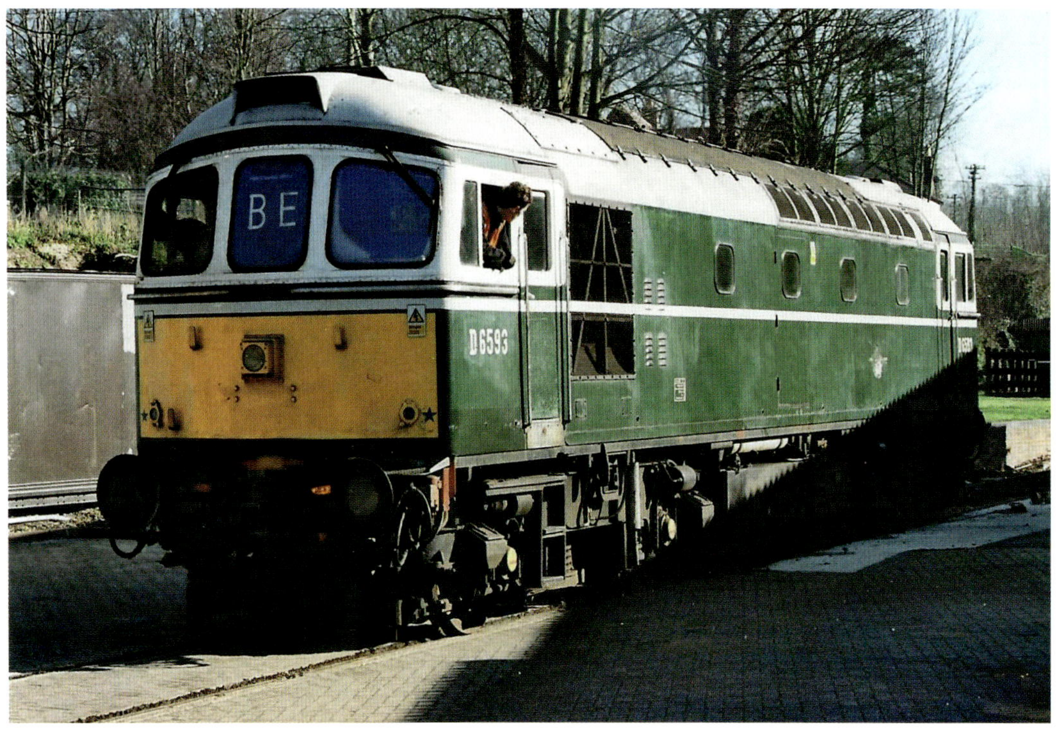

**Preserved Class** 33 No. D6593 (33308) at Alresford on its Mid-Hants Railway home. 13 February 2008. *Robert Carrington – Author's Collection*

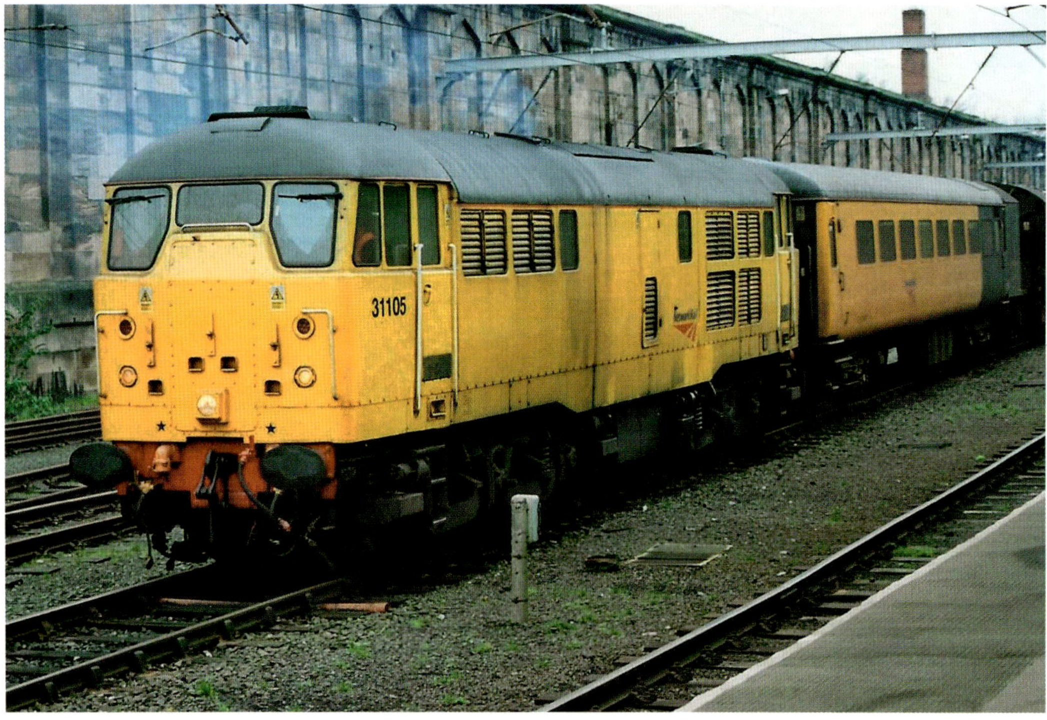

**Class 31** No. 31105 on Network Rail's structure gauging train at Carlisle Citadel, 23 February 2008. *Robert Carrington – Author's Collection*

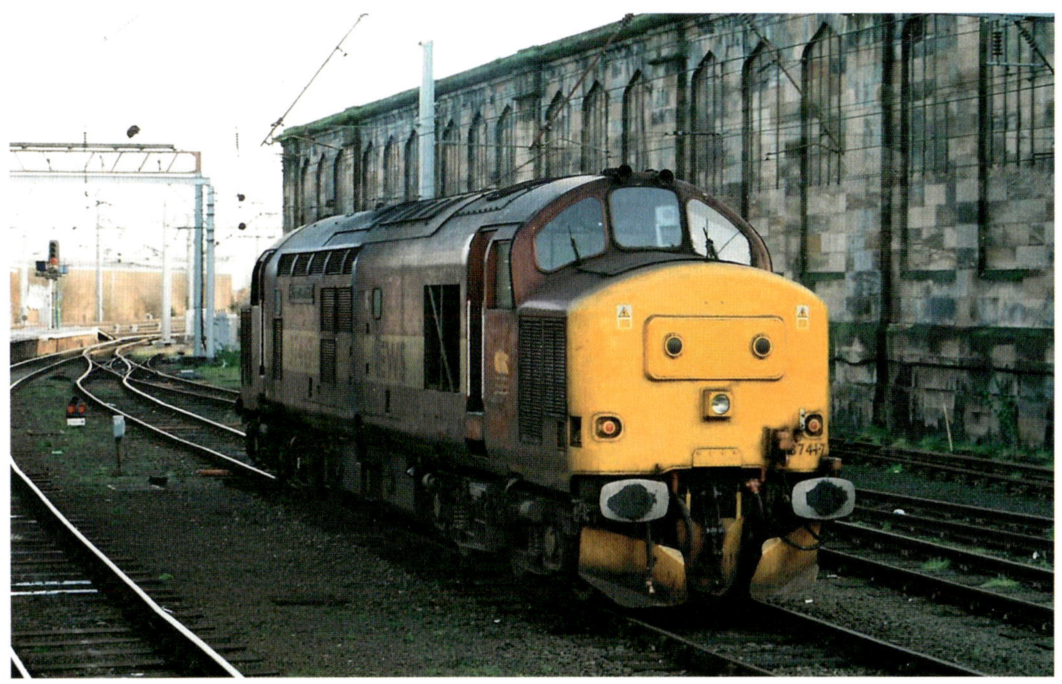

**Class 37** No. 37417 *Richard Trevithick* at Carlisle Citadel on 8 March 2008. The locomotive was named after Trevithick at Methyr Tydfil station on 21 February 2003 to celebrate the 200th anniversary of the Penydarren locomotive. *Robert Carrington – Author's Collection*

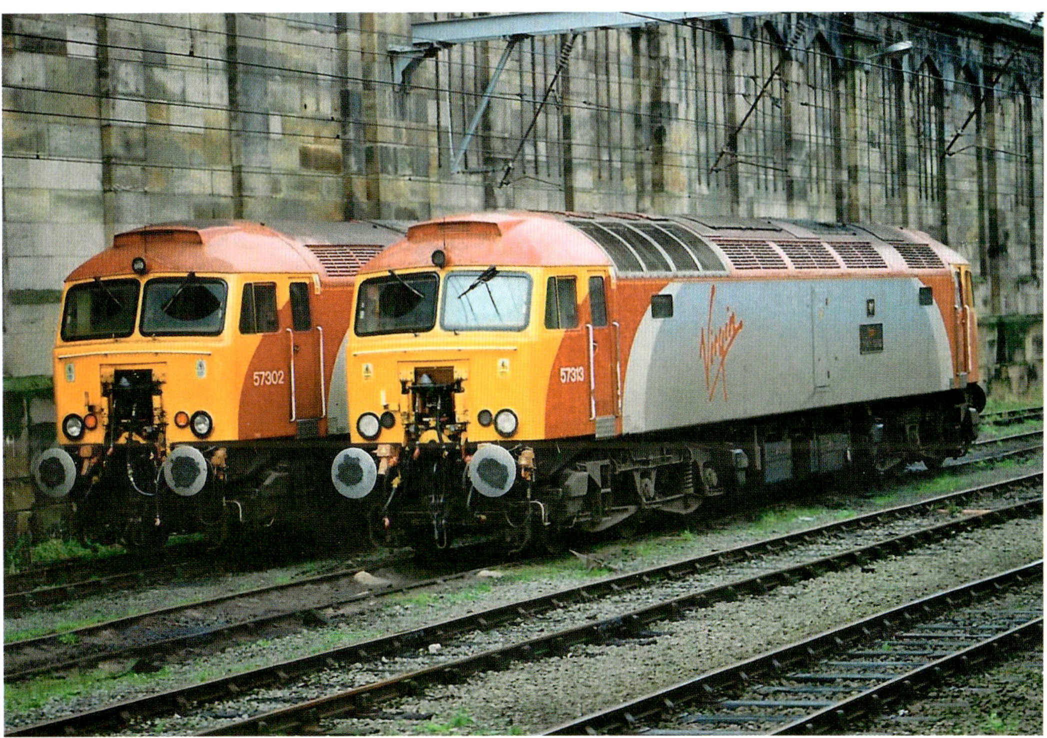

**A pair** of Class 57s at Carlisle Citadel. Nearest the camera is No. 57313 *Parker* whilst behind it is No. 57302 *Virgil Tracy*. 12 January 2008. *Robert Carrington – Author's Collection*

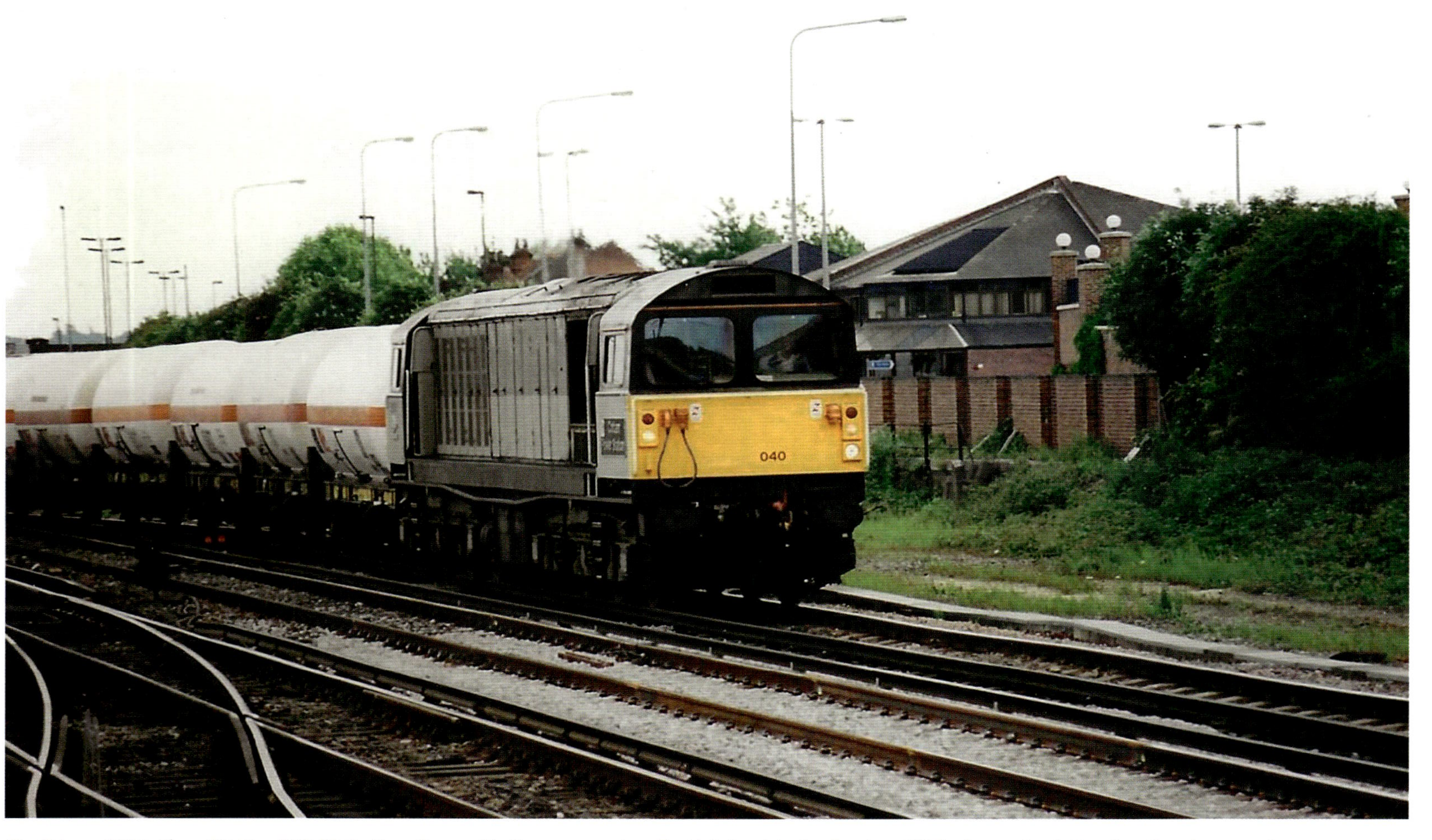

**On 9** June 1995 Class 58 No. 58040 *Cottam Power Station* approaches Eastleigh with the Fawley Oil Tanker train. Following the closure of many collieries in the 1980s, the class were less needed on Merry-Go-Round coal trains and were redeployed to where there was work for them. *Robert Carrington – Author's Collection*

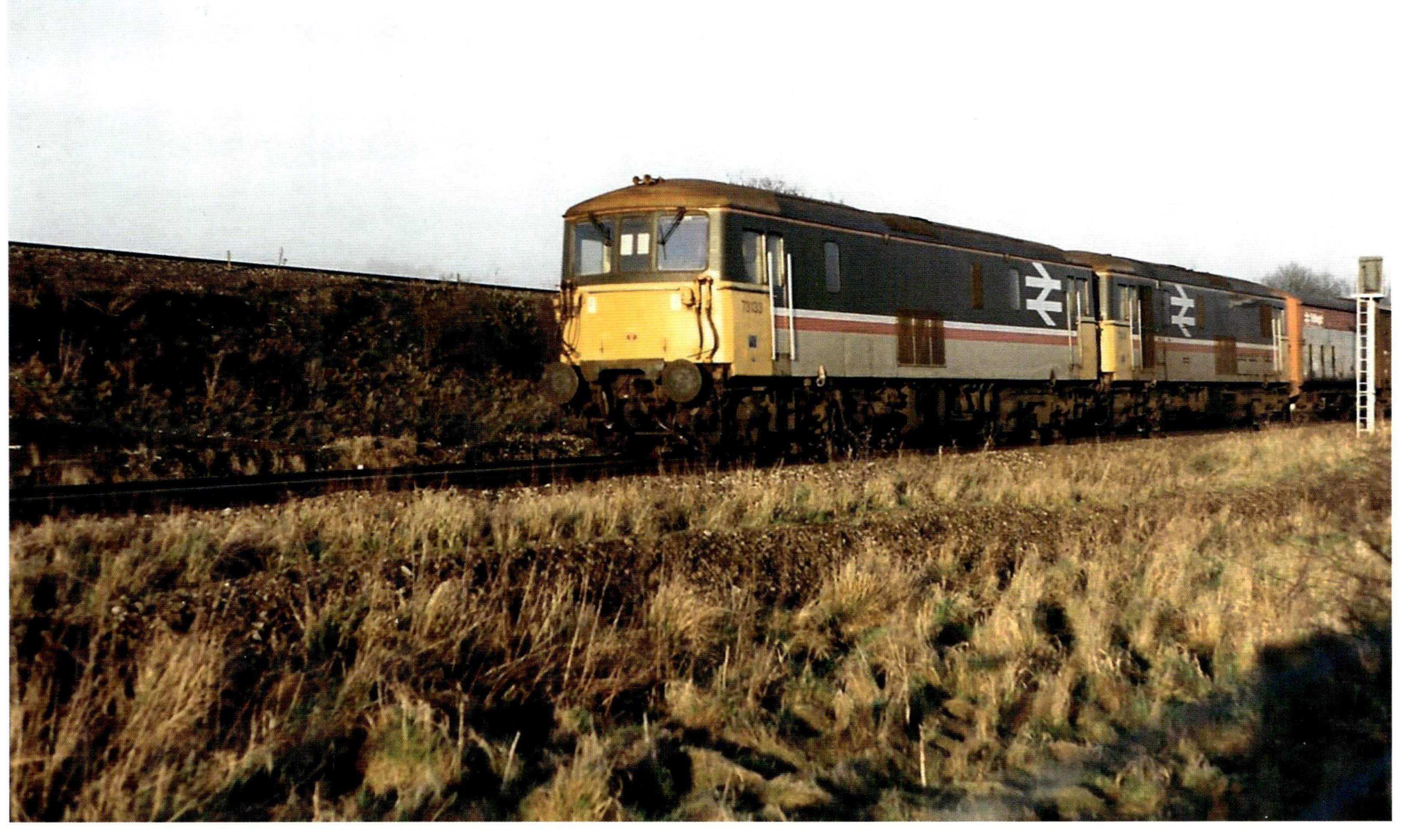

**A pair** of Class 73 Electro-Diesels Nos. 73133 and 73128 pass Worting Junction in the early evening of 17 January 1989. Both are wearing InterCity livery.
*Robert Carrington – Author's Collection*

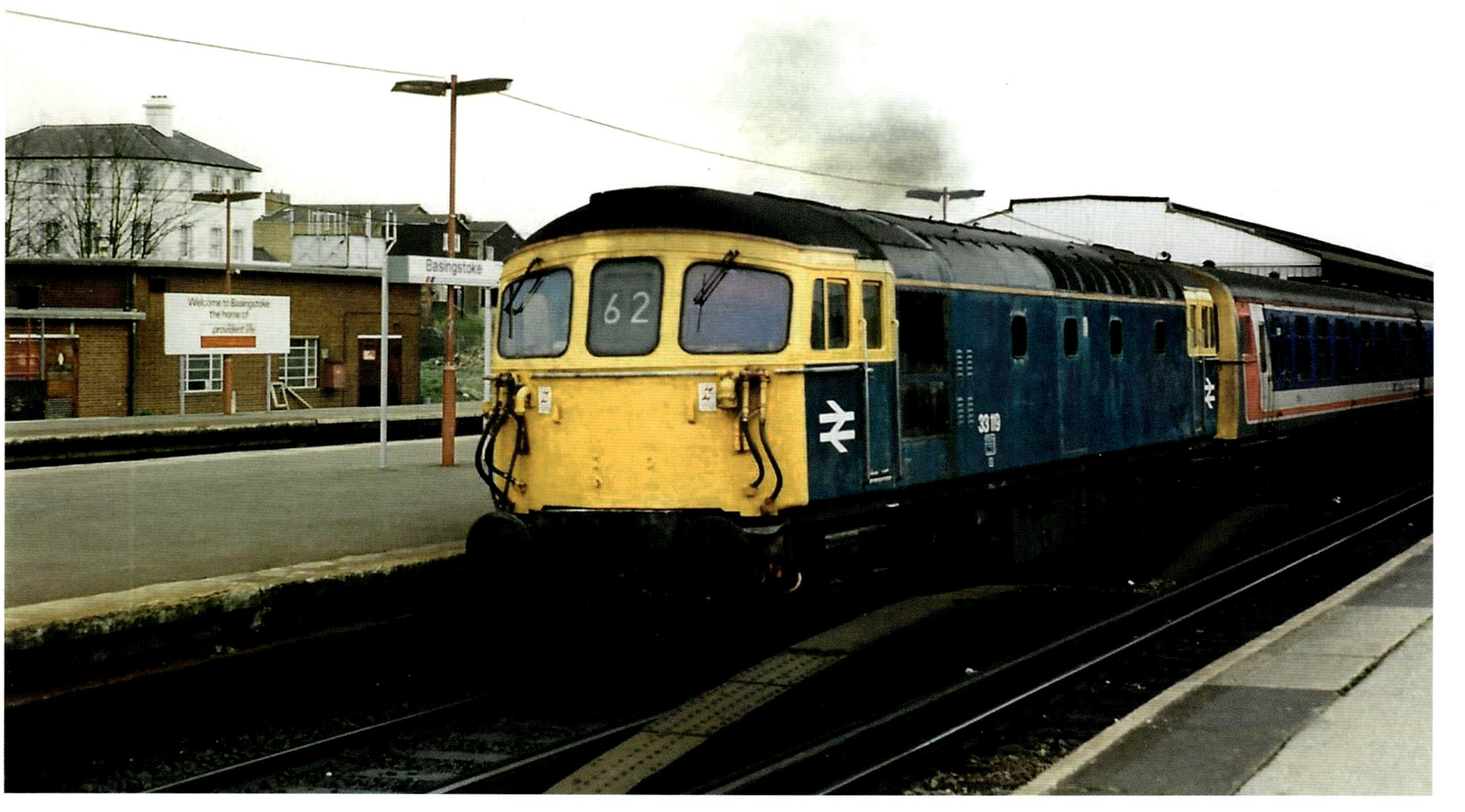

**Class 33/1** No. 33119 accelerates away from Basingstoke on 14 March 1989 with a 4TC in tow. The 4TCs were unpowered coaching stock in set formations with an EMU style driving cab at each end. Often coupled to a 4REP EMU to make up a full train they would either be propelled by the 4REP or, as in this case, hauled by a Class 33/1. The class 33/1 can be identified by the jumper cables on the cab ends for connecting the locomotive to the push-pull driving system in the 4TC unit. *Robert Carrington – Author's Collection*

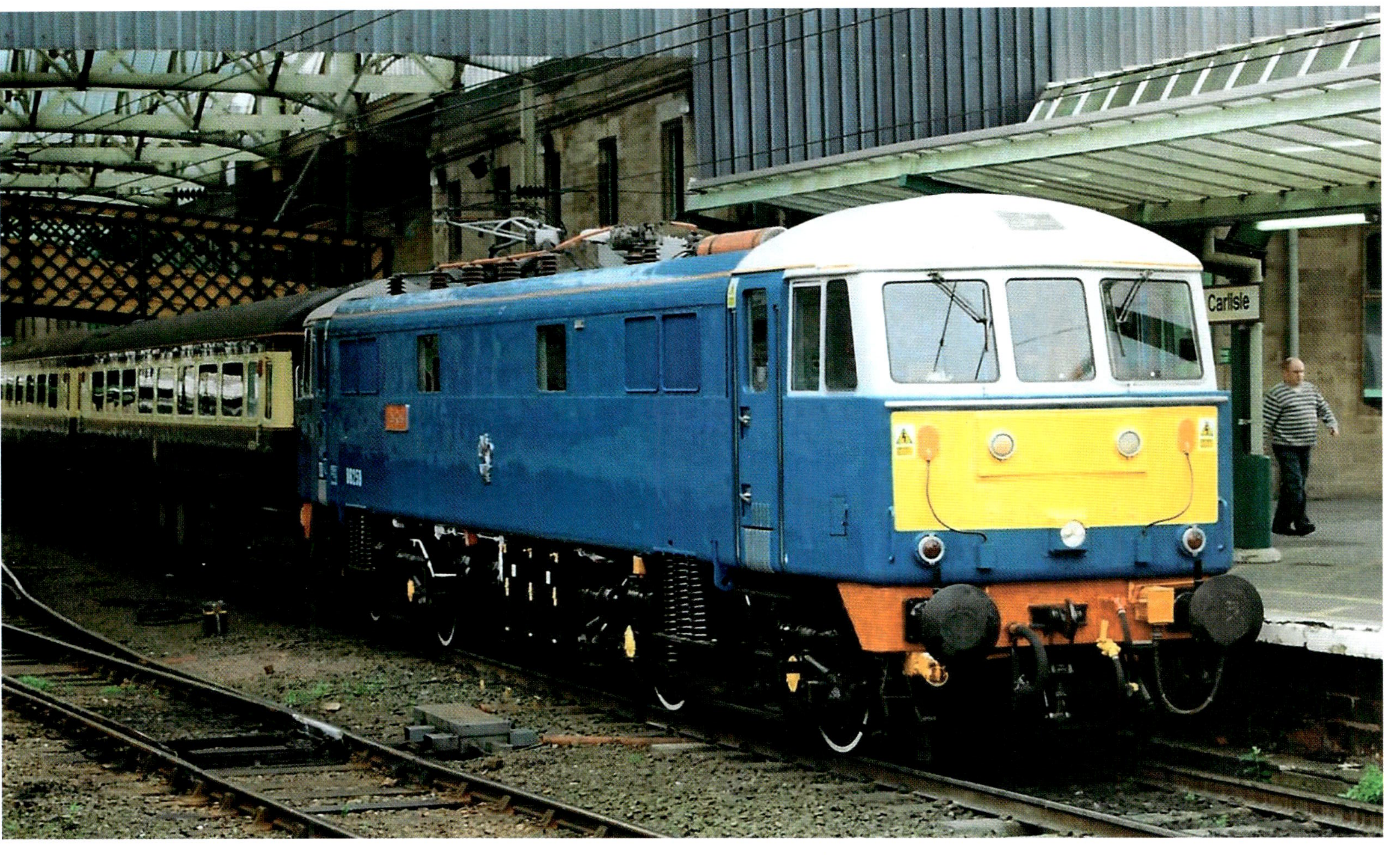


**Class 86** No. 86259 *Les Ross* at Carlisle Citadel on 3 May 2008. The preserved locomotive had been repainted into its original livery although it carried its post TOPS number instead of the original number E3137. *Robert Carrington – Author's Collection*

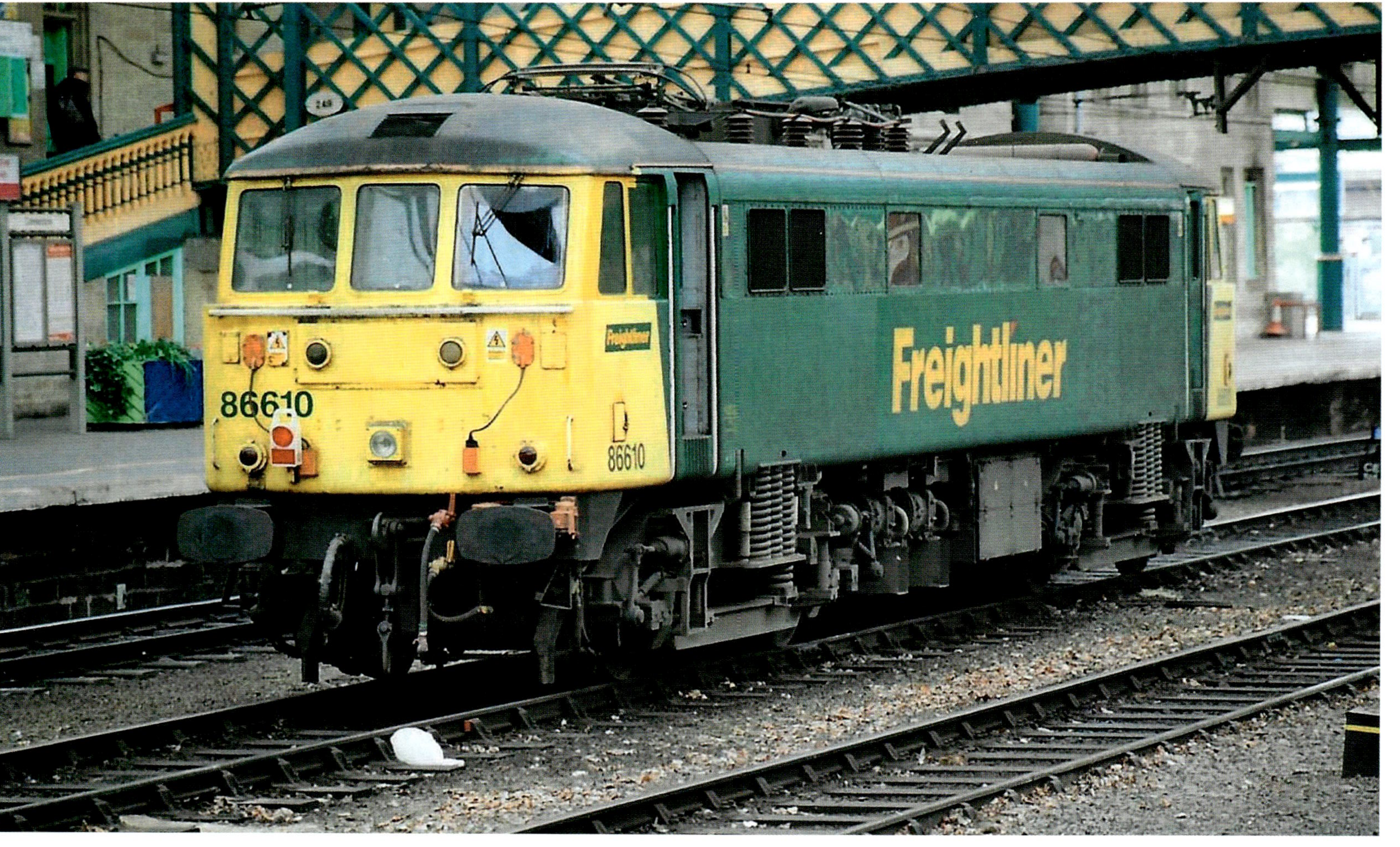

**Class 86** No. 86610 awaiting its next turn on 10 May 2008. The locomotive was kept in traffic for working Freightliner services, often double headed with a sister locomotive. It was one of six owned by Freightliner. *Robert Carrington – Author's Collection*

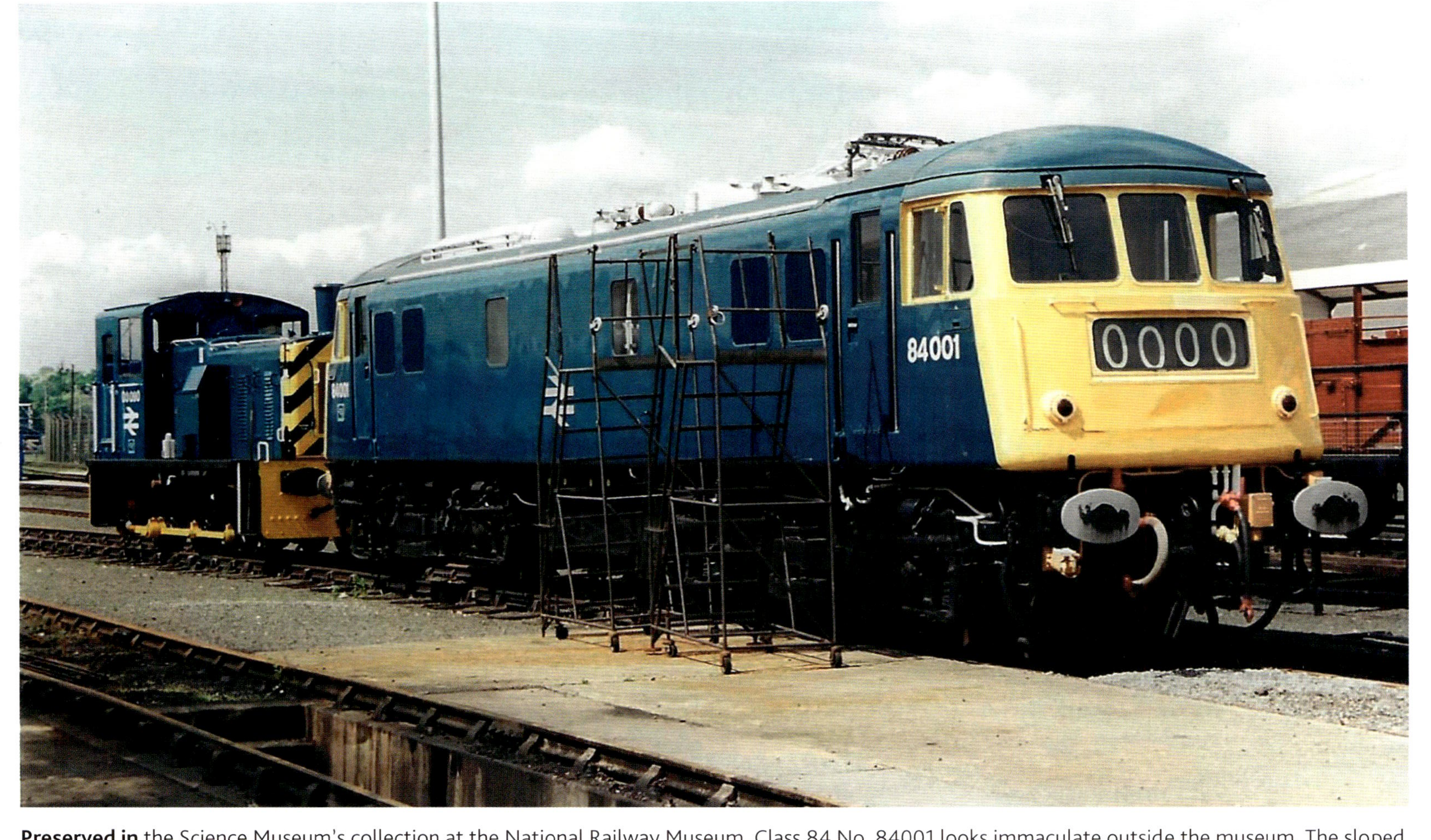

**Preserved in** the Science Museum's collection at the National Railway Museum, Class 84 No. 84001 looks immaculate outside the museum. The sloped front ends of the early west coast electrics are clear to see on this locomotive. The small engine behind is a class 03 No. 03090. The class can be found at a number of other preservation sites, proving ideal for the shunting needs of many heritage railways. *Robert Carrington – Author's Collection*

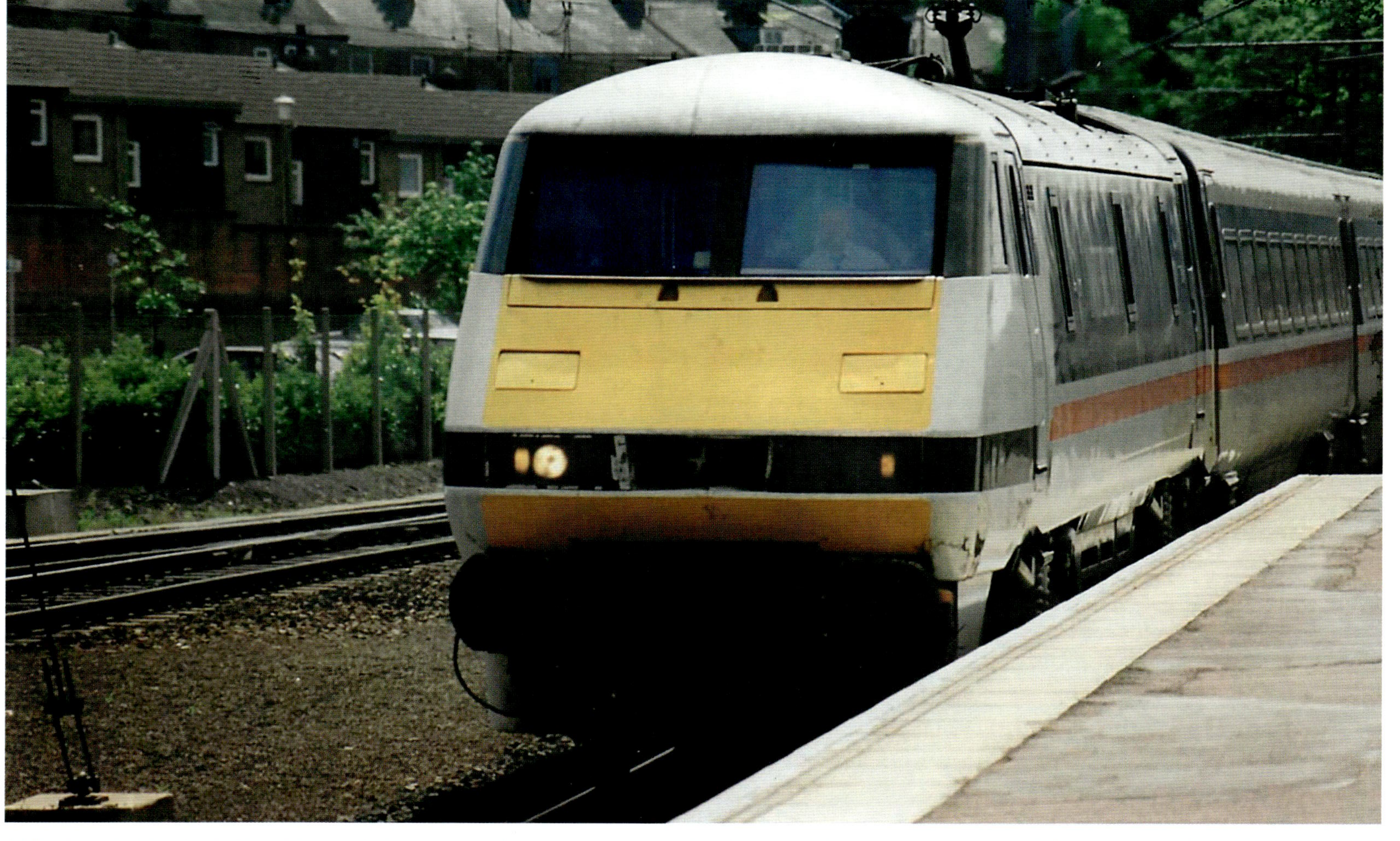

**At York** on 15 May 1995 Class 91 No. 91010 arrives at York on a working to Scotland. It is clear how the rear end of the locomotive has only a simple cab used for moving in yards, the locomotives usually coupled semi-permanently to the coaching stock. *Robert Carrington – Author's Collection*

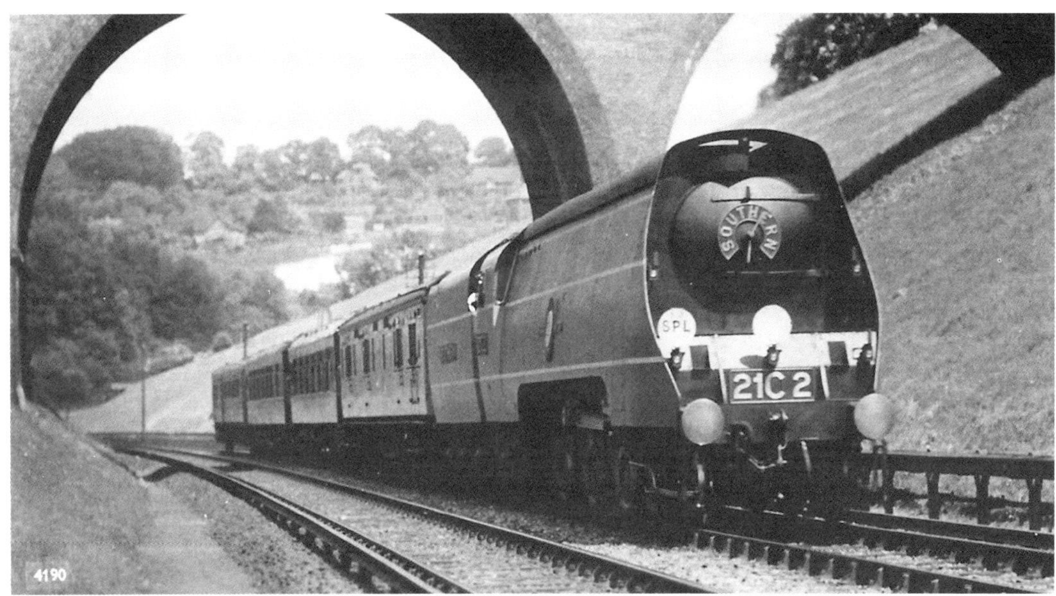

**Bullied 'Merchant Navy'** Class 4-6-2 21C 2 *Union Castle* in its original form. The casing was later changed to allow better airflow. The numbering is Bulleid's own notation based on French practice where the first three letters and numbers refer to the number of axles, '2' on the bogie, '1' on trailing pony truck, and 'C' for three driving axles. The last '2' is the number of the locomotive. *John Scott-Morgan Collection*

**Merchant Navy** No. 35024 *East Asiatic Company* showing the modified form the locomotives were eventually built with. The centre of the large name plate contains the company logo of the shipping line it was named after, as did all the class. *John Scott-Morgan Collection*

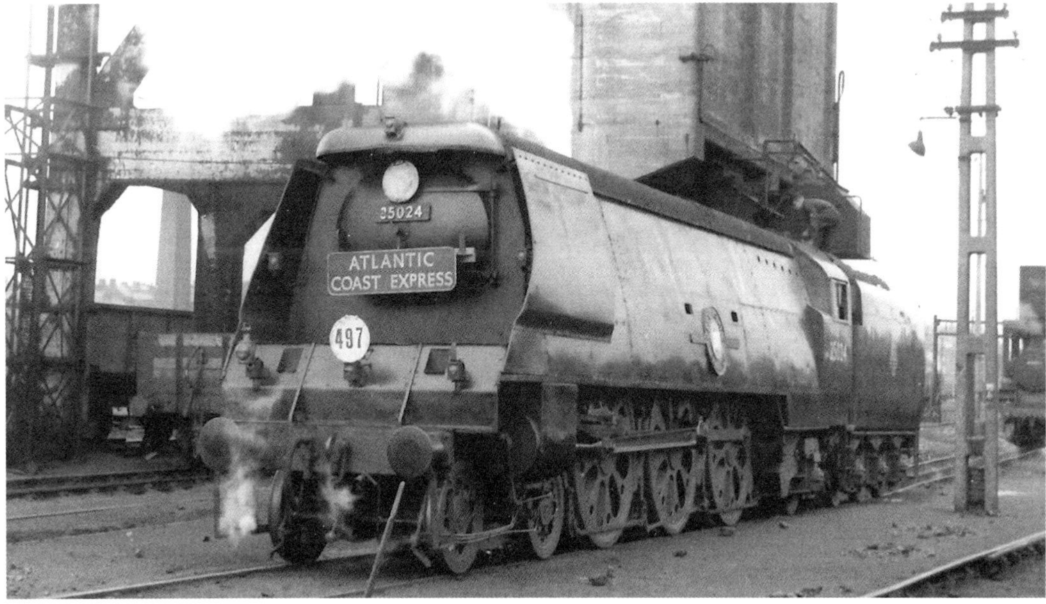

navy had a box shaped casing around the edge of the smokebox, with a slot at the top. The design trapped air and forced it through the slot lifting the smoke and steam away from the engine providing a clear view ahead for the crew. The machines were groundbreaking in other ways too.

The boiler and firebox were partly welded, where traditionally they were of rivetted construction throughout, while the firebox was provided with thermic siphons which were exposed directly to the latent heat of the firebox and naturally self-circulated the water inside, thus increasing the capability of the boiler to produce steam. Fireboxes were constructed with a steel inner firebox as opposed to the more common copper, making them easier to build. Another novel feature could be seen in the design of the wheels which were not spoked as was usual. Instead the wheels were of 'Bulleid Firth Brown' type, which consisted of a single disc with teardrop shaped indentations to give it strength. Wheels of this type distribute weight more effectively and hold the steel tyre which is shrink fitted to the wheel better.

The engines were not only advanced mechanically, thought had also being given to the crew. The cabs were provided with electric lights powered by a steam generator located under the footplate which made working at night easier. External electric lights were placed where the usual route indicator lamps were located on night trains, reducing the workload on the crew when setting the locomotive up for a train working. The fireman was provided with a steam powered treadle which opened the firebox doors when required making stoking the fire easier and saving heat as the doors did not need to be kept open while firing. The cab was completely enclosed by a backplate in the tender which was joined to the cab by a flexible canvas cover, and all the instruments and controls were laid out in groups making it simpler, less tiring and safer to operate the locomotive.

The class were all named after British shipping lines, something that was planned from the outset, hence the name Merchant Navies. The first to arrive in service was named *Channel Packet*, followed by a further twenty-nine locomotives, the final of which, *Elder Dempster Lines*, was built by British Railways in 1949. The Merchant Navies had a relatively high axle loading which prevented them from being used everywhere on the SR network. Something a little lighter was needed.

Bulleid designed a smaller 'light pacific' to the same principles, to fill the gap. The engines looked almost identical to their larger sisters and were mechanically the same. The first left the workshops in 1945, the last in 1951. In total 110 were built at Brighton (104) and Eastleigh (6). The class was split into two groups by virtue of the naming conventions used on them, although there was no difference between them mechanically. The first forty-eight were named after towns and cities in the south west of England and were known as the West Country class. The remainder of the locomotives were named after RAF squadrons, aircraft, airfields and commanders

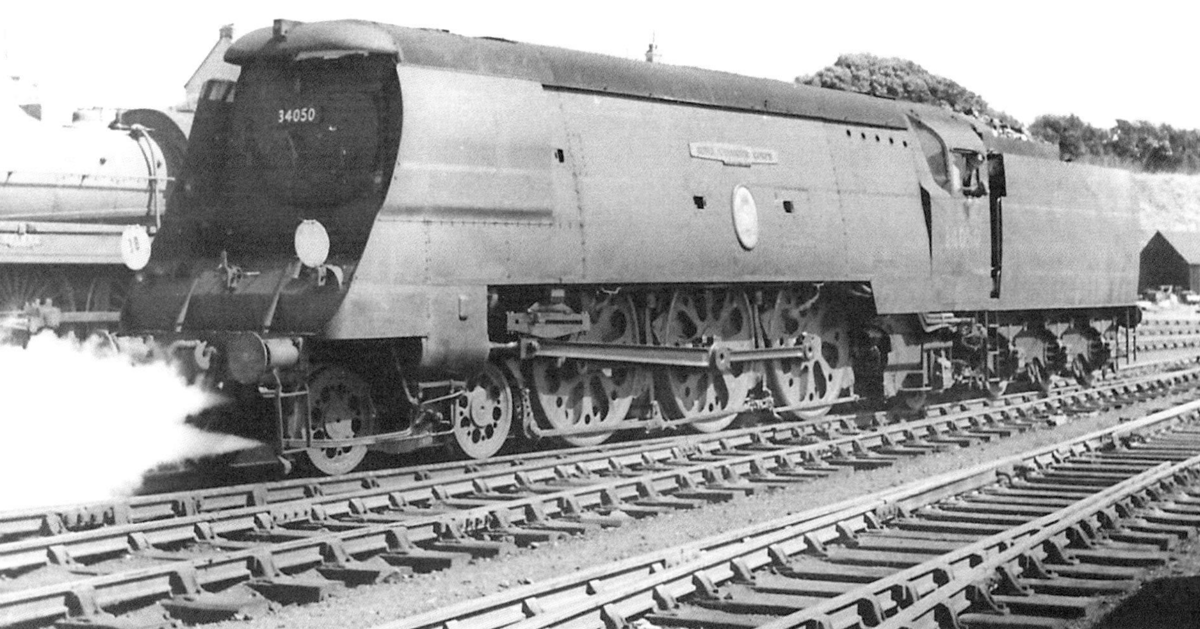

**Battle of Britain** class 4-6-2 No. 34050 *Royal Observer Corps* at Weymouth 19 July 1950.
The locomotive is named after the unit which tracked aircraft over Britain once they had passed
the coastal radar network which could only look outwards. *John Scott-Morgan Collection*

that were linked to the Battle of Britain and were therefore known as the Battle of
Britain class.

In service, the new locomotives were very capable although they had one major
fault. The oil bath became a source of constant trouble as it was often not sealed
properly or was damaged in depots and workshops making it prone to leaking.
Occasionally the oil would be thrown around and soak into the insulation between
the boiler and the casing, which sometimes caught fire. British Railways made the
decision to rebuild them, removing the casing and replacing the chain driven valve
gear with more a conventional system. All of the Merchant Navies were rebuilt, but
some of the West Country and Battle of Britains remained in their original form until
withdrawal by BR in the 1960s.

The new pacifics, with the GWR Kings and Castles, the SR Lord Nelsons and
the LMS Royal Scots were the ultimate expressions of British express passenger
locomotive design, but there was one more type which was built for one purpose.
The LNER needed something for its expresses in Scotland between Aberdeen and
Edinburgh. The route was challenging, with steep gradients and sharp curves
which the existing Scottish locomotives were struggling to cope with in an era of

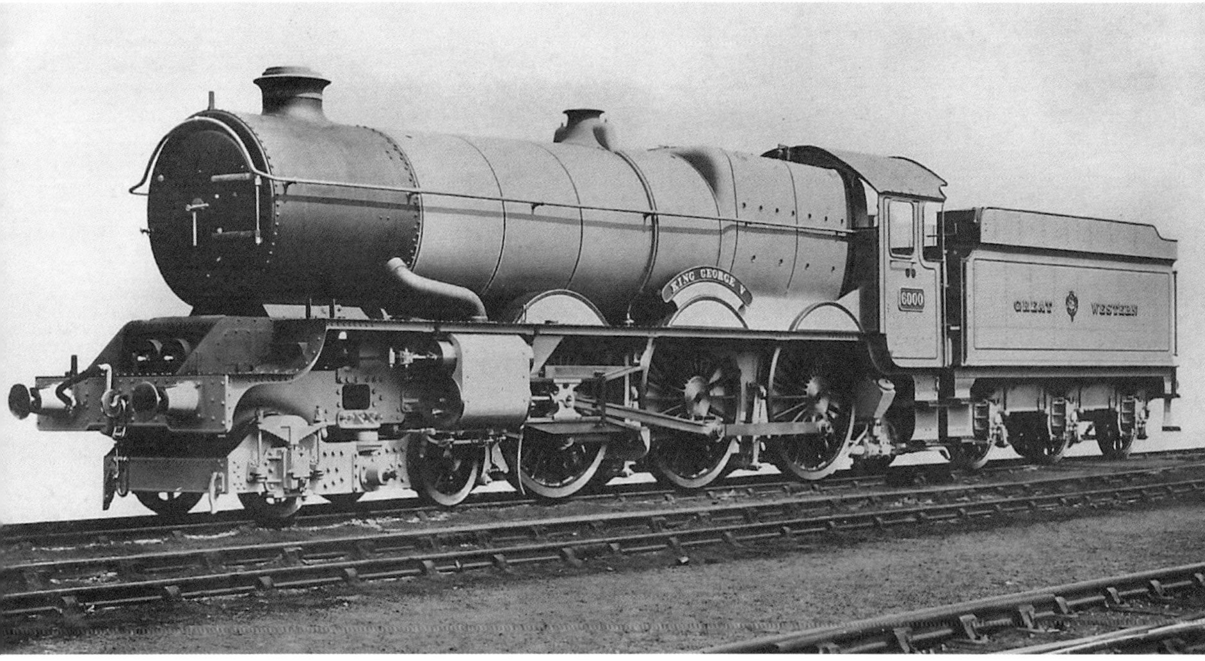


**The first** of Collet and Hawksworth's King class locomotives No.6000 *King George V* in works grey at Swindon. June 1927. Commercial Postcard, *John Scott-Morgan Collection*

increasingly heavy trains. Nigel Gresley designed a small class of engines to resolve the company's problem.

The 2-8-2 P2 class were introduced between 1934 and 1936, with just six examples constructed. The initial two locomotives were streamlined, although not with the A4 nose. The engines had an aerodynamic casing around a conventional smokebox door with a slot around the chimney to create an updraft to clear the soft exhaust caused by the double chimney and blastpipe arrangement. The first engine had rotary cam valve gear, which was unusual on British locomotive, whilst the second had one of the more usual forms of valve gear using the Walschaerts type. The third engine was built in the same form as the A4s and was found to be more effective at clearing the exhaust from the cab and the first two were rebuilt to the same form. The whole class were given names related to Scottish lore. All six of the class were rebuilt by Edward Thompson in 1943 and 1944. The rebuilds became Thompson's A2/2 class of 4-6-2s, although they had major issues including high fuel consumption and crank axle failures. The decision was controversial and sparked much debate which continues today.

The railways had a good selection of express passenger engines but the railways were mainly built to transport freight, for which dedicated types of locomotives were needed.

# Chapter 4

# HEAVY FREIGHT

Much as passenger services increased in load, the size of freight trains also increased during the late nineteenth and early twentieth century. The railway companies were well supplied with 0-6-0 goods engines of various sizes well suited to working goods trains on all sorts of routes, from light branch lines to main trunk routes. Despite this, larger and better freight engines became necessary to meet the operational requirements of the railways by the 1920s.

**Fowler 4F** 0-6-0 No.4547. ETH-Bibliothek Zürich, *Bildarchiv*.

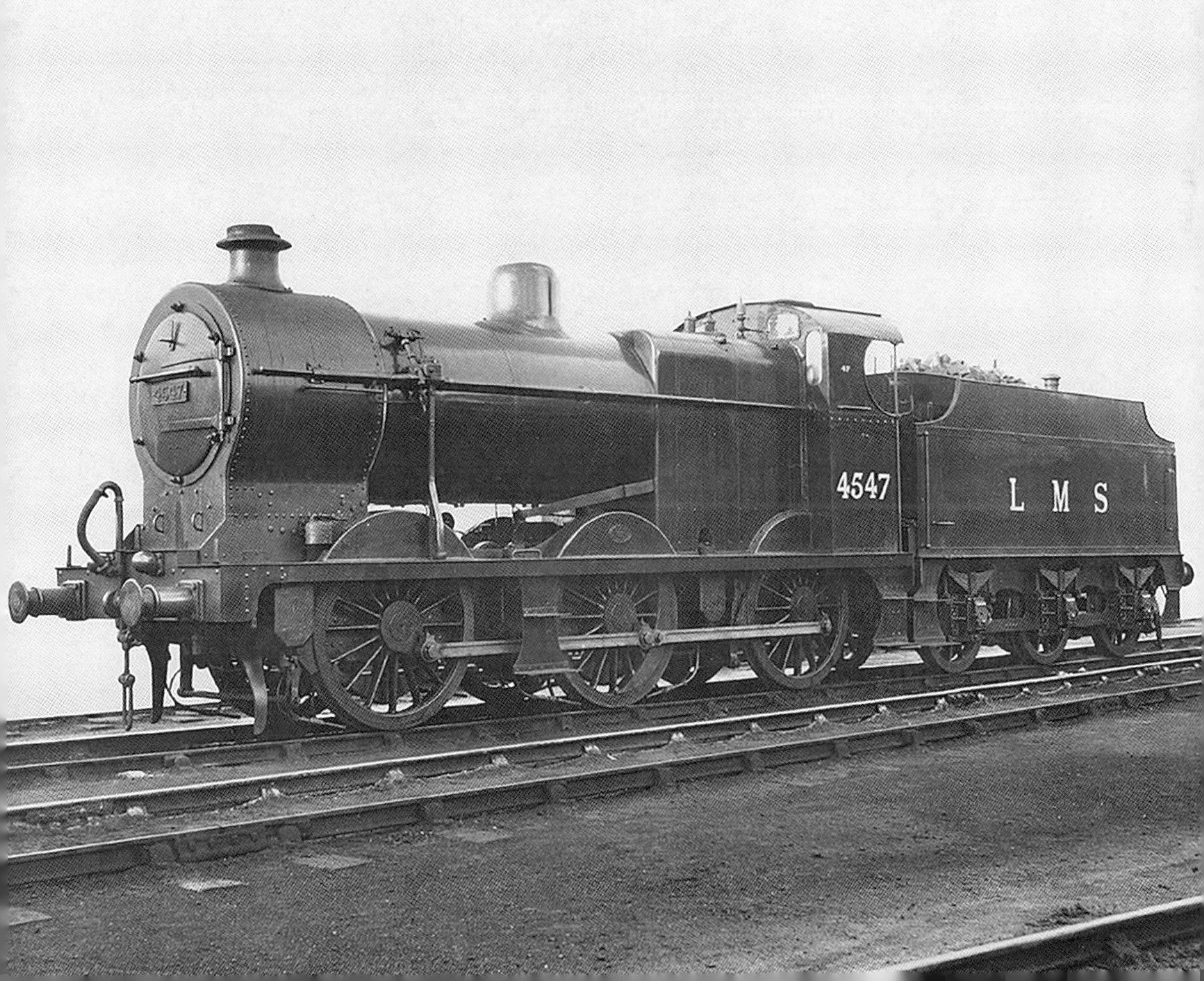

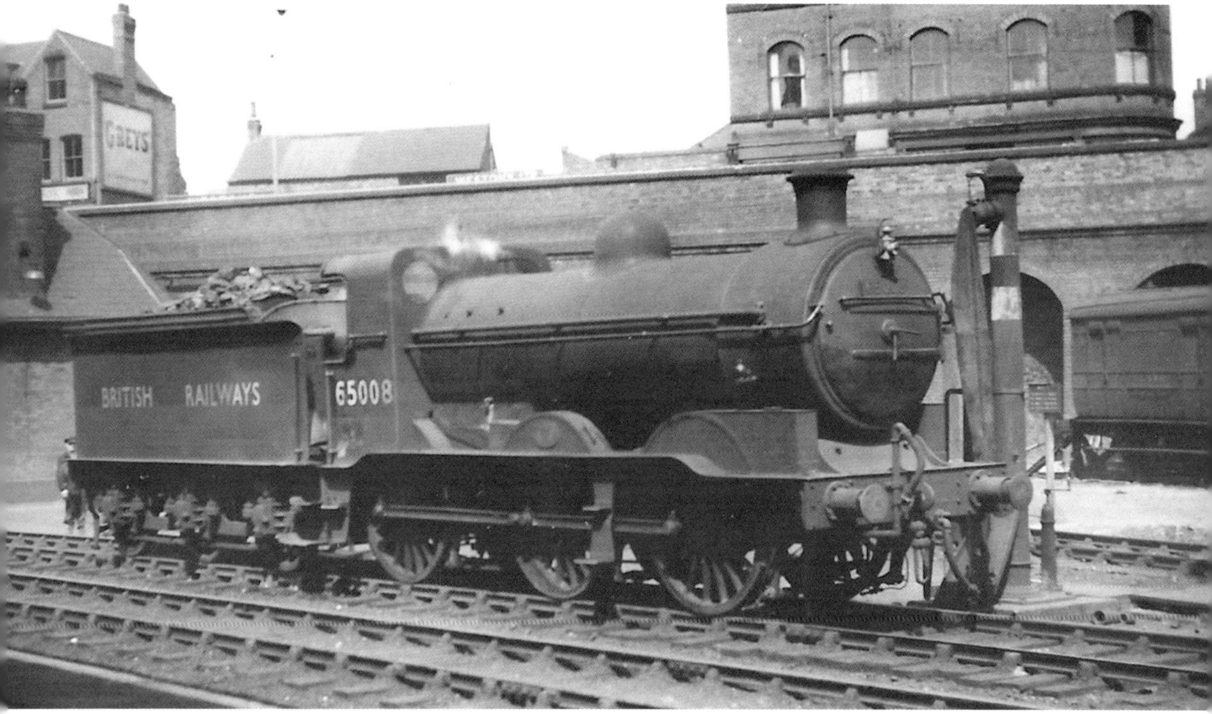

**Ex LNER** Gresley J2 0-6-0 No.65008 at Nottingham Victoria in 1949. *F. Gilford*

**Collett 2251** Class 0-6-0 No.2239 at Porthmadog, Gwynedd in 1962. *Alan Murray-Rust*

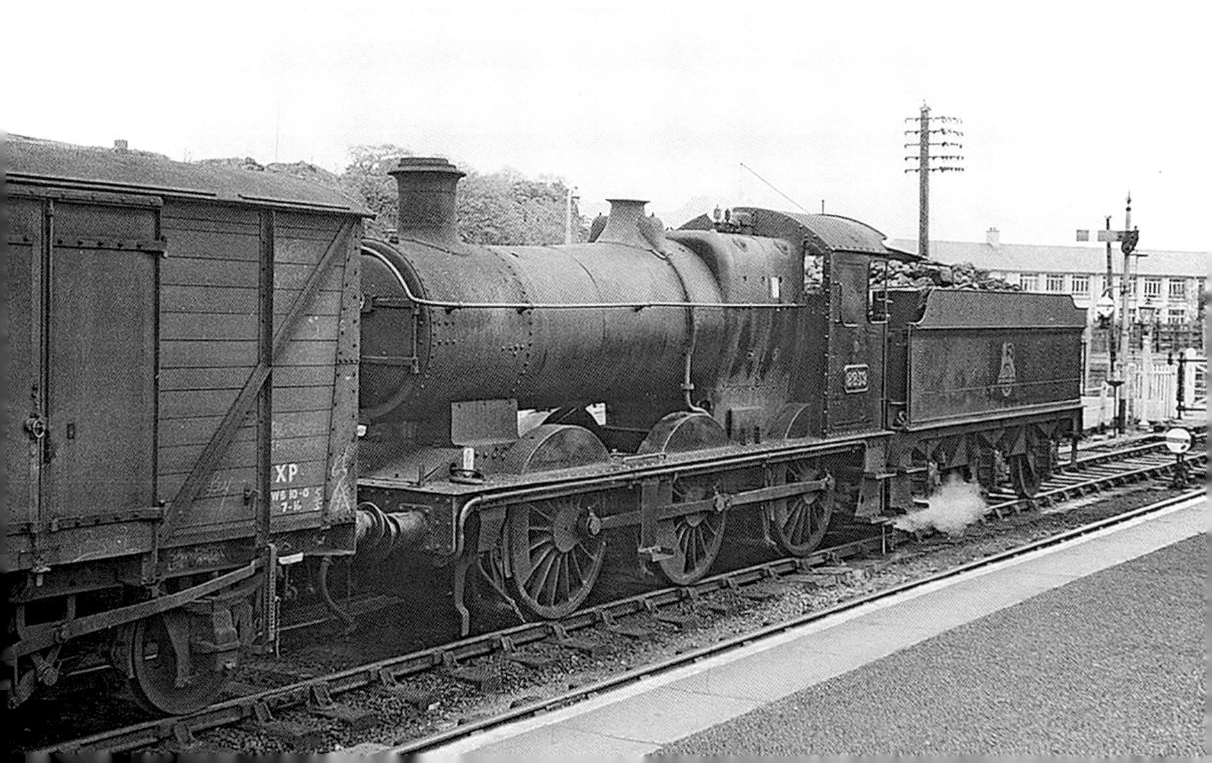

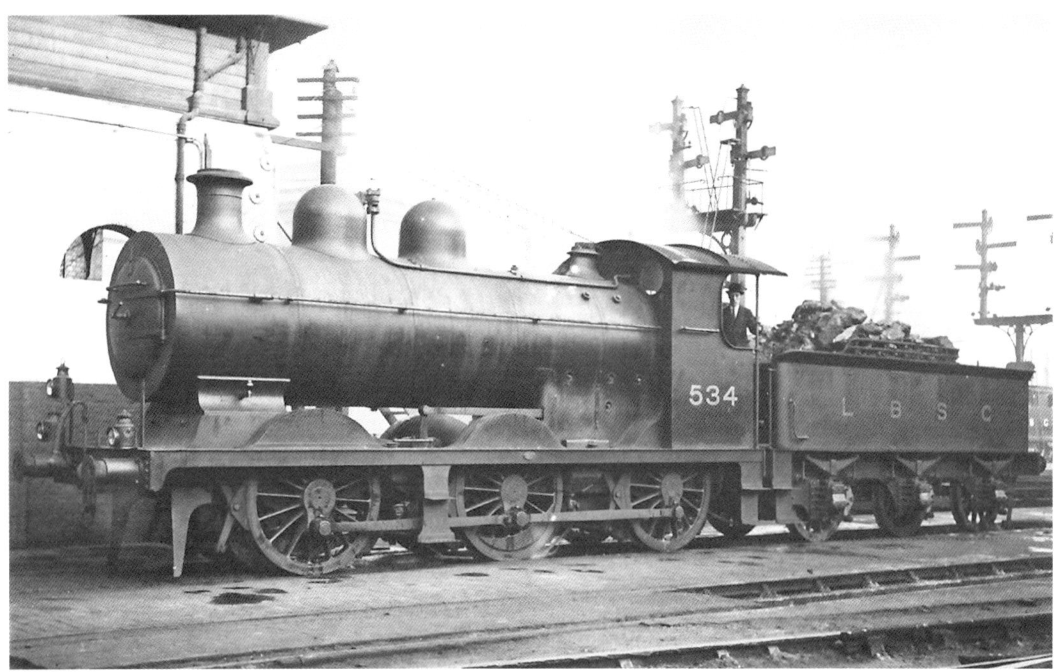

**LBSCR C2X** Class 0-6-0, No. 534. The C2Xs were a 1908 D.E. Marsh rebuild of Billington's C2 class of 1893. *John Scott-Morgan Collection*

The first, and probably most obvious, solution was to build bigger 0-6-0 freight engines, which most of the railway companies did. The Midland built new classes of more powerful mid-range engines with the best, Fowler's 4F Class, arriving in 1924, of which 575 were built. The LNER introduced Gresley's J39 class in 1926, of which 289 were built, whilst the GWR built 120 of Collett's 2251 class after 1930. The three new types modernised these railway's freight fleets, were the ultimate 0-6-0 type and the last of them designed. Things were being done a little differently in the south, though.

The Southern Railway was well supplied with a fleet of capable, although aging, freight locomotives by the three companies which it absorbed. The needs of the company were a little different from the rest of the Big Four. The railway had more of a need for faster freight services, since much of its traffic was perishables from the agricultural areas and fish, although slow heavy freight was still very much present. Richard Maunsell had a different idea to his colleagues at Derby, Doncaster and Swindon, believing that the needs of the Southern would be best met by the existing 0-6-0s of the 700, C2X and O1 classes, with additional 4-6-0 freight engines for the faster and heavier trains.

Maunsell decided to continue construction of an existing design which had been introduced to the LSWR by Robert Urie in 1920. The excellent S15 freight locomotive was a solid and capable engine, which could handle heavy and fast freight trains with equal ease. They were also used on summer holiday passenger trains on which they proved equally adept. The LSWR had already built twenty of the engines by 1921, Maunsell then added another fifteen to a modified design in 1927, with ten more to follow in 1936. The engines were typically paired with one of Urie's eight wheel 'watercart' tenders which allowed them longer range on the Southern.

The SR was finding that some of its more elderly freight engines were starting to need replacement by the late 1930s, so Maunsell designed a new large 0-6-0 for the railway, the Q class. All of the class of twenty were built at Eastleigh works, the first entering service in 1938, with the last arriving the following year. These new engines would serve the Southern well and met all of their needs, almost. One more 0-6-0 would be built for the Southern, a wartime design by Oliver Bullied.

The need for a more powerful locomotive to handle the increasingly heavy freight traffic on the SR during the war was to be met by a new design. Wartime restrictions on the use of 'strategic materials' such as steel caused the design office to look toward removing any unnecessary fittings and features common on traditional designs. Bulleid's design team was also under pressure to create something which could be built quickly with high route availability. The team adopted many new features and weight saving ideas for the design which enabled it to both save material and be used on a large amount of the SR's network. The result was the large Q1 class 0-6-0.

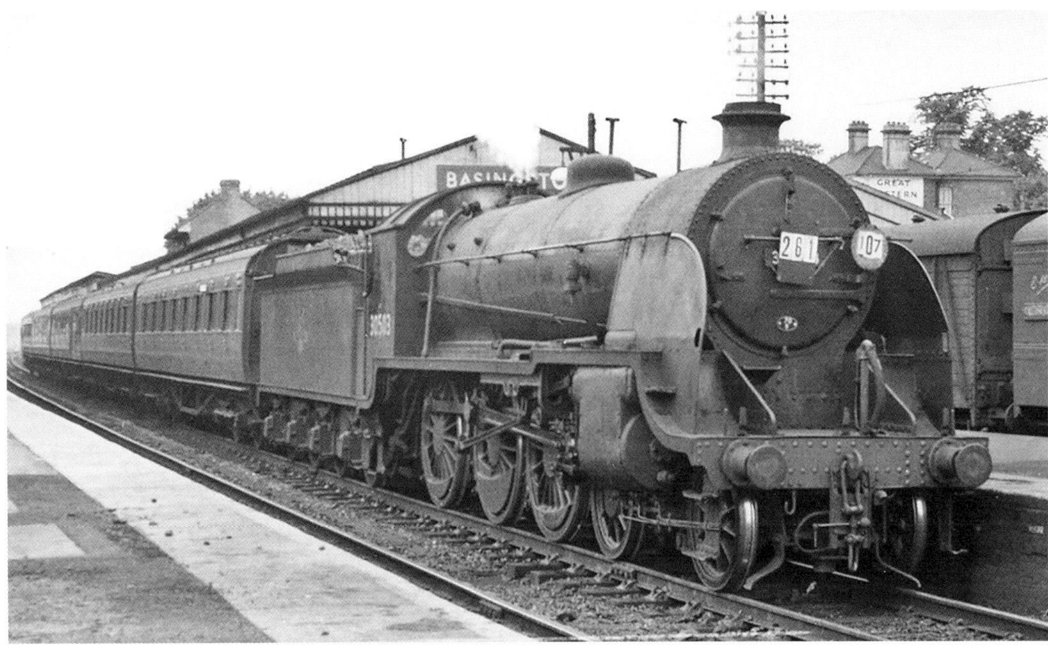

**Slow train** to Waterloo at Basingstoke. Ex-LSW Urie S15 class 4-6-0 No. 30503 is about to leave on the 12.12 all-stations to Waterloo. *Ben Brooksbank*

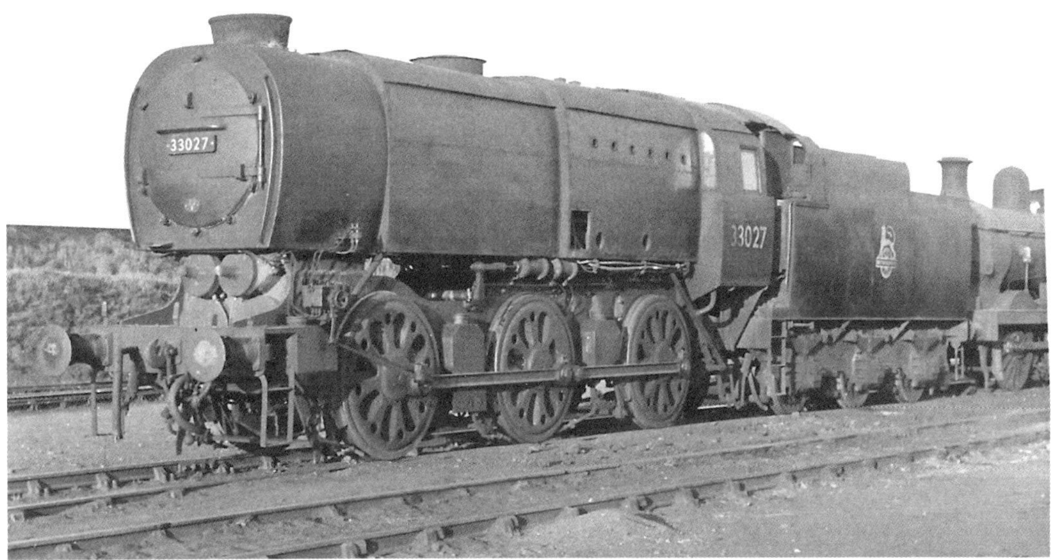

**Bulleid Q1** 0-6-0 No. 33027. *John Scott-Morgan Collection*

The Q1 was probably the ultimate expression of the British 0-6-0 freight locomotive but looked very different to anything that had come before. Every superfluous feature to be found on earlier engines had been removed from the design which gave it an angular look. There were no running plates above the wheels and the boiler casing was a square. The result was a design which divided opinion, particularly around its aesthetics. Despite its looks, the ugly duckling Q1, the most powerful 0-6-0 ever built for Britain's railways was an unreserved success. The forty members of the class were all built in 1942, twenty at Brighton and the remainder at Ashford works.

The other three companies had been finding that their fleets of conventional freight locomotives, whilst fine for most uses, were beginning to struggle with the increasingly heavy mineral trains as the demand for coal and ore increased. As the nineteenth century came to an end, the locomotive works were being asked for something more capable, and the workshops responded by creating larger freight engines with eight coupled driving wheels.

The first large freight engine design appeared in 1893 on the LNWR, the Class A (111 locomotives) designed by Francis Webb, entered service in 1893. The locomotives were 3-cylinder compound designs, which were followed in 1901 by a 4-cylinder compound, the class B (170). Like many of Webb's other designs these were later rebuilt into a more conventional form. The LNWR built a large selection

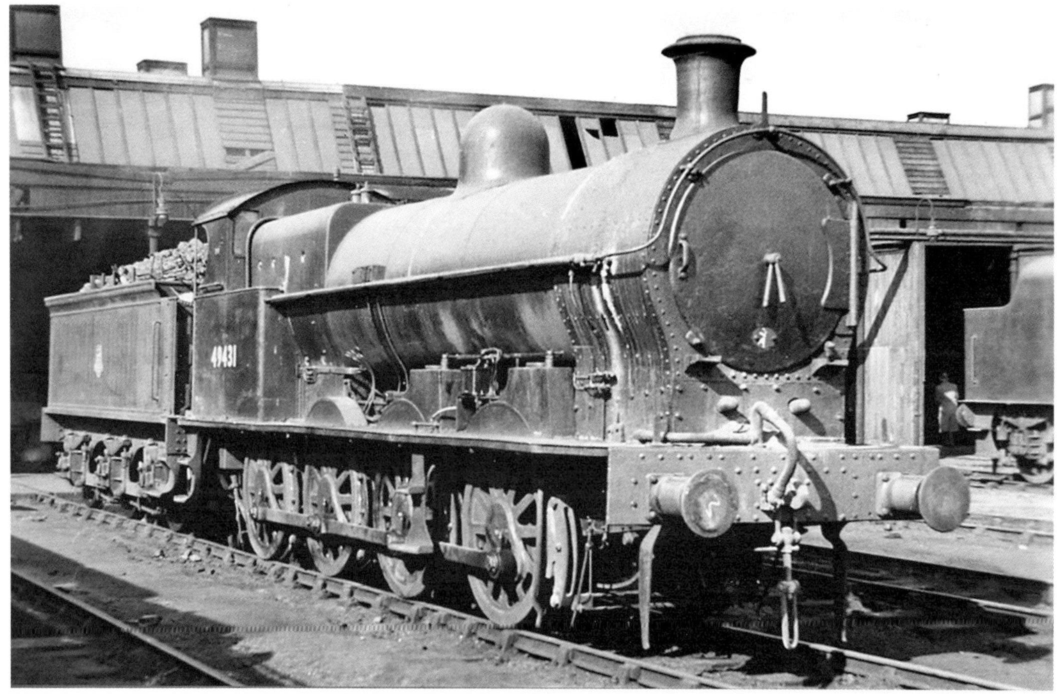

**Ex-LNWR G2** No. 49431 outside the locomotive depot at Rugby, 15 March 1953. *Ben Brooksbank*

of further classes of 0-8-0 freight engines for coal and other heavy freight traffic until the Grouping. The last of the designs were the G2 class created by Hewett Beames in 1921.

Around the turn of the century the GCR and NER were encountering the same need for heavy freight engines. Their response was to adopt the 0-8-0 wheel arrangement. The GCR introduced their class 8A (89) in 1902 for heavy coal trains over the Pennines. In the North-East the NER created three types of eight-coupled heavy freight locomotives, Worsdell's classes T and T1 of 1901 (90), and Raven's T2 of 1913 (120). The L&YR also had a need for engines for coal trains and built ninety-nine of them across three classes. The LMS built the final class of 0-8-0 designed in Britain, the Fowler 7F (175), constructed at Crewe between 1929 and 1932. The engines were not a great success.

The GWR never built any of the type instead opting for a 2-8-0. The company introduced the first of Churchward's 2800 class in 1903. The 2800s were extremely capable locomotives which could be found over most of the GWR's main routes, Swindon building eighty-four. Charles Collett created an improved version, the 2884 class (83 built). The engines were very similar to their predecessors, the most notable differences were outside steam pipes from the smokebox to the cylinders and a large Collett standard cab.

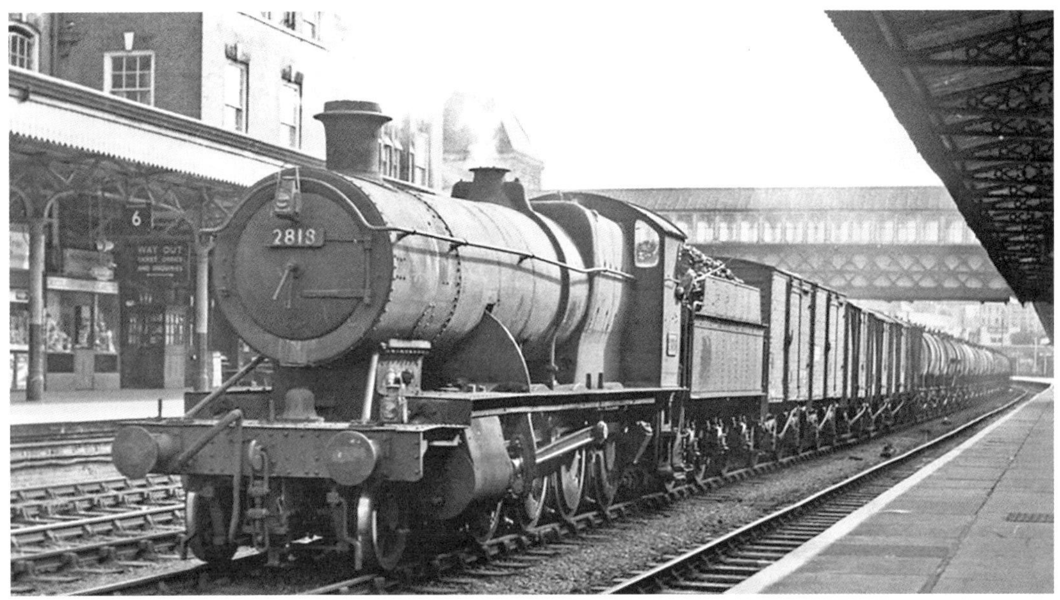

**Ex -WR** 2800 Class 2-8-0 2818 passing through Newport High Street station with a heavy freight train on 14 August 1963. *Ben Brooksbank*

**Ex-GCR 8K** Class (LNER and BR Class 04), No. 63833. The locomotive has the early BRITISH RAILWAYS text on the tender. Note the lack of vacuum brake pipes on the buffer beam which is due to the class only being used on unfitted trains. *John Scott-Morgan Collection*

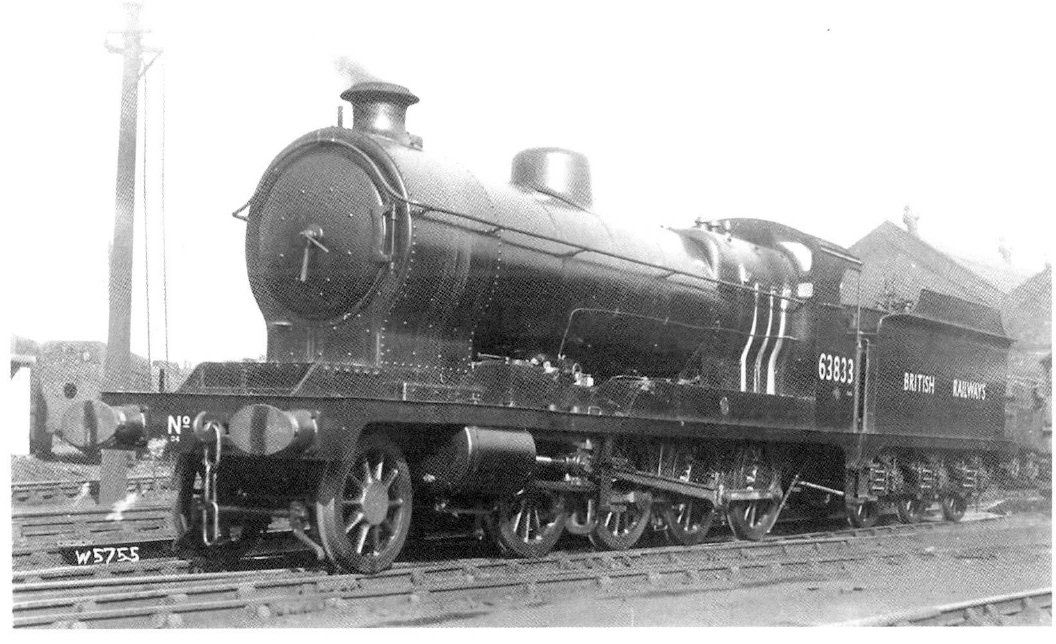

The 2-8-0 arrangement was proving popular and effective on Britain's railways by the second decade of the twentieth century. The GCR built 126 of Robinson's 8K class, the first of which entered service in 1911 with the GNR introducing Gresley's O1 class in 1913, to be followed by the O2s in 1918, all of which were inherited by the LNER in 1923. The Somerset and Dorset Joint Railway (S&DJR) received six of Fowler's 7F locomotives, which were designed specifically for freight traffic over the Mendip Hills, in 1914, with another five following in 1925. The railway was jointly owned by the MR and LSWR, with Derby providing many of the locomotives for the company.

The Robinson 8Ks were not limited to the GCR and could eventually be found on the GWR and LNWR and even as far away as Australia, China and the Middle East. At the outbreak of the First World War, the Railway Operating Division (ROD) of the Royal Engineers needed locomotives to run the railways in France and further afield. A number of locomotives were requisitioned from across Britain's railways but by the middle of the conflict the Royal Engineers had realised that they needed a standard locomotive that could meet all of their needs.

A single type would make training easier and avoid the huge range of spares needed to keep the vast array of types they were using in working order. The army settled upon Robinson's design and 521 were built. At the end of the conflict, Britain's railways were in dire need of repair, and to ease the burden nearly 500 were loaned from the ROD whilst the backlog in locomotive repairs was cleared. The engines were ultimately sold by the British government with the railways buying some, whilst the remainder were exported.

The LMS was particularly troubled during the early 1930s when it adopted the old Midland's small engine policy despite having the LNWR and L&YR's large 0-8-0s of which there simply were not enough to cover the heavy freight on the routes it had inherited from the MR. It was often necessary to double-head using a pair of 0-6-0s which was costly. The railway was still in this situation until William Stanier looked to resolve the problem with a large 2-8-0 freight engine based on his Black 5 design. The first of the new locomotives, the 8F, arrived in 1935 and were an instant success. With the war clouds drawing near once more, the War Department chose the 8F to be its standard freight locomotive, which saw service both at home and overseas. These extra locomotives were built by all four railway companies and three outside contractors. A total of 852 were built.

The Railway Executive Committee (REC) which had been formed to run Britain's railways during the war, although the railway companies still remained independently owned, saw that there was a need for more freight engines by the mid-point of the war. The REC looked to create a quick and cheap to build simplified version of the 8F. The locomotive, designed by Robert Riddles, who would later become the CME of British Railways, entered service in 1943. The official title of the

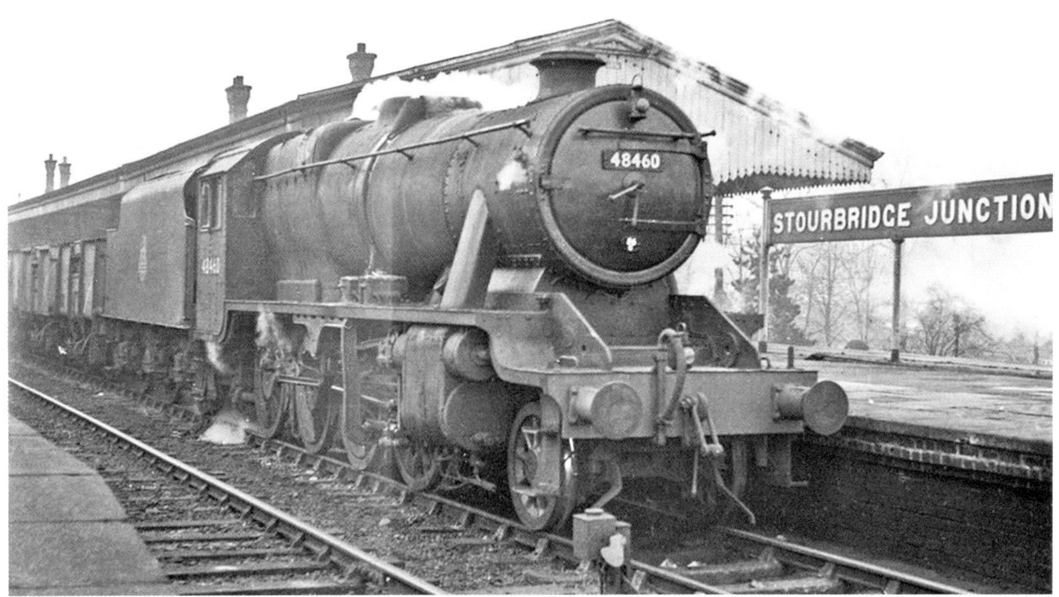

**Ex-LMS Stanier** 8F Class 2-8-0 No. 48460 at Stourbridge Junction working a mineral train on 31 March 1958. The locomotive is one of the batch built at Swindon by the GWR during the Second World War. *Ben Brooksbank*

class was WD (War Department) Austerity, because of the simplified engineering of the locomotives. The last was built in 1945 by which time the two contractors, North British and Vulcan Foundry had completed 935.

Whilst in some aspects they were crude machines, they were nonetheless effective and exactly what a nation at war needed. There was a second version of the design, of which 150 were built by North British, which had ten coupled wheels, but was otherwise identical to the first type. The idea was that the five axles would spread the weight, reducing the load on the tracks which allowed the engines to run on secondary lines.

After the war, 200 of the 2-8-0s were sold to the LNER, with a further 533 purchased by the British Transport Commission for British Railways. One hundred and eighty-four were sold to *Nederlandse Spoorwegen*, the Dutch state-owned railway, to replace locomotives which had been destroyed during the war. A few others were sold to Hong Kong and one was exchanged with the US Army Transportation Corps for an American design. A few of the 2-10-0 type were acquired by British Railways but the majority were sold to the Netherlands, whilst a few were sold to Greece, and Syria. Two each of the 2-8-0 and 2-10-0s were retained by the army for service on the Longmoor Military Railway where they were used to train army personnel on

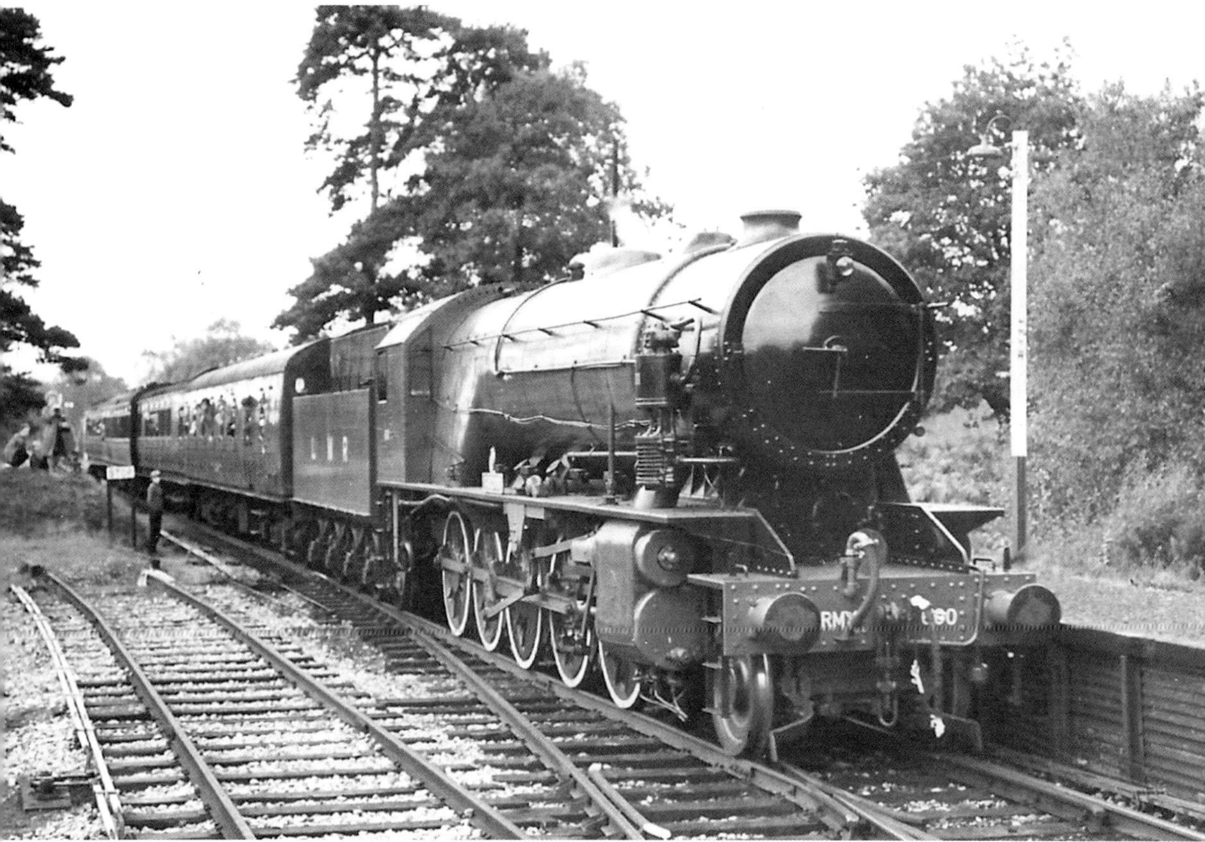

**WD 2-10-0** No. 600 *Gordon*, in service on the Longmoor Military Railway after the Second World War. *John Scott-Morgan Collection*

railway operations. These were not the only unconventional freight locomotives to appear on Britain's railways.

The LMS had looked to address the need for heavy freight locomotives with something different in the late 1920s. Even with the proliferation of 0-8-0s and the introduction of the powerful 4F there was still a gap in the company's motive power which Fowler looked to fill, especially with a view to reducing double heading on the Nottinghamshire to London coal traffic. His design was unusual for Britain's railways, in that it was an articulated locomotive to the Garratt arrangement. The engines were built for the LMS by Beyer Peacock & Co. in Manchester who were familiar with the basic design. Three engines were delivered in 1927 with another thirty in 1930. The design consisted of an articulated chassis with two six coupled engine units with the boiler, firebox and cab located between them on a 'bridge'. The water tank was placed on top of one power unit, the coal bunker on the other. Each unit had a pony truck at the outer end giving the locomotive the unusual 2-6-0+0-6-2 wheel arrangement.

The engines were not without issues when in traffic. The offices at Derby had insisted that standard LMS parts should be used, the most troublesome being the axle boxes which were not suitable for such a powerful locomotive. They were also found to be very uneconomical in traffic with high coal and water consumption common. They were capable and remained in traffic until replaced by British Rail standard designs despite their issues.

Only one other 'Garratt' was used on Britain's mainline railways. Gresley's U1 class was a larger 2-8-0+0-8-2, and was also built by Beyer Peacock. Only a single engine was built as it was designed for a single purpose, banking heavy freight trains over the Worsborough Bank, between Wath and Penistone, on the Woodhead Route from Sheffield to Manchester.

Not all heavy freight locomotives were large tender engines, some machines built specifically for freight use were tank engines. Of particular note were the 0-6-2 classes introduced by the Lambton Railway, TVR, LNWR and GWR. The locomotives had one thing in common, they were introduced mainly to cover coal traffic. The first notable examples of the type could be found on the LNWR in the form of Webb's

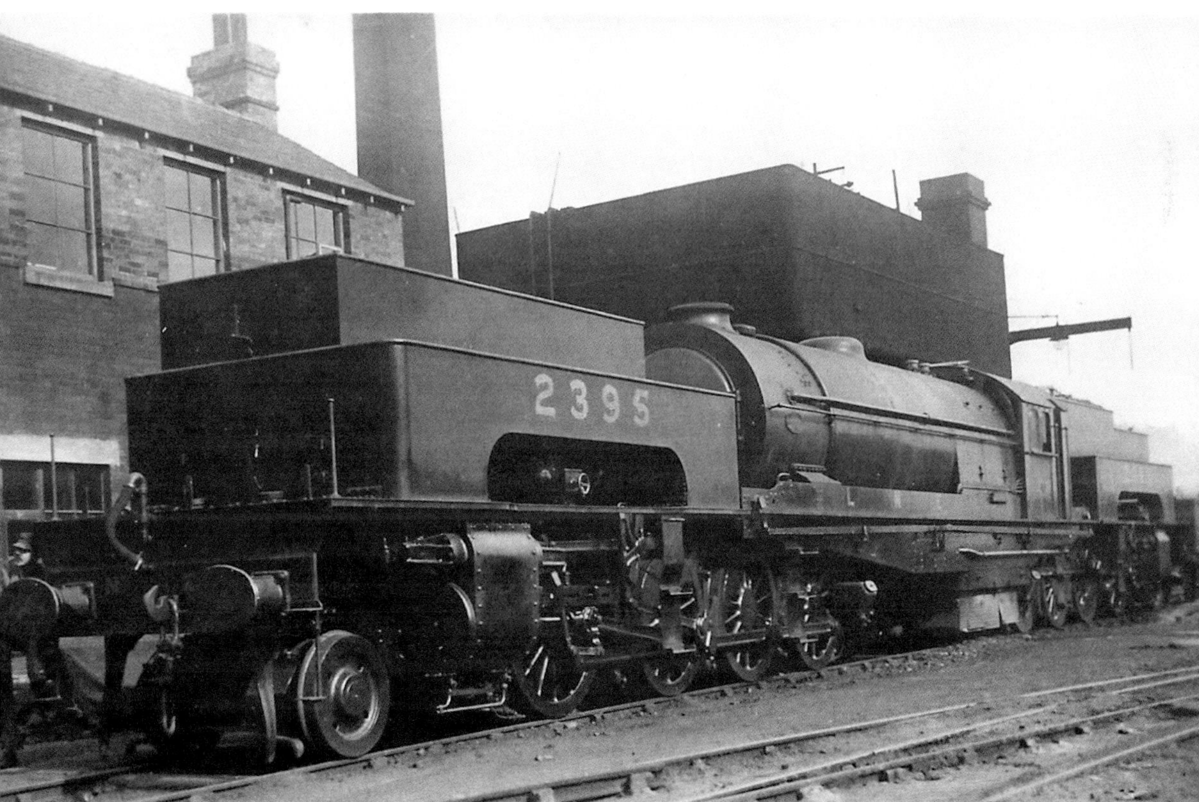

**The sole** LNER Garratt 2-8-0+0-8-2 No. 2395. Commercial Postcard, *John Scott-Morgan Collection*

1881 'Coal Tanks'. The locomotives had cast iron wheels to reduce the cost and a trailing radial axle, which is able to slide from side to side in a curved motion, rather than a pony truck or trailing bogie. The engines were at the lower end of the power scale, classified 2F by the LMS when they received them in 1923. The type was quite successful with 300 built at Crewe. Whilst built for coal traffic, they could often be found on local passenger services on a wide area of the LNWR's system, including their lines in Wales.

The wheel arrangement was very common in Wales, where the combination of large amounts of coal, iron and steel traffic, relatively short distances and the convenience offered by large tank engines drove the adoption of large numbers of them by the Welsh railway companies. The TVR introduced their first 0-6-2 tank engine in 1886 when the first of forty-seven M1 Class engines were introduced, followed by seven of the N (1891) and five of the O (1894) classes. The fleet was expanded in 1894 when the first eight of Tom Hurry Riches's 01 class were delivered from Kitson & Co. in Leeds. They were followed by the U Class of 1895 (eight), and U1 Class of 1896 (seven)

The O1 class engines proved themselves and another six were built by the TVR's own workshops in Cardiff in 1897. Increasing traffic led to the introduction of more 0-6-2 tanks by the TVR. Riches's O2 class of 1899, were followed by the pair of O3 class tank engines, built by Kitson in 1904. The last forty-one of Riches's designs,

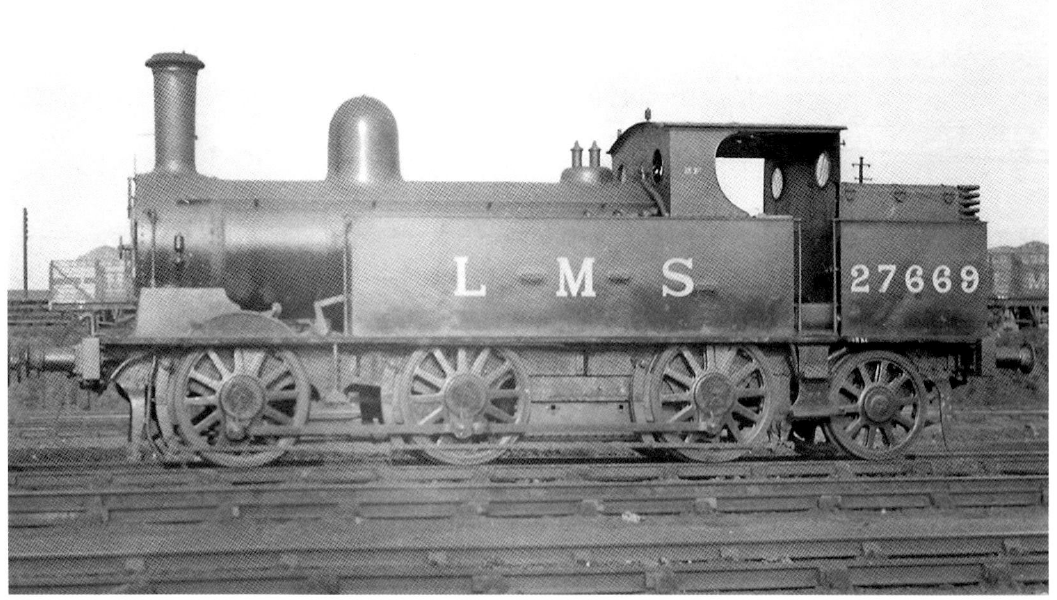


**Ex-LNWR Webb** 2F 'Coal Tank' No. 27669. *John Scott-Morgan Collection*

O4 class, were introduced between 1907 and 1910. John Cameron succeeded Riches in 1911 and continued the theme. The railway introduced the first of his fifty-eight A Class 0-6-2 tank locomotives in 1914, all of which were built by outside contractors.

The 0-6-2 classes, all of which had inside cylinders, dominated the TVR's locomotive fleet; over 200 of a total of 274 locomotives built for and by the TVR were of this arrangement. Despite being designed mainly for mineral traffic most of the locomotives could be found on all types of trains on the TVR.

The Rhymney Railway, like the TVR, built for coal, mineral and steel traffic and one of their great rivals, also adopted the effective 0-6-2 tank engine arrangement for the majority of their locomotives. The first were a pair of L1 class tank engines which were built by Vulcan Foundry in Manchester and arrived in 1890. The twins were followed in 1894 by the forty-seven engines of the K Class, which were unusual in having the water tanks placed over the boiler in a saddle tank arrangement, rather than the more traditional side tanks used on large tank locomotives. Both of the first two classes were designed by Richard Jenkins as were the six M Class tank engines built by Robert Stephenson and Sons from 1904.

With increasing freight traffic, the Rhymney needed more locomotives. To meet the need, the railway's new engineer, C.T. Hurry Riches (son of the Taff Vale engineer), developed two new types. The first of fifteen R Class engines arrived in 1907, followed in 1910 by the first of his twenty-four A Class machines. Hurry Riches's R and A classes and Jenkins's M class were ideally suited to hauling freight on the company's 50 mile long main line.

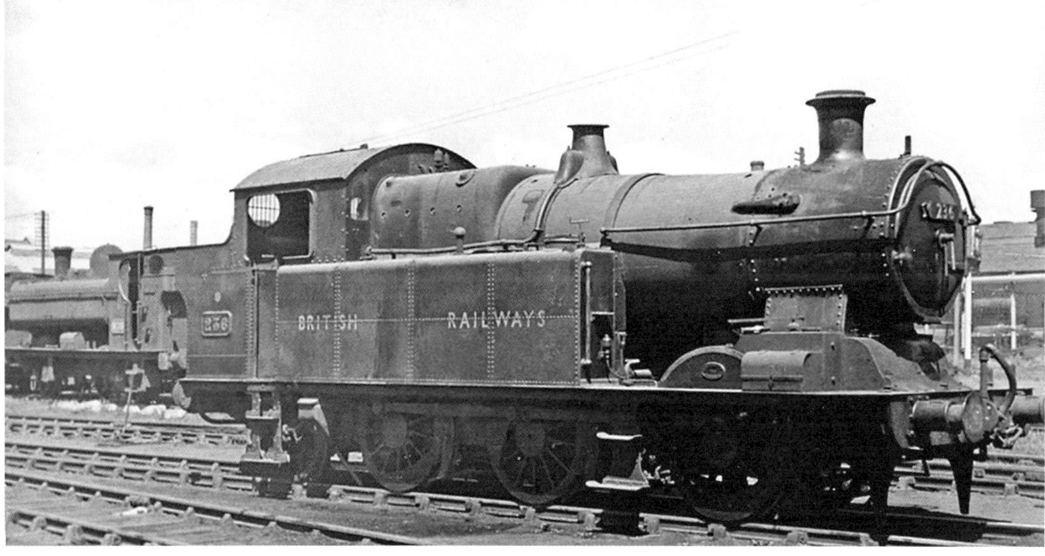

**Ex-Taff Vale** O4 Class 0-6-2 tank No. 236 in Cardiff East Dock yard, 27 July 1950. The locomotive was reboilered by the GWR in 1938. *Ben Brooksbank*

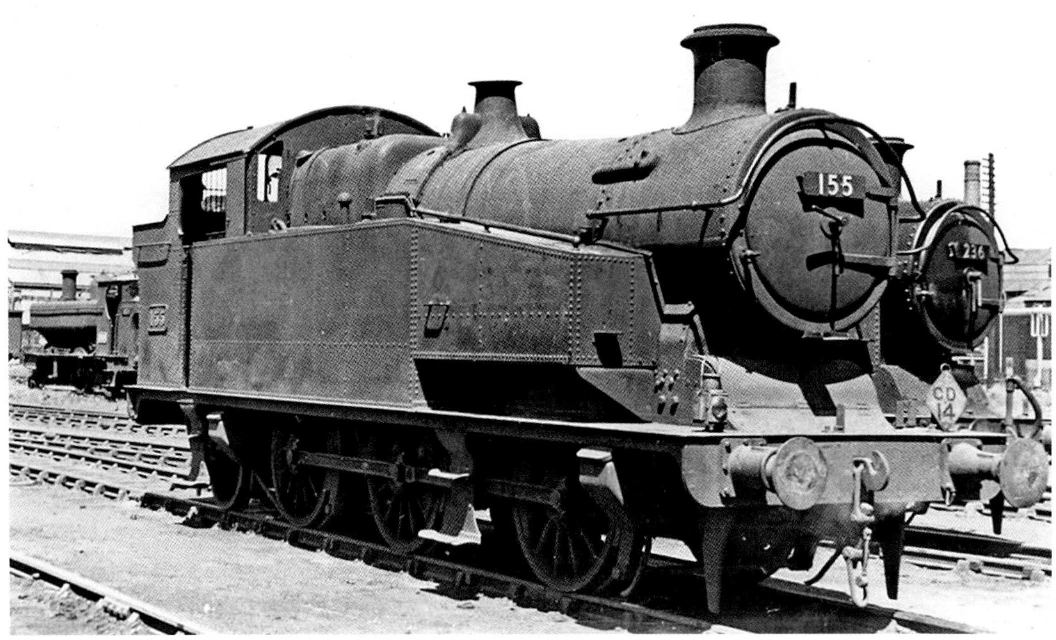

**Ex-Cardiff Railway** 0-6-2 tank No. 155 in Cardiff East Dock yard, 27 July 1950. Photographs of this locomotive are extremely rare as it was the only one of its type built. *Ben Brooksbank*

The arrangement was adopted by most of the other railway companies in Wales. The Barry Railway built two classes, twenty-five of the B class of 1888, followed by forty-two B1 Class (1890). The locomotives were all built by outside contractors since they did not have their own workshops. The B1 Class were unusual in that five of the engines were built by Societe Franco-Belge in Belgium at a time when the vast majority of Britain's railways purchased their engines from British companies. All were passed to the GWR at the Grouping.

The Brecon and Merthyr, Port Talbot (PTR), and Neath and Brecon railways all adopted the 0-6-2 tank engine. The Brecon and Merthyr introduced a class of 12 between 1909 and 1914 which were almost identical to the Rhymney's R Class, and like the Rhymney's version, were built by Robert Stephenson and Company. Robert Stephenson also built three locomotives for the Neath and Brecon in 1904 which were identical to the Rhymney's M Class. These followed the eleven tank engines of an earlier design which Robert Stephenson built for the Port Talbot Railway in 1898. The Cardiff Railway were other adopters of the type, although they sourced their thirteen machines from Kitsons.

The success of the arrangement in Wales, where the 0-6-2s had been seen to be able to easily handle the sharp curves on many of the railway lines in the region as well as the heavy loads, convinced the GWR to build their own version which emerged from Swindon as Collett's 5600 class. Swindon built 200 of the pugnacious locomotives between 1924 and 1928, to replace many of the disparate collection of Welsh locomotives that the GWR had inherited.

The GWR found that the increasing amount of traffic in Wales was beginning to demand a larger locomotive, something which the PTR and Barry railways had already begun to address. The Barry railway was the first to introduce an eight coupled engine, although, like the LNWR, it was a tender engine. The Class D 0-8-0s were a standard locomotive designed by John Waddington Mann at Sharp, Stewart & Co. in Glasgow. The four engines were part of an order for a Swedish railway which was unable to pay for them, so they were offered instead to the Barry Railway in two pairs in 1889 and 1897. All four were purchased. The short 4-wheel tenders were unappealing to larger railways but the lack of water and coal capacity was less of a problem on the shorter Barry line and also meant that the engines could fit on the company's turntables.

More heavy freight engines were needed on the Barry Railway by the mid-1890s and they once more approached Sharp, Stewart. The Glasgow company offered a tank engine design based upon the engines which had become the railway's D class. The new engine had a pony truck at the rear to support the weight of a large coal bunker, and large side tanks. The railway ordered seven of the 0-8-2 locomotives which were delivered in 1896 and became the H Class. All of the D and H classes were inherited by the GWR in 1923, and even though two of the H class were modified, the engines were viewed as non-standard and withdrawn in the late 1920s.

The PTR had identified the same need as the Barry line and also invested in two small classes of eight coupled locomotives. The railway issued a tender for the supply of two 0-8-2 tank engines which was answered by five British and three American engineering companies. The winning tender was submitted by the Cooke Locomotive and Machine Works of Paterson, New Jersey. The two engines were a mix of British and American practice, notably adopting the bar frames common in the United States and outside cylinders. The new engines were strong and able to replace two of the PTR's 0-6-2 tanks on trains, making a significant saving in fuel and staff costs. Both became part of the GWR locomotive fleet at the Grouping, and received new Swindon standard boilers, although both were withdrawn in 1928.

The PTR had an option to buy three more locomotives to the same design from Cookes but chose not to exercise it, instead buying three engines from Sharp, Stewart & Co. The 0-8-2 tanks arrived in 1901. They were extremely large engines but as capable as their American cousins on the railway. All three were passed to the GWR but they were soon withdrawn as non-standard types and replaced by standard 2-8-0 tank locomotives designed at Swindon.

The GWR was presented with a varied collection of Welsh locomotives at the Grouping in 1923, and a need to provide more powerful engines for the heaviest coal traffic. The Barry and Port Talbot engines had proven that an eight coupled tank locomotive would be an ideal response, and a standard GWR design would thus be the answer alongside the new 5600 class. Churchward designed an engine that would fit the bill. The 4200 class started production at Swindon with the first of 105 locomotives emerging in 1910. The class was the first 2-8-0 tank engine to be used in Britain, all of which spent their working lives in Wales. The engines proved to be a good design, ideal for the work, although they were a little thirsty which coupled with the narrow tanks required to fit within the railway loading gauge because of the large boiler meant that frequent stops to replenish the tanks were required.

With a need for more locomotives, Charles Collett designed an improved version of the 4200 class. The 5205 Class (100) began to emerge from Swindon in 1923. They differed from the 4200s in having larger cylinders which made them more powerful, and outside steam pipes to the cylinders from the smokebox. A further twenty locomotives, the 5275 class, were built with curved frames, but were otherwise

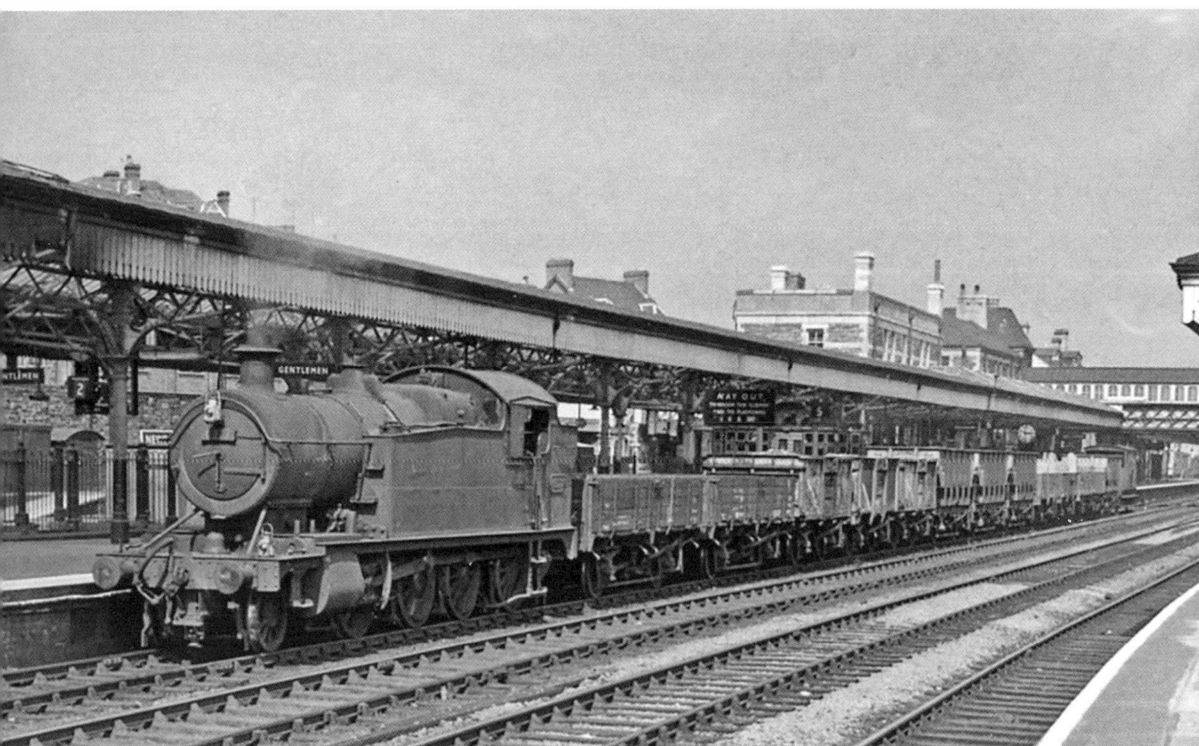


**Ex-GWR 4200** Class 2-8-0 tank No. 4277 at Newport High Street station, 14 August 1963.
*Ben Brooksbank*

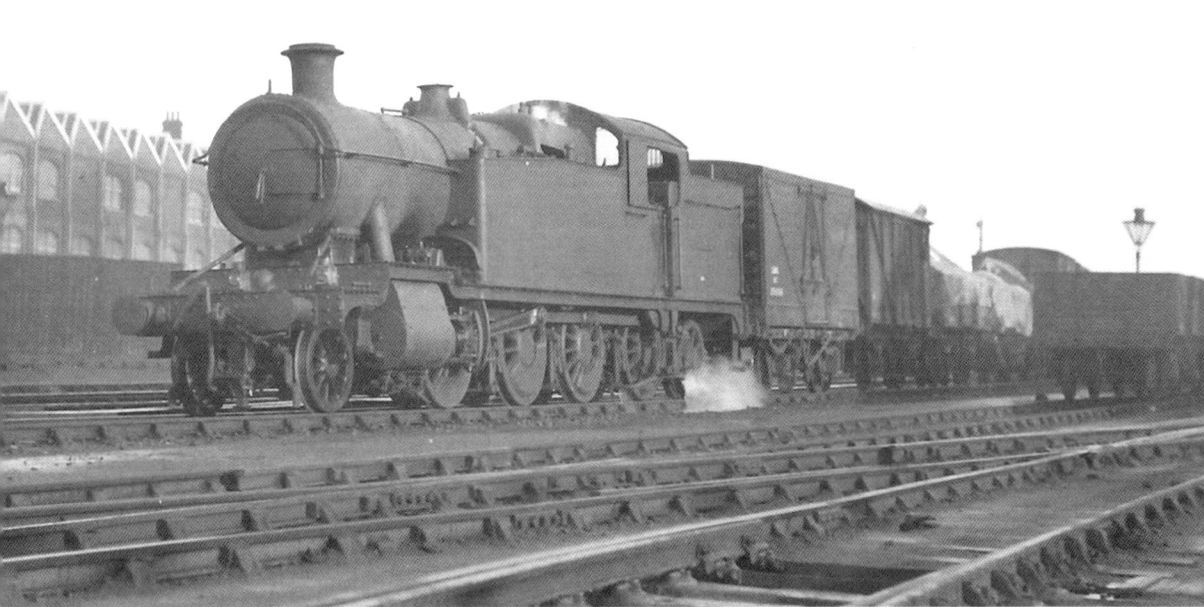

**Ex-GWR 7200** Class 2-8-2 tank. *Photomatic*

identical to the 5205s. All of the 5275s and twenty 5205s were rebuilt in 1934 into the larger 7200 class (fifty-four) of 2-8-2 tank engines which had large bunkers to allow them greater range before needing to refuel. After the 5275s were rebuilt, another ten were strangely built to the original 2-8-0 tank design in 1940, most likely for war work. The 7200s, were the only 2-8-2 tank engines to be built in Britain.

One design of tank engine for the railways of Wales, the Rhymney's P Class 0-6-2s, were not designed for freight, but for local passenger work. The need for suburban and local stopping train locomotives saw the 0-6-2 tank arrangement adopted by many other companies.

# Chapter 5
# SUBURBAN PASSENGER

Ll of the railway companies had comprehensive suburban networks which required short ranged locomotives which could handle intensive services with frequent stops. The networks around the major cities were made up of many local stations only a few miles apart. Fast stopping trains which served most, if not all, of these stations were needed as the populations of the major towns and cities began to move out of the centre and into the suburbs as the nineteenth century drew to a close. The solution were large tank engines which were as capable of running bunker first as they were boiler first, although the mid-range mixed traffic tender engines were often used on the faster suburban services. Some of the earliest designs for suburban tank engines were small 0-6-0 locomotives such as the LBSCR's A1 'Terrier' built to the design of William Stroudley for suburban traffic from London Bridge and London Victoria stations. Most were replaced by larger machines with the older engines cascaded onto lighter duties.

The pre-Grouping companies took a varied approach to providing suburban locomotives. On the LNWR, Francis Webb preferred tank engines of the 2-4-2 wheel arrangement. His first were the 4ft 6in Class of tank engines of which 220 examples were built at Crewe in 1889 and 1890. The class name referred to the size of their driving wheels. The engines were followed in 1890 by Webb's 5ft 6in Tanks, of which 160 were built. They appear to have been successful although were later cascaded onto lighter secondary and branch line services as larger engines took over the suburban routes. Forty-two of the class were fitted for push-pull working, where the locomotive could be driven from a cab in the coaches through a series of mechanical linkages to the engine, by the LMS.

The LNWR's rival the L&YR also adopted the 2-4-2 arrangement for its suburban passenger tanks. Aspinall's 1008 Class of 1889 were the first, but only five were built. The railway would have to wait for more until George Hughes created his 816, and 18 class of tank engines of which forty and sixty-four units were built respectively. The NER also looked to the arrangement for its suburban needs, Worsdell's A Class tanks entering service in 1886, with a total of sixty built by 1892. The engines could be found working suburban traffic but were also successful on the NER's branch lines. The Manchester, Sheffield and Lincolnshire Railway, which became the GCR, took a similar path, building 49 2-4-2 tank engines of the F1 and F2 classes.

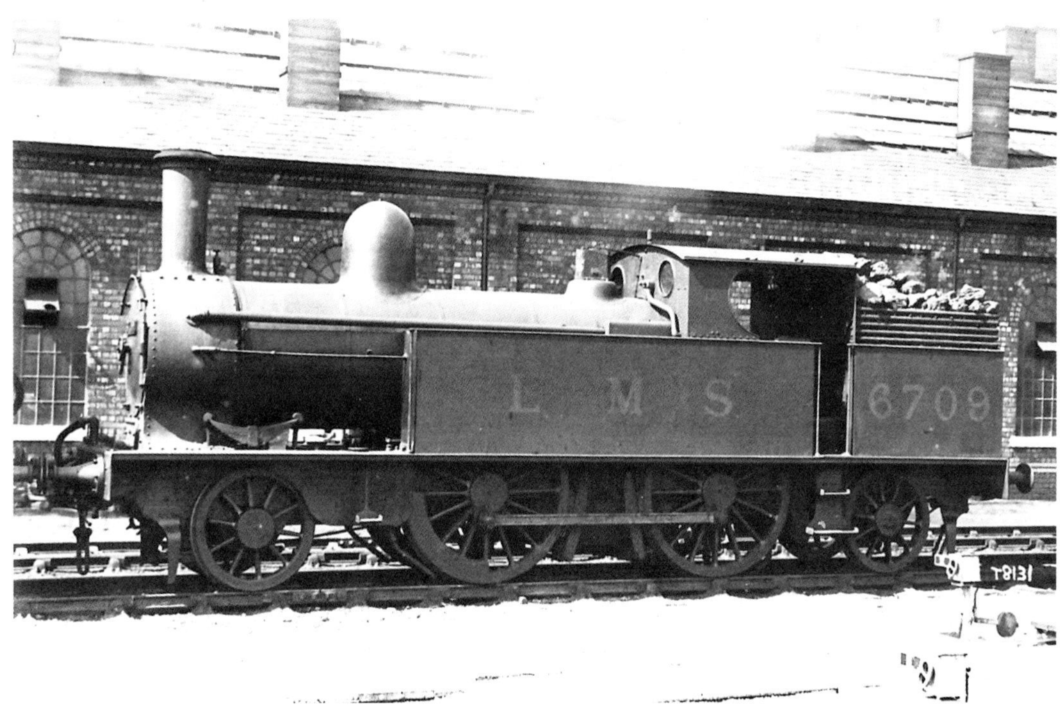

**Ex-LNWR 4ft** 6in 2-4-2 tank in LMS Days. *John Scott-Morgan Collection*

The 2-4-2 arrangement began to fall into disfavour fairly quickly as, whilst the locomotives were useful, their haulage power was limited. Webb designed a class of 0-6-2 tank engines in 1898, the 18in Class. The eighty engines of the type were designed as mixed traffic engines but could often be found on suburban passenger trains, which they managed with ease. They became unofficially known as 'Watford Tanks' due to their use on London Euston to Watford trains.

The LBSCR, GER, and GNR all built a series of powerful 0-6-2 tank engines. The NER had a wide range of 0-6-2 tanks designed for freight, although they were also used on passenger services during their working lives. The LBSCR used the 0-6-2 tank engine layout to provide better locomotives for their suburban and semi-fast passenger services. Billinton's E4 class (seventy-five locomotives), built at Brighton, began to enter service in 1897. The new engines were good machines which were used on freight and branch line work as well as semi-fast passenger services for over fifty years.

The bigger E5 class (thirty) followed, also designed by Billinton and built at Brighton, entering service in 1902. The larger machines were built to cover the increasingly heavy passenger services and all survived to enter SR service, all but two becoming part of the BR locomotive fleet. The E4s and E5s were worn out by the time of nationalisation and were made redundant by the availability of large numbers of BR's standard classes of tank locomotives and were withdrawn.

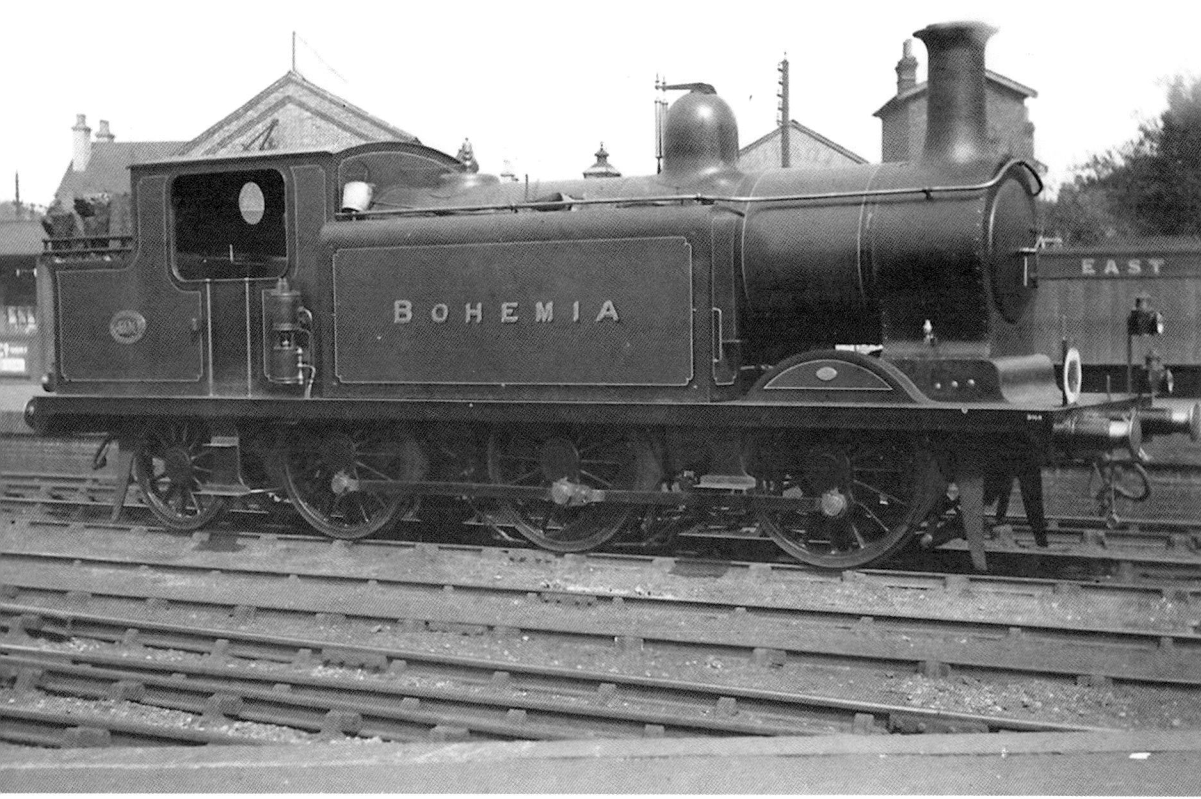


**LBSCR E4** class 0-6-2 tank No 490 *Bohemia* at East Grinstead sometime before 1923.
*John Scott-Morgan Collection*

The GER had a similar need for a large locomotive to take over its local passenger services. The answer was Alfred Hill's L77 class of 0-6-2 tank engine. The class began to arrive on the railway in 1915 and were fitted from the outset with superheated boilers and piston valves which was unusual at the time. They were inside cylinder locomotives, but unlike most other locomotives of that type were fitted with Walschaerts valve gear. They were intended for the company's London suburban passenger trains, and as such were fitted with Westinghouse air brakes. The GER had adopted air braking for its passenger stock instead of the more common vacuum braking applied to almost all other railway coaches.

A small selection of the class were fitted with condensing apparatus which took some of the steam from the exhaust and passed it back into the water tanks where it was cooled back into water. The equipment was fitted to allow the engines to work through the Metropolitan and East London Lines tunnels, but it was removed in the 1930s. The locomotives were an excellent design and the LNER's chief

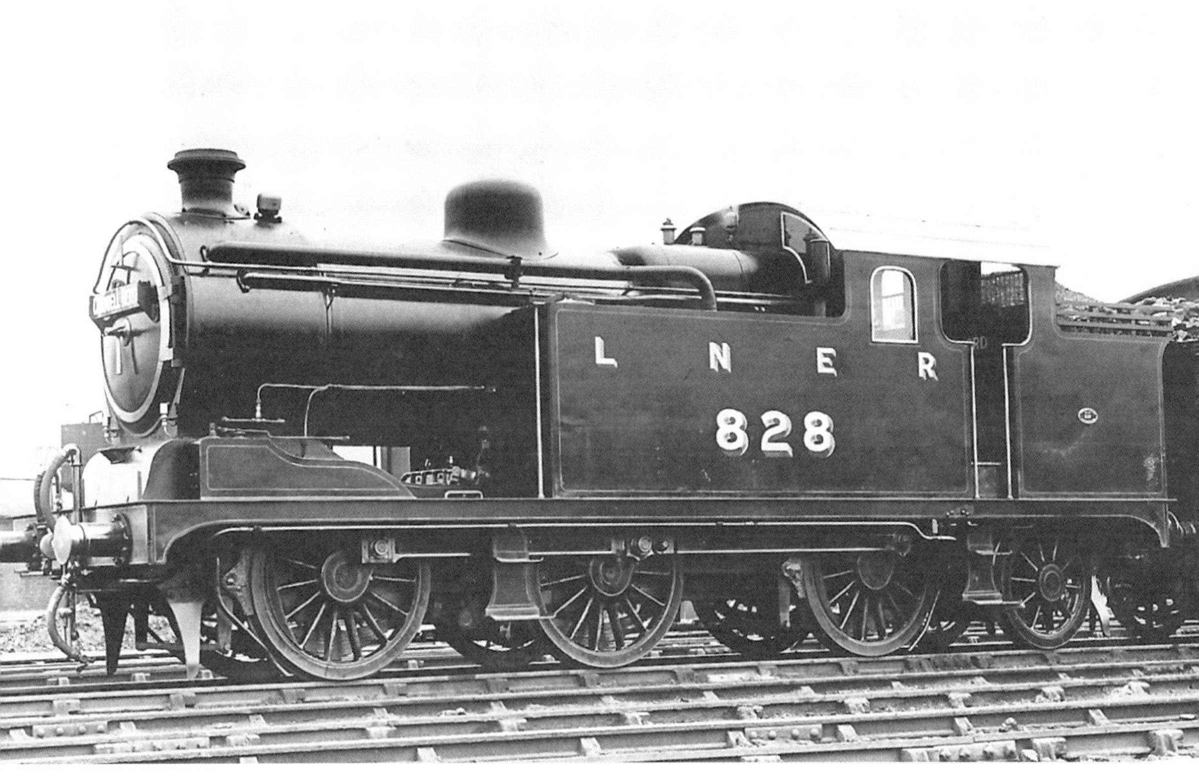

**Ex. GER** L77 Class (LNER N7) 0-6-2 tank No. 828. Commercial Post Card. *John Scott-Morgan Collection*

mechanical engineer, Nigel Gresley, continued to build them after the Grouping. The class, reclassified as N7, eventually numbered 134 with the last coming into traffic in 1928.

The GNR found they had a similar need for their suburban services from London King's Cross. This was addressed by Henry Ivatt's N1 class, fifty-six of which were built at Doncaster between 1906 and 1912. All of the class were fitted with condensing apparatus to enable them to work the GNR's branch to Moorgate. The engines could also be found working cross London freight services, as well as empty coaching stock trains around King's Cross. A larger engine was soon needed for these services.

Gresley designed a new 0-6-2 tank engine for the GNR, the large N2, which was introduced in 1920. A total of 107 were built at Doncaster works as well as subcontractors North British, Beyer Peacock, The Yorkshire Engine Company (Sheffield), and Hawthorn Leslie and Company (Newcastle upon Tyne). Some were fitted with condensing

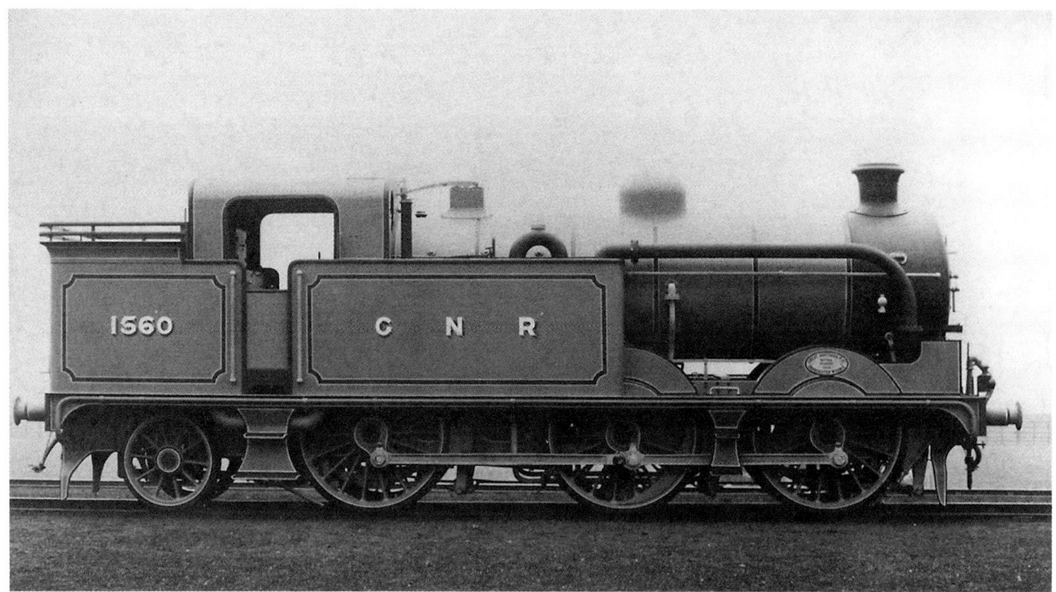

**GNR N1** Class 0-6-2 tank No.1560. The pipe leading from under the smokebox into the tanks is part of the condensing apparatus which reduced steam emissions in London's tunnels. Commercial Postcard, *John Scott-Morgan Collection*

apparatus to allow them to work the Moorgate branch. The locomotives could often be found working passenger trains, made up of Gresley's articulated 'Quad Art' coaching stock, to New Barnet and Hertford. They were spread over the network and were to be found as far away from London as Glasgow and Edinburgh.

The 0-6-2 tank engine was not the only type used on local and intermediate distance passenger trains. Four other arrangements were adopted, 0-4-4, 2-6-4, 4-6-2 and 2-6-2 tank engines. All these arrangements proved popular although the GWR would prefer the 2-6-2 alone. Britain's first standard gauge 2-6-4 tanks appeared on the GCR in 1914. Robinson's inside cylinder 1B class design was an improvement upon the Class D 0-6-4 tanks inherited from the Lancashire, Derbyshire and East Coast Railway designed by Robert Thom. Thom was Robinson's assistant on the GCR by 1914 and may have had some influence on the design of the new engines. A total of twenty of the solid looking machines, fitted with a large superheated boiler, were built by the GCR's workshops at Gorton. All were inherited by the LNER, with nineteen becoming part of BR in 1948.

The 1B class was reclassified as L1 by the LNER, changed to L3 in 1945 to make way for Thompson's new locomotives of the same wheel arrangement. The first new L1 was built by the LNER, but the remainder of the 100 engines were built by British Railways and outside contractors. The locomotives were well equipped with electric lighting on the front and rear of the machine and in the cab to improve the

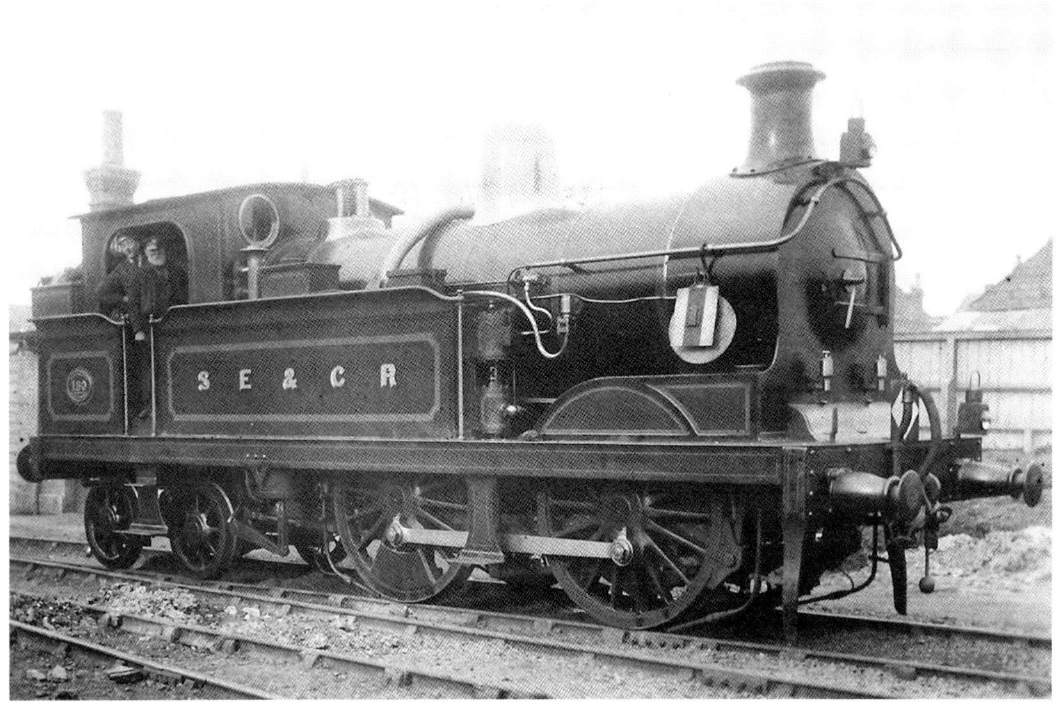

**SE&CR Q1** Class 0-4-4 tank No. 140. The Q1s were Harry Wainwright (1864-1925) rebuilds of the SER Q class. The class is a good example of the 0-4-4 tanks which were used by most companies for suburban work before being replaced by larger locomotives. The white square and disk hanging from the handrail are route indicators which would be placed on the leading end of the locomotive to indicate its route. *John Scott-Morgan Collection*

working environment for the crew. The engines have divided opinion, despite being more economic than many of the other locomotives used on the same services. They were criticised by crews for being rough riding and needing careful handling due to the poor drafting of the boiler and suffered from overheating axle boxes. It seems that the older Robinson's design was much preferred.

The LMS produced a series of good 2-6-4 tank engine designs. All of the various types had the same power classification, 4P, which was changed to 4MT by British Railways. The first was designed by Henry Fowler, the initial locomotive entering service in 1927, with a total of 125 built at Derby. The engines were used on commuter trains around London, Manchester and other large towns. The locomotives were well received with a number allocated to Tebay depot to bank trains on the fearsome Shap incline.

The old LT&SR lines from Fenchurch Street were in need of an improved passenger engine by the early 1930s, and William Stanier designed such a machine. The new design, also a 2-6-4 tank, differed from Fowler's locomotives in having three cylinders. The more complex arrangement was needed to give the new locomotives the better acceleration from station stops needed to meet the tight schedules on the line. The increased maintenance the design needed was deemed to be undesirable for traffic elsewhere, and so only thirty-seven of the class were built. Instead a simpler 2-cylinder design was produced for work elsewhere. The new 2-cylinder Stanier tanks entered service in 1935, a total of 206 built when production ended in 1943.

Stanier retired in 1944 and was replaced as chief mechanical engineer on the LMS by Charles Fairburn. His short tenure was marked by just a single steam locomotive design, although as Stanier's deputy his earlier influence was probably more important. The new engines were another 2-6-4 tank, which were very closely based on Stanier's design, but with a shortened coupled wheelbase and lighter construction, both of which increased their route availability. The new locomotives were very good machines, and a total of 277 were built up to 1951. BR continued to build the design, with Brighton works taking on construction of some of the class for the nationalised railway.

The GCR, LBSCR, LNWR and CR all built bigger locomotives for heavy intermediate distance suburban and general passenger traffic. All were large 4-6-2

**Ex-LMS Fairburn** 4P Class 2-6-4 tank No. 42118. The British Railways standard class 4 were based on Fairburn's design, with which they bear an uncanny resemblance. *John Scott-Morgan Collection*

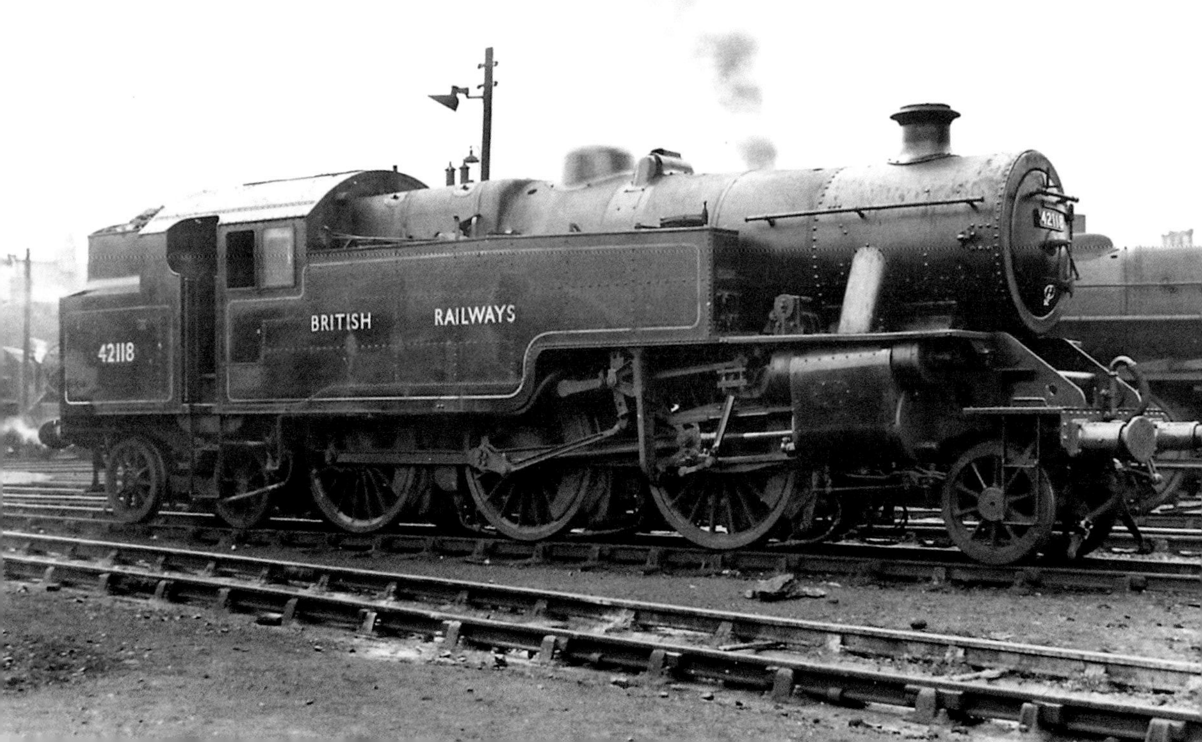

types with impressive dimensions. The LNWR and LBSCR both introduced pacific type tank engines in 1910. The LNWR's *Prince of Wales Tank* class of forty-seven locomotives, designed by Bowen Cooke, were built between 1910 and 1916. They seem to have been successful, all of the class passing on to the LMS at the Grouping. The engines were later replaced by the more modern Fowler and Stanier tank engines, withdrawals starting in 1935.

The LBSCR's pacific tanks were designed by Douglas Marsh and his successor Lawson Billinton, who produced two types, the J1 and J2 classes. The single J1 was an enlarged version of Marsh's I3 class 4-4-2 tank engines which was intended to haul the very heaviest London to Brighton expresses. After modification following trials which aimed to reduce coal and water consumption, the engine proved to be a success. A second was ordered but Marsh left the railway and work ceased.

Lawson Billinton restarted work on the engine, but with a number of design improvements. The changes made the locomotive so different from the first that it was classified J2. The single locomotive was completed in 1912 and like its sister engine was a great success. Both worked the heavy Brighton trains until the Grouping, although no more were built. The class were replaced by the SR with capable King Arthur class tender engines and the ill-fated River tanks and were transferred to haul Eastbourne trains. They both entered service with British Railways but were replaced by new Fairburn tanks built at Brighton and scrapped.

The GCR was the last company to opt for a 4-6-2 tank for its longer distance heavy suburban trains. Introduced in 1911, the Robinson designed, inside cylinder, 9N class (LNER A5) were typically large engines. Twenty-one of the class were built at the GCR's Gorton workshops before the Grouping, with another batch of ten that was ordered before 1923 completed under the auspices of the LNER. The 9Ns were ideal for the GCR's needs, so much so that the LNER ordered a further thirteen in 1925, although to a slightly modified design. All bar one were passed to British Railways in 1948.

The GWR's suburban needs were met through the adoption of the 2-6-2, or 'prairie' arrangement. The first prairie tanks came in 1903 with the introduction of Churchward's 3100 class (later reclassified as 5100) of which forty were built. The design was improved upon and resulted in the 3150 class of 1906 which used the larger standard No.4 boiler giving them greater capacity for steam, but at the expense of greater weight which limiting route availability. The forty-one members of the class were used on heavy suburban traffic.

Charles Collett looked to improve upon the useful prairie tanks, his 5101 or 'Large Prairie' class were designed as medium sized tank engines which could cover the GWR's suburban and local passenger trains across the whole network. The first left Swindon works in 1929, the last of the 140 engines entering traffic in 1949. A second class of 2-6-2s developed by Collett were the improved 6100 class of which seventy examples were built. The new class was an improvement on the 5101s, the boilers having a higher maximum pressure, giving them greater power. They were designed purely for commuter trains around London Paddington and could be found on trains to Aylesbury, Oxford, Windsor, Reading and Basingstoke. The class were allocated to the GWR's depots at Old Oak Common (London), Southall, Slough, Reading and Aylesbury, rarely straying further afield.

The LMS created only two classes of 2-6-2 tank engine for heavier trains, Fowler's 3P class of 1930 (seventy examples) which were followed by Stanier's development of the design. The 139 Stanier engines were built between 1935 and 1938 at Crewe and Derby. Both the Fowler and Stanier engines were used on stopping suburban passenger services as well as branch line duties. The Fowler types were the better of the two classes, the Stanier engines seemingly worse at creating steam. The LMS created one more 2-6-2 design, the excellent 2MT tanks designed for branch line and secondary work. The LNER also had a pair of 2-6-2 tank engine designs, Gresley V1 and V3 classes. The V1 (eighty-two units) and V3 (ten) were produced for the same traffic for which the LMS and GWR had built theirs.

These were the mainline locomotives that made up the fleet which would be inherited by BR in 1948 but this was not the whole story. Locomotives had been needed to assemble trains and operate Britain's rural branch lines.

**Ex GWR** 5101 Class 2-6-2 tank No. 4158 in Wellington locomotive yard, 12 April 1960. *Ben Brooksbank*

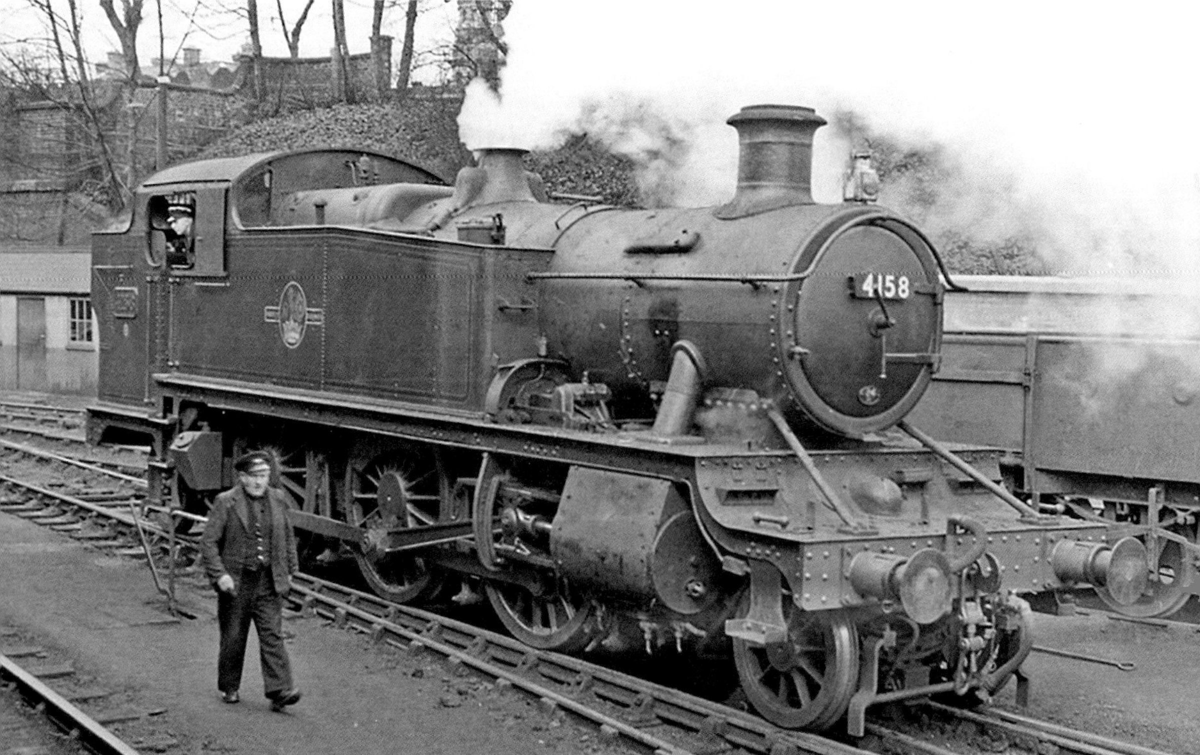

# Chapter 6

# SHUNTING AND BRANCH LINES

The railway was about more than just the mainline trains. In the days before the advent of fixed formation trains, it was necessary to shunt coaches and wagons to make up train formations. Whilst most coaching stock was kept in sets, extra coaches often needed to be added to the consist, or a faulty coach removed and replaced. At terminuses, coaches needed to be taken away to release the train engine so that it could be made ready for its next trip. Freight trains needed to be formed in marshalling yards for long distance transport of goods. Shorter trains then had to be created to deliver the wagons to the correct goods yards at wayside stations on both main and branch lines.

Industry also relied on rail for its supply of materials, and the transport of finished goods. Mines were no different, the extracted coal and ore needing to be sent away to customers or for processing.

Britain's railways were richly provided with relatively short local branch lines which radiated out from junction stations all over the country. Local passenger and goods services were key reasons for the construction of such local arteries.

The locomotives already discussed were mostly too large and heavy for the lightly constructed branches and unsuitable for shunting in yards. A particular type of locomotive was needed for these jobs. A mixture of engines built by the railway companies' own workshops and some bought in from independent manufacturers met the demand. In industry the majority of the shunting locomotives were built by independent companies, although at the end of steam in Britain some engines, such as the GWR pannier and LMS 3F tanks were sold to collieries and other sites with large private networks.

Shunting was mostly the preserve of small 0-4-0 and 0-6-0 tank engines. In many instances the tight curves to be found in industrial sites and docks meant that only the smallest of engines could be used, mostly of a short wheel base 0-4-0 type. Built with very small wheels, and with the weight of the water tanks directly over the driving wheels these little engines were much stronger than they looked. Britain's mainline railway companies built a range of small four coupled shunting engines, among the first were the 0-4-0 saddle tanks built for the Caledonian Railway in 1853 to the design of Robert Sinclair. The most notable though are probably the LSWR's B4, and L&YR Class 21.

The LSWR B4 class were introduced by Adams for the LSWR in 1891, with a total of twenty-five built at the company's workshop at Nine Elms in London. The engines were outside cylinder side tanks designed for dock shunting and station pilot duties. They were initially allocated to major stations throughout the LSWR system but in 1892 the company purchased Southampton Docks with its internal railway. The existing dockyard railway contained a large number of sharp curves, usual for most industrial settings, and so fourteen of the short wheelbase B4s were sent to operate the docks railway as the resident engines became worn out. They became associated with Southampton and served well until they were replaced by larger American army surplus tank engines after the Second World War. The Southampton engines were all given names relating to the common destinations of ships which then sailed from the Docks. The remainder of the class were occupied working other depots and docks around the LSWR.

The L&YR's Class 21 0-4-0 saddle tanks were designed by Aspinall and introduced in 1886. The first three locomotives differed from the rest of the class, having a longer wheelbase, a smaller cab, and the saddle tanks stopping short of the smokebox. Like the B4s they were developed to work in sharply curved sidings and were allocated to industrial areas and in the docks at Goole, Liverpool and Salford. The

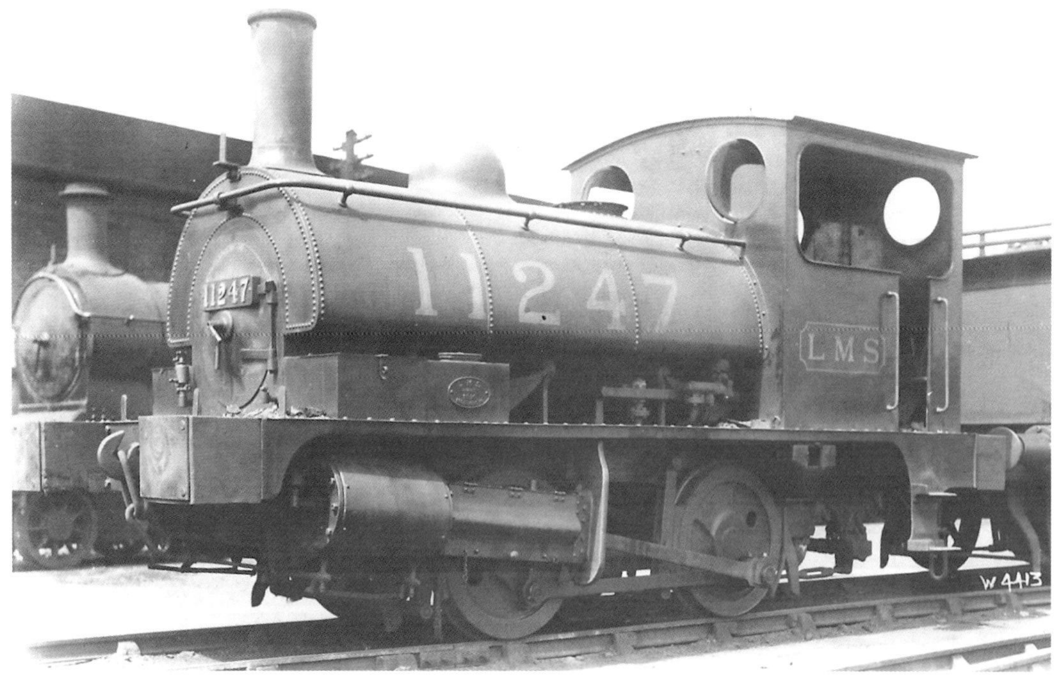

**Ex L&YR** Class 21 0-4-0 saddle tank, No.11247. *John Scott Morgan Collection*

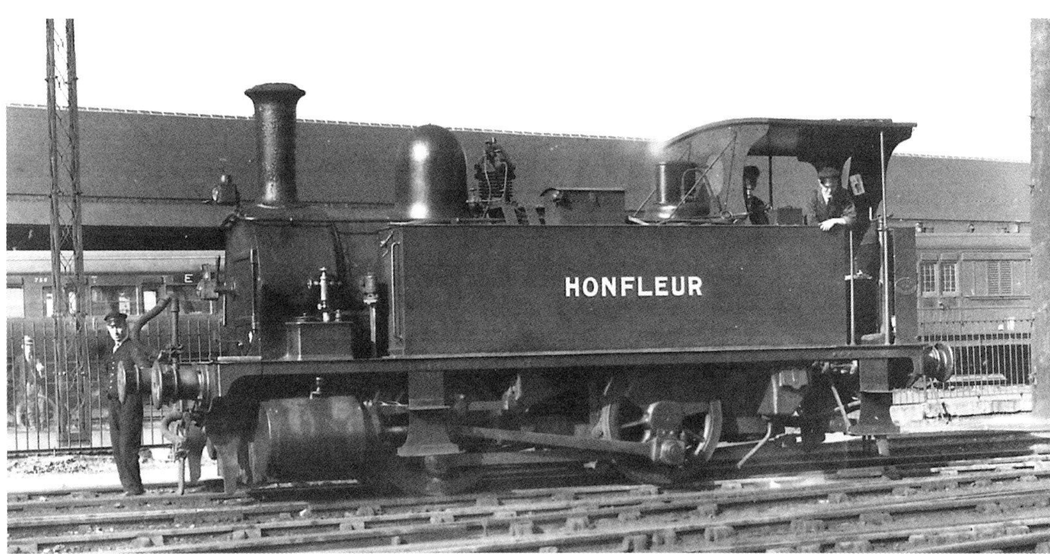



**Ex-LSWR B4** Class 0-4-0 tank No. 95 *Honfleur* at Southampton Docks September 1934. Honfleur is in the Calvados department of north-west France. *Author's Collection*

little engines were capable of handling much of what was needed although the LMS began to withdraw small numbers after 1924. Twenty-three still remained in service on 1 January 1948 but withdrawals steadily continued.

Bizarrely, BR decided to build an old shunting engine design in 1953. The LMS had purchased five small 0-4-0 saddle tanks from Kitson in 1932 and BR decided to build another five at Horwich but to a modified design. The Horwich locomotives appeared unbalanced with the cab located well behind the rear driving wheel and the saddle tank stopping short of the firebox leaving a gap between it and the cab.

The 0-4-0 saddle tank design was a favourite of the independent locomotive manufacturers who made many shunting engines for industry. Many of the large collieries, breweries and factories in Britain had their own railway networks and were good customers for companies such as Peckett and Sons (Bristol), Hunslet (Leeds), Andrew Barclay (Kilmarnock), Robert Stephenson & Hawthorn (Newcastle upon Tyne), Hudswell Clarke (Leeds), Manning Wardle (Leeds) and many more who also exported locomotives in large numbers.

The locomotive builders provided a range of different sized 0-4-0 saddle tanks to these companies depending upon their needs, but all were outside cylinder engines, although the valve gear was often placed between the frames. The engines were often built to a basic design, which then had a suite of options that a customer could select, much as extras can be added to a modern car. The engine manufacturers would also paint the engines in the house liveries of the customers.

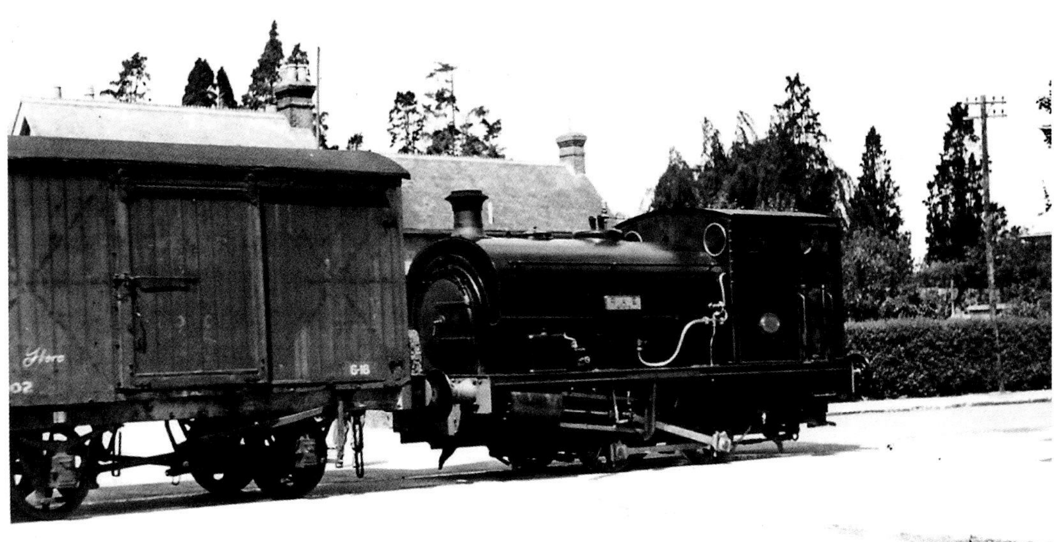

**Hudswell Clarke** 0-4-0 saddle tank, *RAE* No. 7 taking a train through the streets of Farnborough to the Royal Aircraft Establishment c.1950. The locomotive is an example of the small locomotives developed by British engineering companies for industrial use. *John Scott-Morgan Collection*

For heavier work all of the locomotive builders offered larger versions of their designs to an 0-6-0 wheel arrangement, and whilst many were saddle tanks, some were offered with side tanks. The larger engines were also able to accommodate inside cylinders. The larger engines tended to be attractive to the collieries where the heavier trains required bigger engines. Regardless of whether a customer opted for a little 0-4-0 or a larger 0-6-0 engine, the locomotives had one thing in common. They were designed to be robust and simple to operate and maintain.

One company decided to enter the market and offer a completely different form of shunting engine. Aveling and Porter, a firm of traction engine builders, saw an opportunity to provide a small engine that would fill a gap in the market. The locomotives, used for shunting and on light tramways, were essentially a traction engine with flanged railway wheels and no steering. They were cheap and easy to operate with minimal training, which made them attractive to customers with simple needs.

The increasingly heavy demands on shunting locomotives as freight traffic increased, and the need for trip workings between local yards and factory sidings off the main railways resulted in the railway companies finding the same need that heavy industries were finding. Larger engines were needed, and the larger 0-6-0 tank engine was seen as the answer. A mixture of types were built by the railway companies, some with saddle tanks, some with side tanks, but all with inside cylinders. Many of the classes were also used on light branch line passenger work.

The archetypal shunting locomotives are most probably the LSWR's G6 (1894); LBSCR's E1 (1874) and E2 (1913); SER's R (1888); MR's 1377 (1878) and 2441 (1899); NER's E1 (1898), and GNR's J13 (1897) classes. All bar the GNR J13, a saddle tank, had side tanks. All were built for shunting and local trip workings and proved very successful. The third most produced of these were the GNR J13 (LNER J52) of which eighty-five were built to Ivatt's design by Doncaster works. The NER built the second largest class, its E1 (LNER J72) class numbering 113 examples, although 28 were built by BR between 1949 and 1951. The most produced pre-Grouping shunting locomotive class were the MR's 1377 Class (LMS 1F) of which a total of 185 were built by the time production ended in 1892.

Whilst these engines were built in large numbers they paled in comparison to locomotives that came later. The MR had introduced its 2441 class in 1899, building a total of sixty up to 1902. Samuel Johnson's design was perfect for the work, and his successor Henry Fowler based his own shunting locomotive on it. The improved design emerged from the workshops in 1924 and became the LMS's standard shunting locomotive, the 3F Jinty. Four hundred and twenty-two were built by 1931 and they could be found all over the LMS system.

The GWR did things differently. They saw that side tanks got in the way of accessing the inside motion for preparation and maintenance, whilst saddle tanks

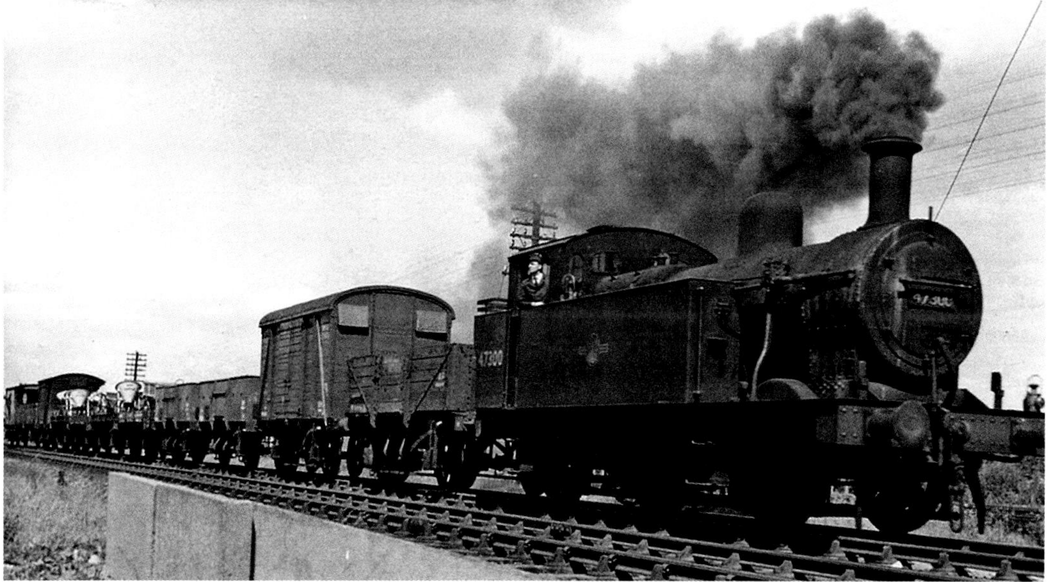

**Former LMS** 3F 0-6-0 tank No. 47300 on the old Midland main line at Walton, near Peterborough on 15 August 1959. *Ben Brooksbank*

were difficult to fill with water. The answer was to use pannier tanks, which were located either side of the boiler. The tanks were also much easier to form than saddle tanks, which made manufacturing cheaper and easier.

The first GWR pannier tanks were rebuilds of older saddle tank designs undertaken by Churchward, the most notable being the 2021 class of 140 locomotives which were gradually converted from saddle to pannier tanks, although not all were rebuilt. The 1854 class were rebuilt from saddle to pannier tanks between 1909 and 1932, with open cabs.

The first new design was Collett's 5700 Class of 1929. These were based on Churchward's rebuilt 1854 and 2021 classes and became the most built pannier tanks, Swindon and numerous subcontractors producing 863 units for both the GWR and BR by 1950. A subclass, the 6700s, were produced without the GWR's Automatic Train Control (ATC) safety system, vacuum brakes and steam heating. They were intended purely for shunting and just fifty were built.

The 9700 class of just eleven locomotives were built to work the London Underground line from Paddington to Smithfield Market. The tanks were shortened to make way for the condensing apparatus the engines were fitted with to reduce steam emissions in the tunnels. The engines were fitted with London Transport trip cocks to work with the safety system on the underground.

In 1930, Collett's 5400 class began to come out of Swindon. The class of twenty-five were all fitted with the required equipment (autofitted) to work with the GWR's auto coaches that were used on branch line services. The 6400 class that followed in 1932 were all autofitted, and 40 were built. The similar 7400 class were introduced in 1936, and whilst similar to the 6400s outwardly, were not autofitted and had a boiler rated to a higher pressure. The smaller wheels of the 6400s made them better suited to working in hilly locations than the 5400s and were thus allocated to work in South Wales. They also worked the branch lines in Devon and around Plymouth until the 1960s.

It was realised that a lighter version of the 5400 was needed for lightly built branch lines and short distance freight as well as shunting. The answer was Hawksworth's 1600 class. The design was completed just before nationalisation and were built by British Railways between 1949 and 1955. A total of seventy engines were built but their service lives were very short, the first withdrawal occurring in 1959. Two were sent to Scotland to work the Dornoch Light Railway and two were sold to the National Coal Board (NCB) in 1959 and 1965.

Hawksworth's 9400 class of 1947 were the last steam engines built by the GWR, although only ten of the eventual 210 were built prior to nationalisation. They were allocated all over the old GWR system, although many were concentrated in South Wales and at Old Oak Common for working empty coaching stock at Paddington. Seven of the locomotives were transferred to work as banking engines on the Lickey Incline when it became part of Western Region.

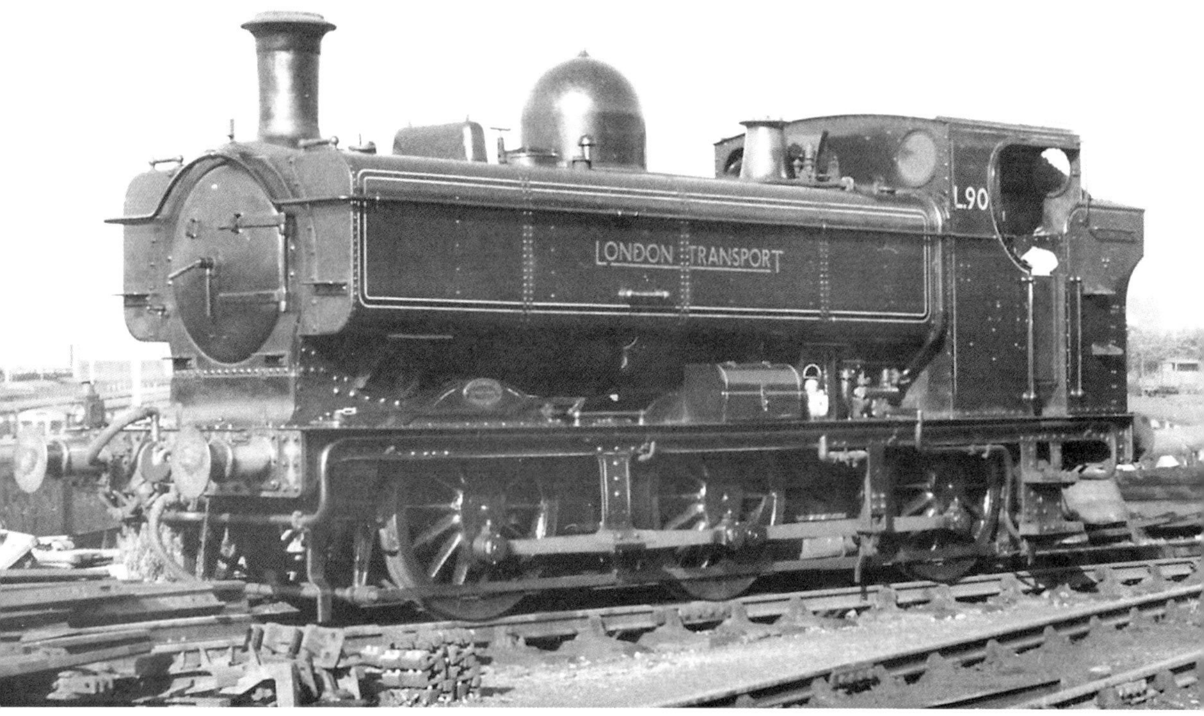

**Ex GWR** 5700 Class Pannier Tank No. L90 (ex 7760) at London Transport's Neasden depot in October 1952. This is the first 'L90' sold to LT by British Railways identifiable by the brackets on the smokebox for the old GWR number plate. The engine was swapped with BR for another due the firebox being in poor condition. *John Scott-Morgan Collection*

Two classes of pannier tank were designed purely for shunting, trip goods and station pilot duties and unlike their cousins did not work light passenger services. The 1366 class of 1934 were the first of these. Collett created a short wheelbase, lightweight engine which made the six engines extremely useful for working dockside railways. They were one of only two classes of GWR pannier tank with outside cylinders.

After nationalisation, three of the class were sent to work at Weymouth Harbour and a need later arose from the class to replace the three aging ex-LSWR 0298 class 2-4-0 tank engines which had been built to a Joseph Beattie design in the nineteenth century.

The three old LSWR engines were the only locomotives that had been found to be capable of working the sharply curved Wenford Bridge freight branch which carried china clay traffic to the main line at Bodmin, and had being doing so for almost a century. One of the small panniers was sent on trial to Cornwall and proved more than able to cope with the conditions on the branch, and two more were sent to accompany it, after which the Beattie tanks were withdrawn. The 1366s were in turn replaced by diesel shunters.

The last class of panniers were the ten outside cylinder 1500 class. Designed by Hawksworth before nationalisation, they were all built by BR. Most were confined to working empty stock around Paddington, with a small number working the yards around Newport, Cardiff and Ebbw Junction. Their short wheelbase and high weight made them unsuitable for fast running or for use on light branch lines. They were soon ousted by dieselisation of their duties, and three were sold to the NCB where they were used at Coventry Colliery, ironically doing exactly the work they had probably been designed for.

The GWR and LMS built a series of 2-6-2 tanks for light branch and secondary work. On the GWR, Churchward's 4400 class led the way, the company building eleven of the useful engines. Their small wheels made them ideal for use on lines with many gradients and the class were particularly associated with the Princetown (Devon) and Much Wenlock (Shropshire) branches. All were withdrawn and scrapped between 1949 and 1955.

The larger 4500 class (seventy-five), also designed by Churchward, first entered service in 1906. They were meant for light mixed traffic work, mainly on branch lines where their larger driving wheels gave them a good turn of speed. The 4575 class which followed in 1927 were a development of the 4500s. Designed by Charles Collett, the larger side tanks fitted to the new engines gave them better range, a small number were also fitted with the apparatus to work the GWRs push-pull auto trains. One hundred were built between 1927 and 1929, complementing the small prairies already in service.

George Ivatt's class 2 tank engine was built to replace elderly pre-Grouping light mixed traffic engines used on branches and other light work. The LMS introduced the class in 1946, although the majority of the 130 useful little engines were built under BR ownership.

# Chapter 7

# MIXING IT UP AND SETTING THE STANDARD

The railway companies had already adopted a degree of standardisation long before nationalisation. Standard types of boilers were common, which were interchangeable across classes, although many older types that were still in service had unique units which could only be fitted to sisters in the same class. The GWR was different, Swindon adopting complete standardisation of parts where possible across the entire fleet. The drive to standard components was led by Churchward who proposed a fleet of six classes with interchangeable parts in 1901. The scheme created the 2800, 6800 Grange, 2900 Saint, 5100 2-6-2 suburban tank engine, 2221 County 4-4-2 tank, and 3800 County 4-4-0 classes. Whilst there were some differences in the designs, many of the parts were interchangeable. Even boilers became standardised, a series of numbered designs being created which could be used on different classes.

The move to standardisation, taken to its logical conclusion by the GWR but adopted in all of Britain's railway workshops to a degree, made manufacturing easier. It also reduced the size of spare part stocks which needed to be held in workshops and maintenance depots, and made training engineers simpler.

The GWR, like the LMS and LNER who followed, adopted a 4-6-0 and 2-6-0 design as their standard mixed traffic locomotives. Collett's 4300 class 2-6-0, of which Swindon built 342 between 1911 and 1932, were based upon existing standard components and so no prototype was built. The combination of the outside cylinders of the Saint class, wheels of the 5100 class tank engine, and the standard No.4 boiler with superheating, created an extremely useful engine which could cover everything from local stopping goods trains to express passenger trains. The engines were so useful that a number were requisitioned by the ROD during the First World War.

Collett's 4900 or 'Hall' Class which followed, was a capable engine able to cover most of the mid-range work on the GWR. The first left Swindon works in 1928, the last of the 258, in 1943. All of the class, other than the first engine which was named *Saint Martin*, were named after country houses which had the hall suffix in the name. Frederick Hawksworth succeeded Collett at Swindon and created a new mixed traffic engine, the 6959 or 'Modified Hall' class. The seventy-one engines of the class, whilst outwardly similar to the Collett Halls, were completely new engines of a design which contained radical departures from standard Swindon practice. The engines were as capable as their predecessors, and also adopted the same naming convention, some unusual 'Halls' appearing in the list, some of which were actually colleges of the University of Oxford rather than country houses.

All of the companies adopted a set of standard designs for mixed traffic duties. The LMS adopted Stanier's 'Black 5' (842) and the earlier 2-6-0 designed by George Hughes in 1926, of which 245 were built in two batches. George Ivatt succeeded Stanier at the LMS and added a further class of mixed traffic engines, his 2-6-0 Class 4 designed for use on secondary routes. One hundred and sixty-two were built between 1947 and 1952, and were used across the whole of the LMS network.

The LNER created a series of standard mixed traffic locomotives. Gresley's B17 design of 4-6-0 (seventy-three) were built between 1928 and 1937 mainly to replace the old GER B12 class on express trains in East Anglia. The 3-cylinder design was light enough to work the old GER lines, but still able to work the heaviest expresses. The class were all named either after stately homes and British army regiments with a connection to East Anglia, or professional football clubs. Two of the class, *Norwich*

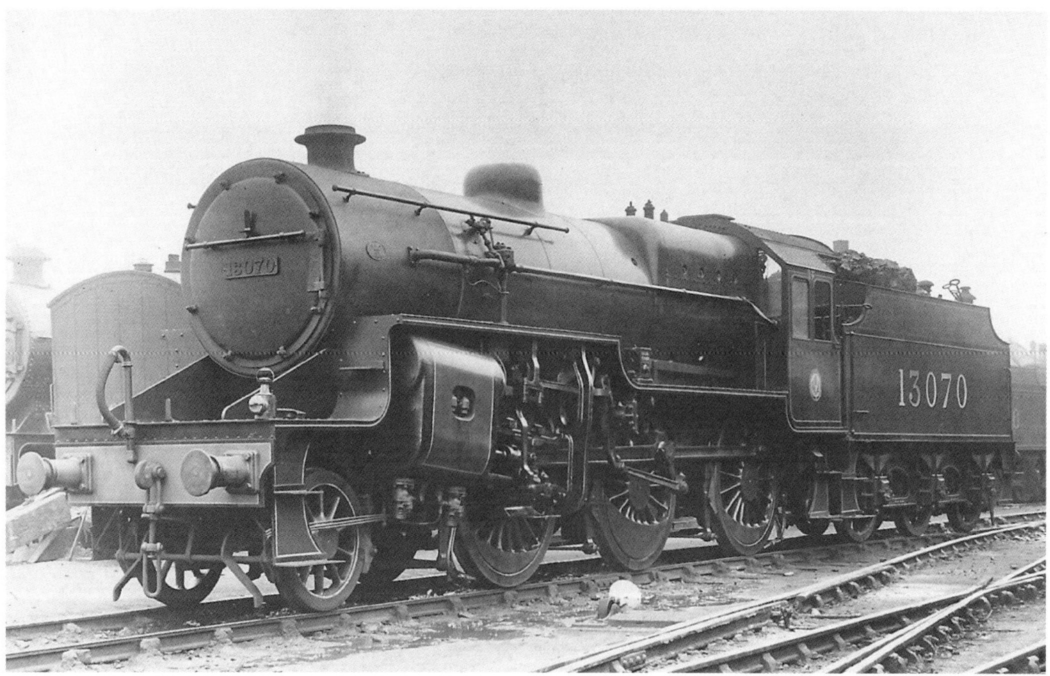

**LMS Hughes** 2-6-0 No. 13070. Commercial Postcard. *John Scott-Morgan Collection*

*City* and *Tottenham Hotspur,* were streamlined in the same manner as the A4s and renamed *East Anglian* and *City of London.*

Gresley also designed a class of locomotive designed for express mixed traffic work. The 2-6-2 V2 class arrived in 1936, with 184 built up to 1944. The engines were more than capable of covering the majority of the company's fast work, including deputising for a pacific on occasions.

Edward Thompson succeeded Gresley at the LNER and in 1942 created his most successful design, the 4-6-0 B1 Class (410 locomotives). The engines could be found across most of the LNER's lines and, like the LMS Black 5s, replaced a disparate group of small pre-Grouping classes. The B1s proved capable and useful locomotives, British Railways continuing to build them up to 1952.

The SR was well provided with mixed traffic locomotives when the railways were grouped in 1923. The LBSCR contributed seventeen of Billinton's K class 2-6-0, whilst the SE&CR added Maunsell's very capable N Class 2-6-0 to the fleet. The SR continued to build more Ns, a total of eighty being constructed at Ashford Works. Maunsell designed a second mixed traffic 2-6-0, the U Class, which entered service in 1928. In total, fifty of the class were built.

The first twenty engines were rebuilds of his K class 2-6-4 tank engines which had experienced trouble on the SE&CR's lines due to water surging in the tanks causing them to roll excessively. One of the class, *River Cray,* was involved in the Sevenoaks

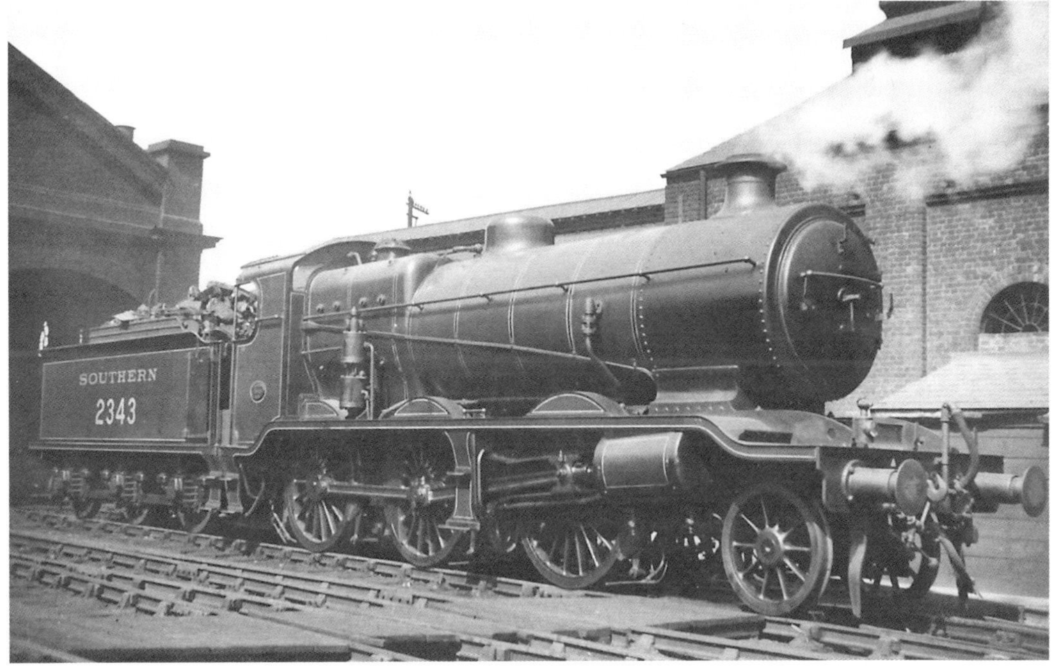


**LBSCR K-Class** 2-6-0 No. 2343. *John Scott-Morgan Collection*

railway accident caused by the locomotive derailing at speed as it passed Dunton Green railway station on 24 August 1927. The whole class were withdrawn due to concerns about their stability and rebuilt.

In 1948, British Railways was created, the vast majority of the country's railway companies becoming part of a single nationalised railway. Whilst BR inherited a fleet of modern locomotives, they also received a collection of aging engines which needed replacement. Whilst they continued to build pre-nationalisation designs, the railway's chief mechanical engineers, Robert Riddles and his assistants Roland Bond and Ernest Cox, sought to create a series of new 'standard' locomotives. The 'standards' were made up of eleven classes of locomotives, most mixed traffic, although some express passenger classes, and one dedicated freight locomotive class were included. All of the engines bore a strong family resemblance with, where possible, standard components used.

All of the BR standard classes had a common feature, ease of maintenance. All had high running plates and outside cylinders which made accessing the machinery for preparation and maintenance much easier. The cabs were improved over many earlier designs, with a much more ergonomic layout.

The BR standards included two class 2 locomotives. The little 2MT 2-6-2 tank engines were a new version of Ivatt's tank engines for branch line and light mixed traffic use, whilst the 2MT tender engines where based upon the same designers tender locomotive equivalents designed to have longer range. Only thirty of the tank engines were built as BR had continued to build the earlier design. The last thirty of the original version, built at Crewe, were allocated to Southern Region where they proved extremely useful. There was more of a need for the tender version, so BR built 65 of the Riddles version to add to the 128 that had been built by the LMS and by BR after nationalisation. The two types of Class 2 were able to work anywhere, which, with their good turn of speed and acceleration, made them very important additions to the fleet.

Riddles designed a pair of class 3MT locomotives. The tank engine version was also a 2-6-2, all forty-five of which were built at Swindon between 1952 and 1955, and were allocated in small numbers to all the regions apart from the North East and Scotland. The twenty Class 3 tender engines, also built at Swindon, were all allocated to Scottish and North Eastern regions, although one example was transferred to Southern Region, working out its final days based at Guildford depot. The Class 3s were built for traffic which was declining, so thus had very short working lives, and the need for them to have been built at all is often questioned.

Much more successful were the three classes of 4MT locomotives, one tank engine and two tender engines. The class 4 tank engine was a 2-6-4 based upon Fairburn's extraordinary design for the LMS. The nationalised railway had inherited large fleets of big GWR, LMS and LNER tank engines all of which were more than capable of handling commuter and outer suburban as well as secondary line passenger trains.

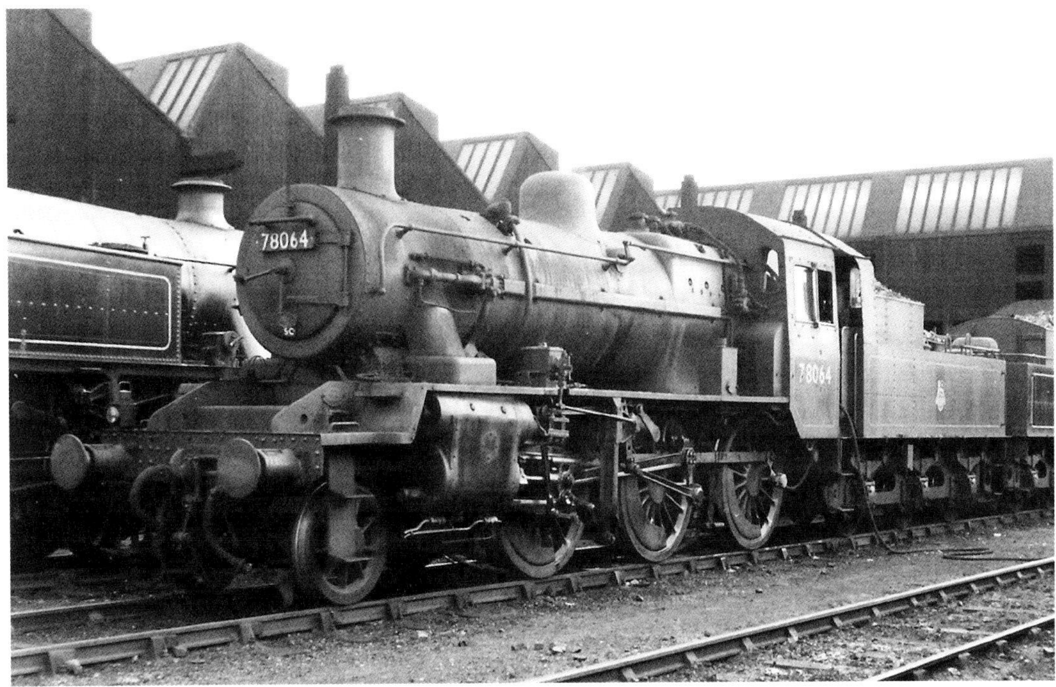

**British Railways** Standard Class 2MT 2-6-0 No.78064 at Wigan shed in 1957. *John Scott-Morgan Collection*

Whilst those regions were well provided for, Southern Region and the old LT&SR lines were lacking in modern motive power for these services.

Electrification of the London suburban network which had been gradually extended further afield by the SR resolved some of the issue but may also have been responsible for the problem BR inherited. Outside of the areas where electrification had reached the commuter and secondary services were being handled by older, often pre-Grouping, classes which were struggling with increasing weights and frequencies of services. Whilst the U and N class 2-6-0s were more than capable of handling the work, they were insufficient to cover the region's needs. The new Class 4 tank engines were ideal solutions to the gap in the fleet. With design work being undertaken at Brighton under the supervision of Riddles, it made sense for 130 of the 155 engines to be built at Brighton.

The class was allocated across the entire BR network but became particularly associated with the commuter services out of Fenchurch Street as well as fast trains to Southend which they were equally at home on. The 4MT tanks were used on the old LBSCR routes which had not yet been electrified and were common on services in East Sussex and Kent. A further group, allocated to Polmadie depot, were good performers on the Glasgow commuter services.

The two class 4 tender engines were built to a 2-6-0 and 4-6-0 design. The 2-6-0s were designed at Doncaster works, who built 70 of the 115 engines, with the remainder built at Horwich, all between 1952 and 1957. One of the class, 76114, was the last steam engine to be built at Doncaster, and another, 76099, was the last built at Horwich. The engines were a variant of the Ivatt Class 4 and was designed mainly for freight work. Their light axle loading allowed them to work on nearly all of the network and they were allocated across every region of BR, apart from Western Region which had no need of them, the work being covered by existing GWR designs. The engines allocated to Southern Region received the larger BR1B tender to allow them to work on the region's longer distance trains.

The last of the class 4s were the larger 4-6-0 design which were built at Swindon between 1951 and 1957. The eighty locomotives of the class were used for mixed traffic duties on secondary lines where the larger Black 5s and BR standard class 5 were too heavy. London Midland, Western and Southern Region received the class, the group intended for Southern Region, like the 2-6-0s, receiving the larger BR1B tender which made their route availability less broad due to the tender having a higher axle loading than the engine. The rest of the class received the smaller BR2 or BR2A tenders.

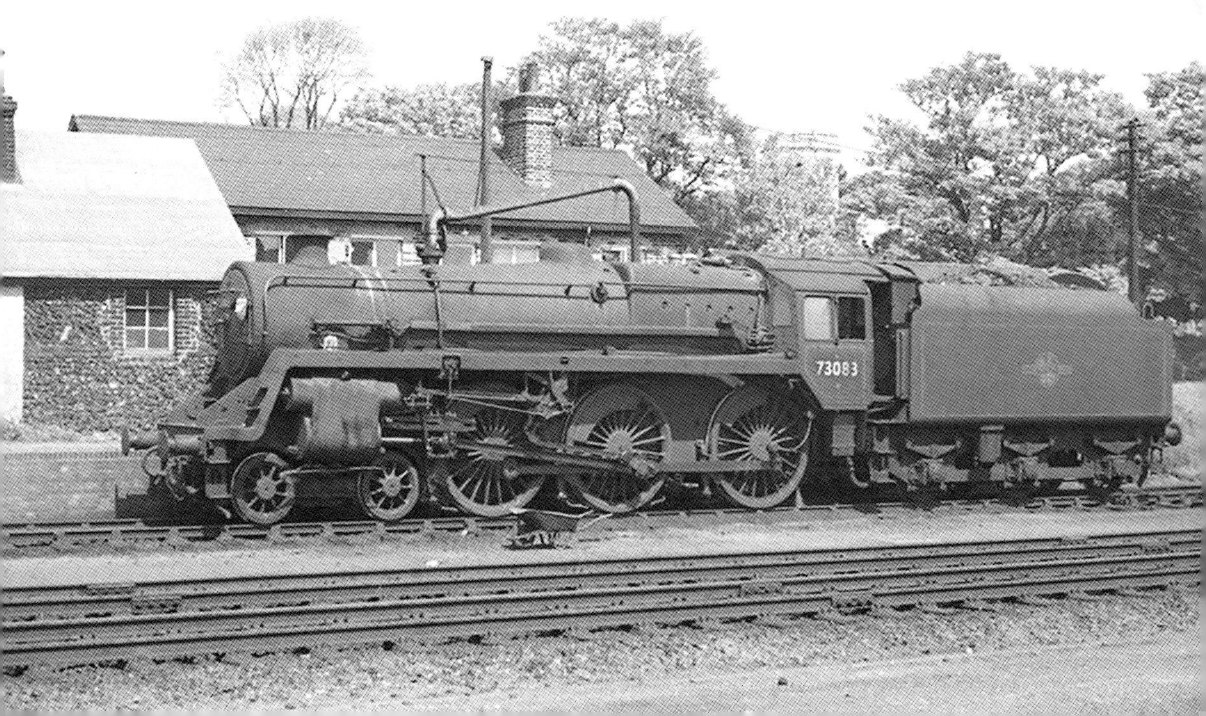

**British Railways** Standard Class 5MT 4-6-0 No.73083 heading towards Basingstoke Shed after arriving with a freight working in the summer of 1964. Note the large BR1B tender which was used for Southern Region standard class tender engines. *Barry Lewis*

The standard class 5MT was very similar to the Stanier Black 5 upon which it was based. The class were built at Derby and Doncaster, with 172 entering traffic on BR. They were fitted with labour saving devices such as self-cleaning smokeboxes and rocking grates to make disposing of the locomotive after a 'turn' easier for the crew. The Class 5s proved to be as good as their LMS predecessors and were as popular with crews. The engines were equally at home on fast expresses as on slow freight. Like the Class 4s, the 5MTs, some of which also carried names from withdrawn King Arthur class locomotives, intended for Southern Region were fitted with the large BR1B tender.

BR designed three classes of 4-6-2 for express work. The first were the fifty-five locomotives of the Class 7 Britannias. The Class 7s were all built at Crewe between 1951 and 1954. The design, unlike the pacifics which preceded them, was a 2-cylinder locomotive, although they still proved capable in service. The engines were a combination of the best engineering developments achieved by the

**British Railways** Standard Class 7 4-6-2 No.70013 *Oliver Cromwell* at Carnforth Shed on 10 August 1968 on the eve of the end of steam on British Railways. Note the painted on nameplates, the originals having been removed for 'safe keeping'. *Hugh Llewelyn*

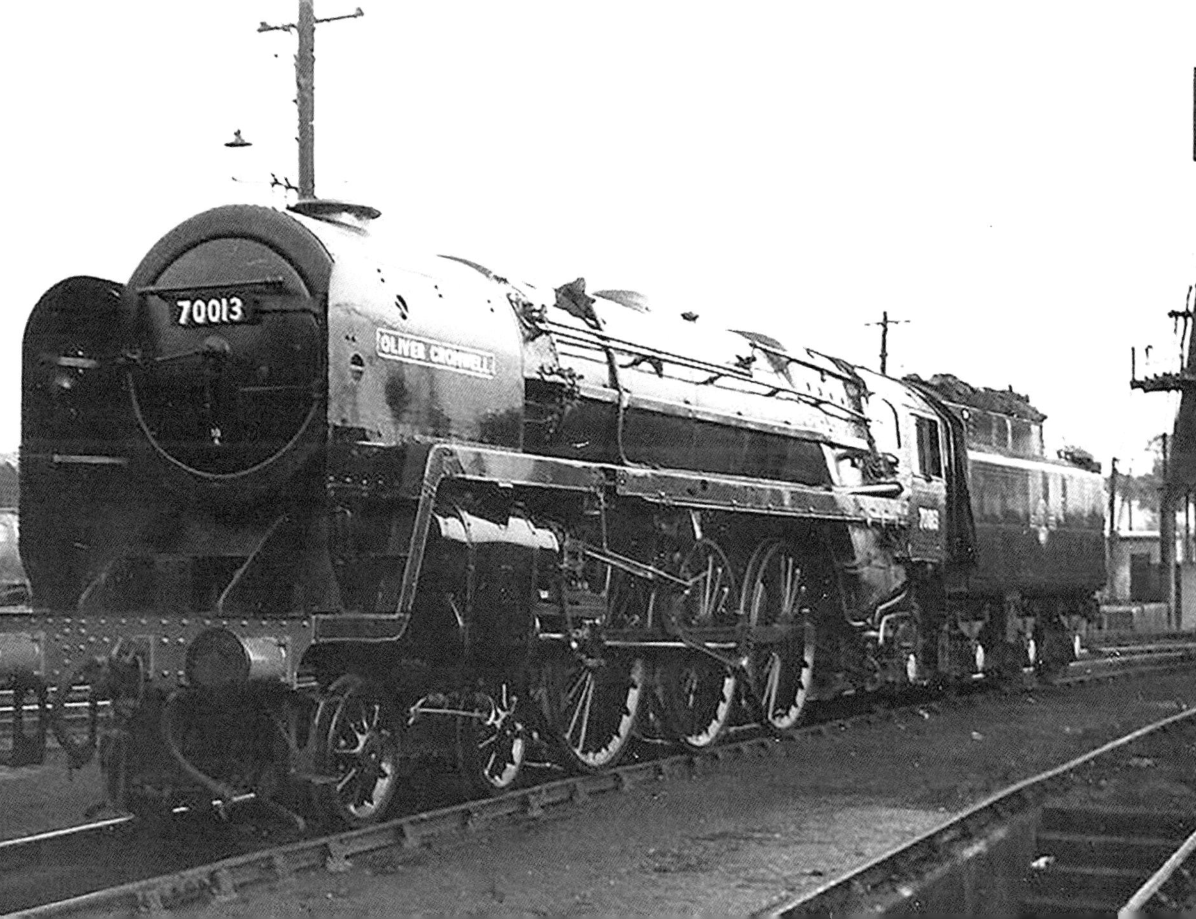

pre-nationalisation companies, and they generally received good feedback from crews. Most were named, the first, *Britannia*, giving the class its name.

The improvements in design and materials enabled the locomotive to have a lower axle loading, allowing them to be used on routes upon which large pacifics had previously been barred including Eastern Region, the first time pacifics had been available for the more lightly built East Anglian lines. The crews who received them at Stratford and other East Anglian depots gave them glowing reports, the high power and easy operation of the class providing the crews with an engine they could get good results from. They were equally popular across the rest of Britain, apart from Western Region.

Crews at Old Oak Common and Plymouth Laira disliked them intensely. This may have been down to a degree of partisan preference for GWR designs, since Cardiff Canton crews achieved good results with them in South Wales. The general dislike of the Class 7 in Western Region may also have been caused by the new engines being left side drive as opposed to the GWR designs which had all been right drive. The signals on Western Region were all situated for right drive engines, and were more difficult to see from a left seat. The handrails on the smoke deflectors were also claimed to reduce visibility which was partly agreed to have caused the Milton crash in 1955, so the engines allocated to Western Region had them removed and replaced with hand holds in the deflector plates.

Southern Region received no Britannias as they already had large classes of Bulleid's pacifics, although seven were loaned to the region after the crank axle on Merchant Navy *Bibby Line* fractured at speed and the whole class was withdrawn for checks.

The Class 6 or 'Clans' were a smaller version of the Britannia class intended for the west of Scotland where a light but powerful engine was needed. They were liked by the Scottish crews who regularly worked them and had got used to the way to fire and drive them, but when trialled elsewhere they were unpopular. The locomotives all took names from withdrawn ex-Highland Railway Clan Class engines and only ten were built, all at Crewe. BR had planned to build a further fifteen of the class, the first five of which were intended for Southern Region, although why remains a mystery given that the more capable Bullied pacifics were available. The last ten were to continue with the Clan naming convention and were destined for Scotland. They were never built as the works order was cancelled after the publication of the 1955 Modernisation Plan.

One final pacific class was built, although it consisted of just a single prototype locomotive. The large class 8 pacific, named *Duke of Gloucester*, was built at Crewe in 1954, and differed from all of the other standard classes as it had three cylinders instead of the usual two. It was built as a replacement for Princess Royal class locomotive *Princess Anne*, which was written off after it was involved in the Harrow and Wealdstone crash. Riddles had been lobbying for a new state of the art class 8 pacific class, but the Railway Executive Committee continually refused to make budget available. It seems that the availability of budget to build the new engine after the Harrow crash was taken advantage of in other ways, since the new engine contained a host of new developments including the rare use of 'Caprotti' rotary cam driven valve gear.

A small group of Claughton class engines had been fitted with a version of the system by the LNWR in 1928, but they were not an improvement over an unmodified engine. The LNER tried the system in 1929 and again in 1938 but with the same result. In the 1950s the system was improved and fitted to the last two Black Fives built by BR as a trial. The last thirty of the Standard class 5s which followed were also fitted with the new system.

The 'Duke' was built with three cylinders despite Riddles' attempts to keep the bigger locomotive to the 2-cylinder arrangement favoured on all the standards. The power requirements for a class 8 engine would have meant large cylinders that took a 2-cylinder machine out gauge. The only viable option was for Riddles to reluctantly adopt a 3-cylinder design, with all the maintenance complexities that involved. The design team felt that the issues traditionally associated with 3- and 4-cylinder locomotives could be mitigated through the adoption the Caprotti system. The system not only offered a more maintenance friendly option but promised precise control of steam let in to the cylinders and better exhausting of the used gas. In theory the system could provide a more freely steaming locomotive, which would be more economic on fuel, and able to work hard for long periods of time on the heaviest trains.

Sadly the engine proved a disappointment in BR service. It was found that a lots of design errors and deviation from the drawings during construction had undermined what should have been a fine locomotive. The workshops had also ignored the advice of L.T. Daniels, who represented the British Caprotti Company, when he recommended the installation of a Kylchap blastpipe as fitted to four of Gresley's A4s, including world record holder *Mallard*, and all of Arthur Peppercorn's A2 class pacifics built for the LNER. The Kylchap could have coped with the fierce exhaust blasts that were generated by the Caprotti system, but instead Crewe elected to fit a standard GWR double chimney which was installed before Riddles could stop them. The result was poor draughting since the blastpipe was too small for the high-pressure exhaust which stifled the boiler and prevented it steaming correctly. The firebox was also faulty in design, the ashpan was incorrectly dimensioned and the dampers, which let air into the fire through the grate were too small, both being departures from the drawings. The fire thus received too little air when working at speed reducing the ability of the fire to heat the boiler water.

The locomotive was also being built whilst the BR Modernisation Plan was being created which raised questions over whether the engine was even needed since steam would be soon dispensed with. Despite the scepticism and issues with the built machine, it appears that Riddles was actually right, and the Duke should have been an exceptional machine. The engine survived into preservation, where it was fitted with the Kylchap blastpipe and larger chimney that it should have had, and better ashpan and dampers in accordance with the original drawings. The valve timing was also very carefully set to ensure the best possible gas flow into and out of the cylinders. When the locomotive returned to steam it was a revelation, proving that the basic design was sound.

The last of the standard classes was a heavy freight locomotive designed to improve upon what already existed in BR's locomotive fleet. The 9F class were intended for use on long distance fast freights, but were often found on passenger services, particularly on the steeply graded Somerset and Dorset line. A total of 251 of the class were built at Crewe and Swindon between 1954 and 1960 and could be found across most of the mainline and secondary routes in Britain. The use of a ten coupled arrangement with leading pony truck (2-10-0) spread the weight without losing power due to the small diameter of the driving wheels. The 9Fs had an interesting design feature to address potential issues with such a long wheel base on sharper curves. The centre driving wheels had no flanges, allowing them to drift across the top of the rail stopping them derailing.

Despite the undoubted excellence of the design, efforts were made to improve them still further. In 1955, ten locomotives were built with a non-standard experimental Franco-Crosti boiler. These had a feed water pre-heater that used the residual heat of the exhausted steam to heat water prior to it passing into the boiler through the injectors, thus making the engine more efficient. The devices fitted to the 9Fs took the form of a drum under the boiler barrel in which the water was preheated. The exhausted steam, and smoke passed through the tubes of the secondary boiler and into a second smokebox from where they were exhausted through a rectangular chimney toward the rear of the main boiler. In order to alleviate the soft exhaust, the usual smoke deflectors fitted at the front of a normal 9F were moved backwards. The result was an ungainly looking engine, which fell into the old engineers' maxim that if a design looks right it is right. They didn't and weren't, the hoped for improvements in efficiency were minimal and didn't justify the complexity in maintenance and expense of fitting the system to the locomotives.

The 9Fs had one last claim to fame; the very last steam locomotive to be built by British Railways left Swindon Works in March 1960. To mark the occasion, the works fitted the locomotive with a copper capped chimney, bringing back memories of the days of the GWR. It was also painted in BR Locomotive Green livery, usually reserved for passenger engines. The railway decided that the locomotive should be named to mark the occasion and Western Region staff magazine ran a competition to decide the name that the engine should carry. The winning suggestion was

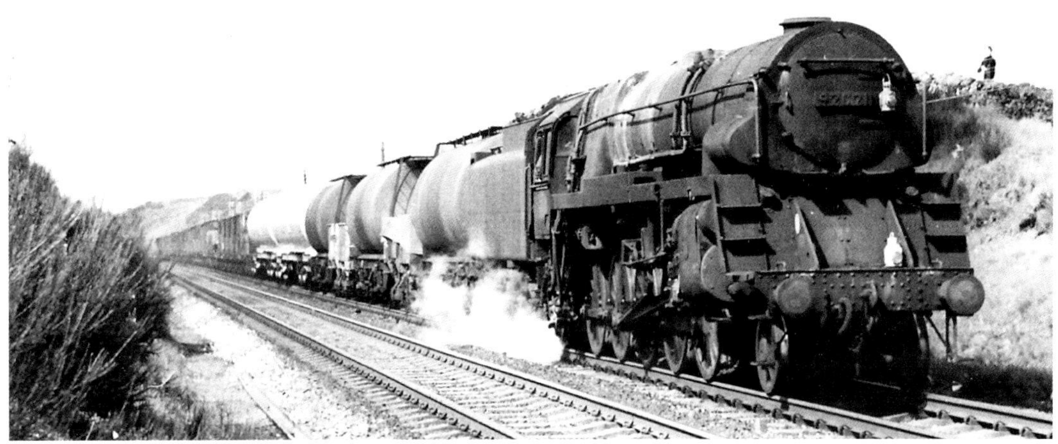

**British Railways** Standard Class 9F 2-10-0 No. 92021. The locomotive was built with a Franco-Crosti boiler but later rebuilt and the pre-heater removed. *John Scott-Morgan Collection*

*Evening Star*. *Evening Star* was the only 9F to be named whilst in BR service although some have since received names in preservation.

BR built 999 of the standard classes as well as pre-nationalisation types, none of which would have a long service life. The controversial 'Modernisation Plan' which sought to replace steam with diesel and electric traction made steam locomotives with only a few years of service redundant.

# Chapter 8

# THE MODERN RAILWAY

As the 1950s dawned, Britain's railway management and politicians were giving thought to how the country's railways could be brought up to date. The result, published in December 1954, was the 'Modernisation and Re-Equipment of British Railways' report (Modernisation Report). The report advocated the electrification of some principal main lines, the replacement of steam with diesel traction, closure of a small number of duplicated lines and the construction of new rolling stock. The result was the creation by BR of the 'pilot scheme' for the construction of a series of diesel locomotives spread across three power categories. The locomotives were ordered from six independent manufacturers, some of whom had no experience of railway engine construction. British Railway's own workshops were partly involved in the programme but most of the new locomotive classes came from outside the railway.

The irony of the report was that the pre-nationalisation railways had already been embarking on the introduction of electrification and experiments with diesel traction were well underway. The L&YR and Mersey Railway electrified their suburban lines around Liverpool in 1903 and 1904. The LBSCR had started to electrify the south London suburban lines in 1909, while the LNWR undertook a similar project on its London inner suburban network. The LSWR followed suit in 1917.

The NER also embarked on a wide programme of electrification after 1904. The suburban lines around Newcastle upon Tyne were provided with electric multiple units (EMUs) by the NER which ran on a 600V DC third rail supply, which was uprated to 630V in 1934 by the LNER who expanded the electrification around the city. The NER's Newcastle Quayside freight branch was also electrified but with overhead power lines to make working in the dockside yards safer for staff involved in shunting wagons. Two light freight and shunting locomotives were built specifically for the ¾ mile lines, the ES1s. The engines were BO-BO electrics with a large centre 'steeple cab' which allowed for good visibility, essential in the quayside yards. Both survived until 1966 when BR withdrew them.

In 1914 the NER electrified the Newport to Shildon line with 1500v DC overhead catenary. Darlington works built ten electric freight locomotives, class EF1, to haul coal traffic on the line between 1914 and 1919. The success of the two projects convinced the NER directors that their mainline between Newcastle and York could be viably electrified and a project was put in motion to do so. Raven designed a prototype electric locomotive for the planned scheme, which was built at Darlington. The engine had a leading and trailing bogie and six driving wheels powered by electric traction motors, giving it an unusual 2-CO-2 arrangement. The plan was dropped in 1923 after the Grouping and locomotive was stored. It remained in store until 1950 when BR sadly scrapped it.

The GCR had also looked to electric traction as a means to improve its services. The 'Woodhead Route' from Sheffield to Penistone and Manchester had opened in 1845, but the railway was finding difficulty in operating heavy coal trains over the route using steam traction. The GCR didn't proceed with electrifying the route, but the idea did not go away. The LNER, who inherited the line from the GCR, continued to plan for the modernisation of the line. In 1936 final plans were drawn up and Gresley designed two types of locomotives for the route. The project began but was interrupted by the Second World War. Electrification recommenced after the war with the addition of a new tunnel at Woodhead. The plan was complete by 1955.

Gresley's two locomotives were the EM1 (BR Class 76) and EM2 (Class 77). The EM1s were a class of 58 BO-BO electric locomotive with pantographs to collect power from the overhead power catenary. The prototype was built in 1941 at Gorton Works, the main class following between 1950 and 1953 from Doncaster. The

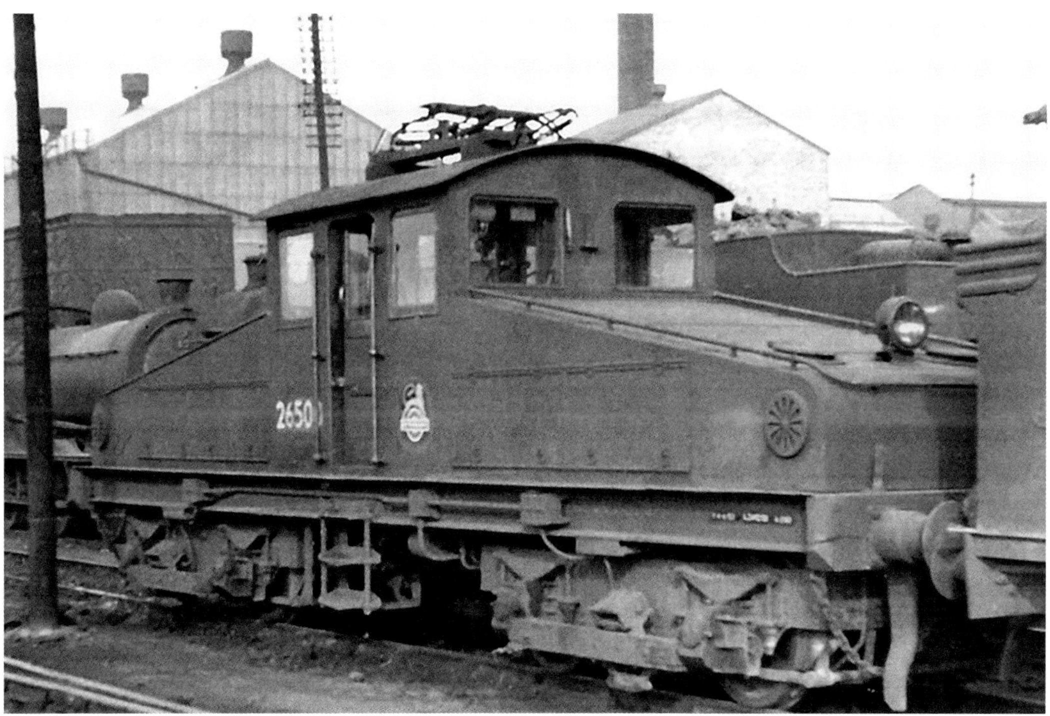

**Ex-NER Electric** ES1 No. 26500 at Heaton depot on 30 June 1954. *Ben Brooksbank*

engines were intended for freight, often working in pairs on coal trains, but were regularly used on passenger trains. The EM2 class, built in 1953 and 1954, at Gorton works numbered just seven units. The large CO-CO engines were used on express passenger services on the Woodhead route but unlike the EM1s which survived until the line was closed in 1981, the EM2s had a relatively short working life in Britain, all being withdrawn in 1968 and sold to Netherlands State Railways.

The pre-nationalisation railways had not only looked towards electric traction but were also experimenting with diesel traction. The GWR had introduced a series of thirty-eight diesel railcars in the early nineteen thirties and were examining a pair of diesel shunting locomotives in 1933 and 1936. The LMS were likewise looking at the possibilities offered by replacing steam shunting engines with diesel units, which had the advantage of simply being switched off when not in use.

The LMS rebuilt a steam locomotive in 1932 to become the first diesel shunter. It was not entirely successful but convinced the company that the idea had promise. A selection of experimental prototypes were commissioned from outside contractors, the company eventually settling on a design which was echoed in form by Maunsell on the Southern who was undertaking an independent study. The LMS and SR designs both had a large bonnet a single cab at one end, and an 0-6-0 chassis. The designs influenced the British Rail Class 08 which is still in service in 2025 in small numbers on the national network.

**Ex-LMS 0-6-0** Deisel Shunter No. 12000 (renumbered from LMS 7074) at Crewe South, 8 April 1962. *John Scott-Morgan Collection*

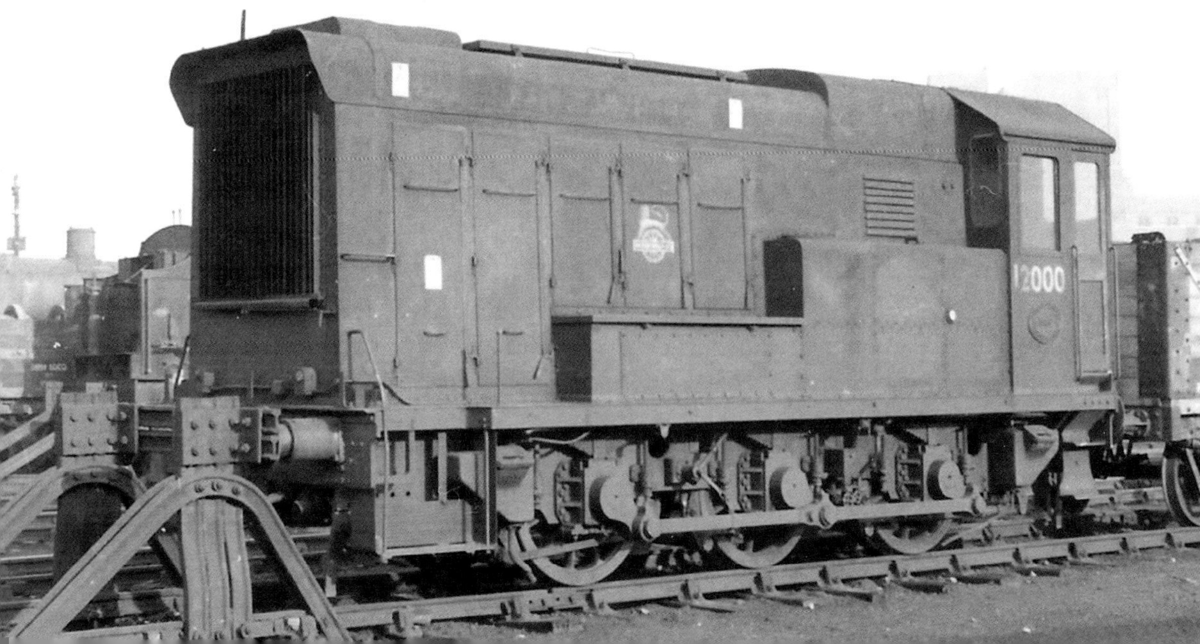

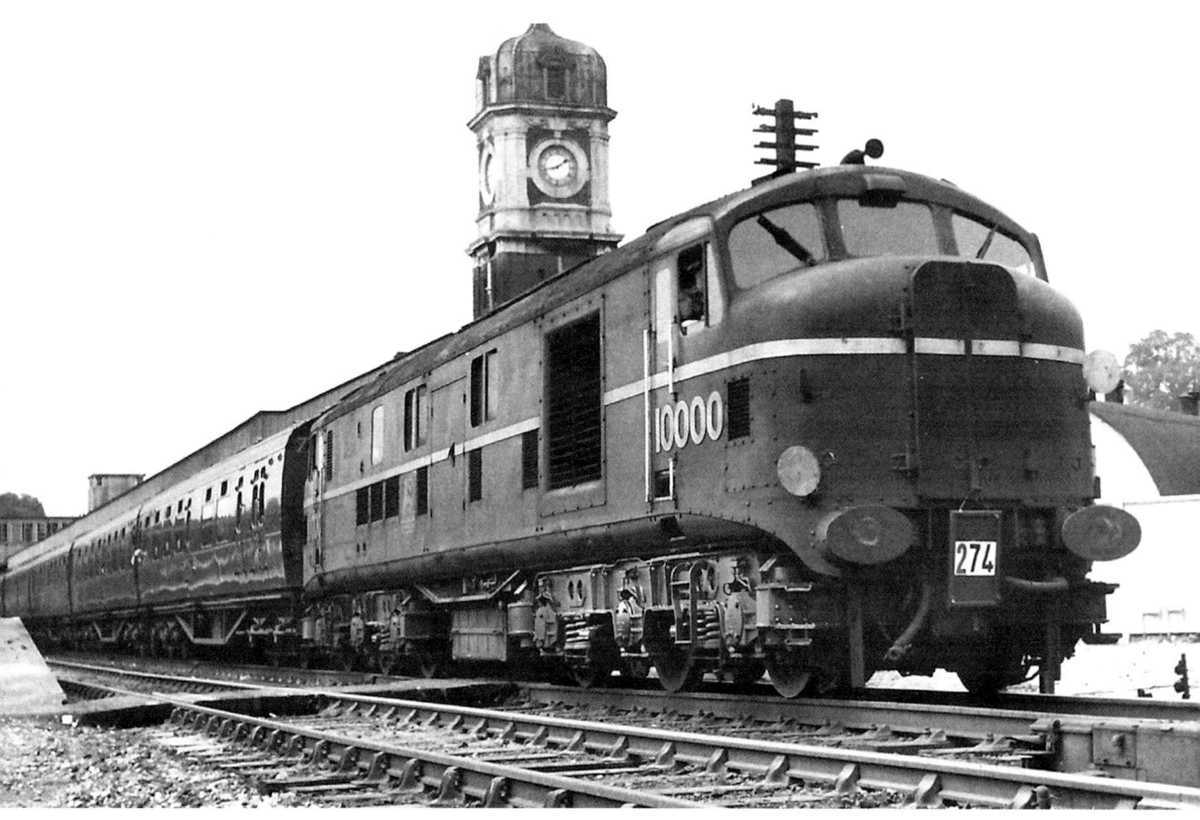

**Ex-LMS CO-CO** Diesel No. 10000 at Southampton on 1 August 1953. *John Scott-Morgan Collection*

The LMS and SR had also created prototype diesel locomotives for mainline work. The LMS built a pair of identical CO-CO diesels. The two engines were built at Derby, emerging in 1948. The machines were influenced by American designs, having a bonnet at each end in front of the cabs, whilst the power units and associated equipment were located in a flat sided body. The 'twins' became BR Class 16/1 and were trialled on former LMS lines, often working together. In 1953 the pair were sent to Southern Region for trials against Bulleid's mainline diesels. Bulleid's diesels were designed in 1947 but were not complete until 1948, becoming BR class 16/2. The Southern diesels were quite different from the LMS machines, with a flat front cab similar to the designer's electric locomotives. Both had considerable influence on designs that would follow.

The SR had embarked on a rolling plan of electrification, gradually expanding the third rail west. As a result it had become clear that electric locomotives would be required to replace steam, although the use of EMUs was being examined at the same time. Bulleid's designs, of which three were built, were CO-CO electrics collecting power from the third rail. The design aesthetic seems to have been influenced by the Southern's 2-HAL EMUs introduced in 1938 with which they bore an uncanny resemblance. The three electric locomotives proved a success and became BR Class 70 but were withdrawn by 1969.

It seems extraordinary that BR would exclude their own workshops from large parts of the Pilot Scheme given that they already had experience of working with new technologies which BR had halted investment in. This may explain why the scheme under which 174 locomotives were purchased was such an abject failure. There were, however, some successes and Swindon once more chose to find their own solutions.

The discussion that follows will use the Train Operations Processing System class numbering adopted after the computer system was adopted in the early 1970s for clarity.

The plan purchased locomotives, such as the class 14, 15 and 16, for which work was rapidly declining before they were built. The Class 14 was an 0-6-0 design with a large central cab of which fifty-six were built at Swindon (1964-65). The engines were designed for shunting and trip working and were much more reliable than many other designs of the time. They were withdrawn, like many other pilot plan locomotives after very short working lives, although a number were sold to the NCB and British Steel where they undertook exactly the work they had been designed for and proved popular. The class 15s and 16s were

**Bulleid CO-CO** Electric No. 20003, built by British Railways at Eastleigh in 1948. *John Scott-Morgan Collection*

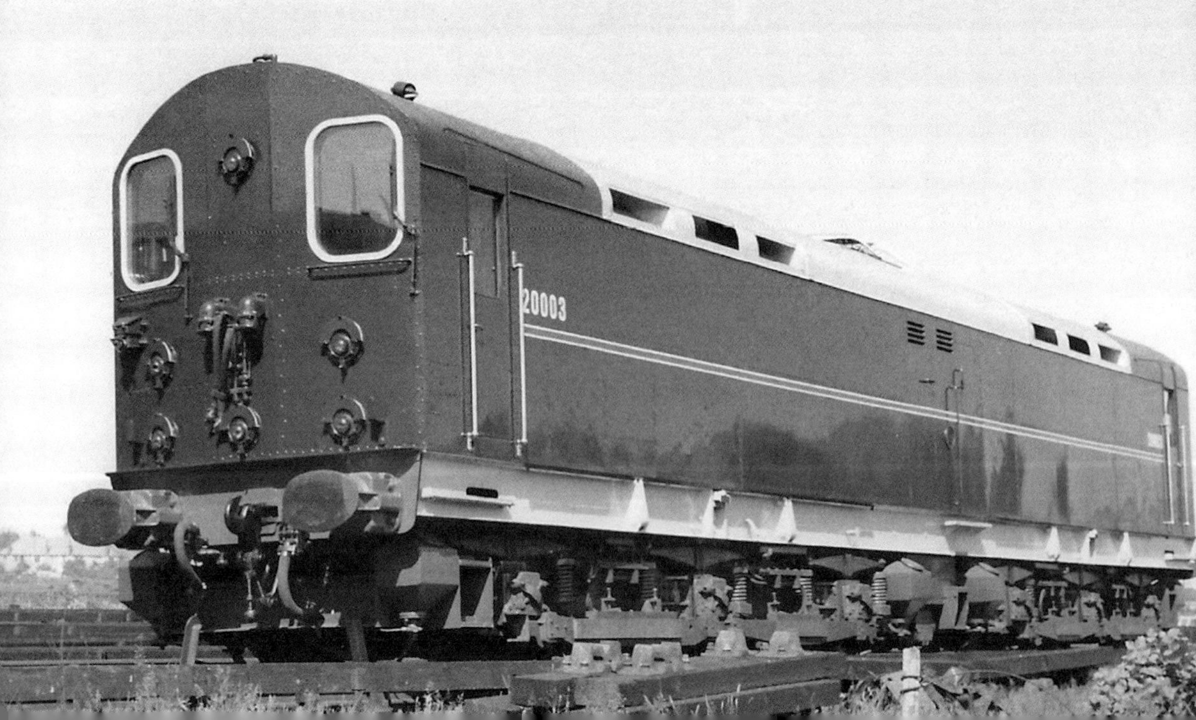

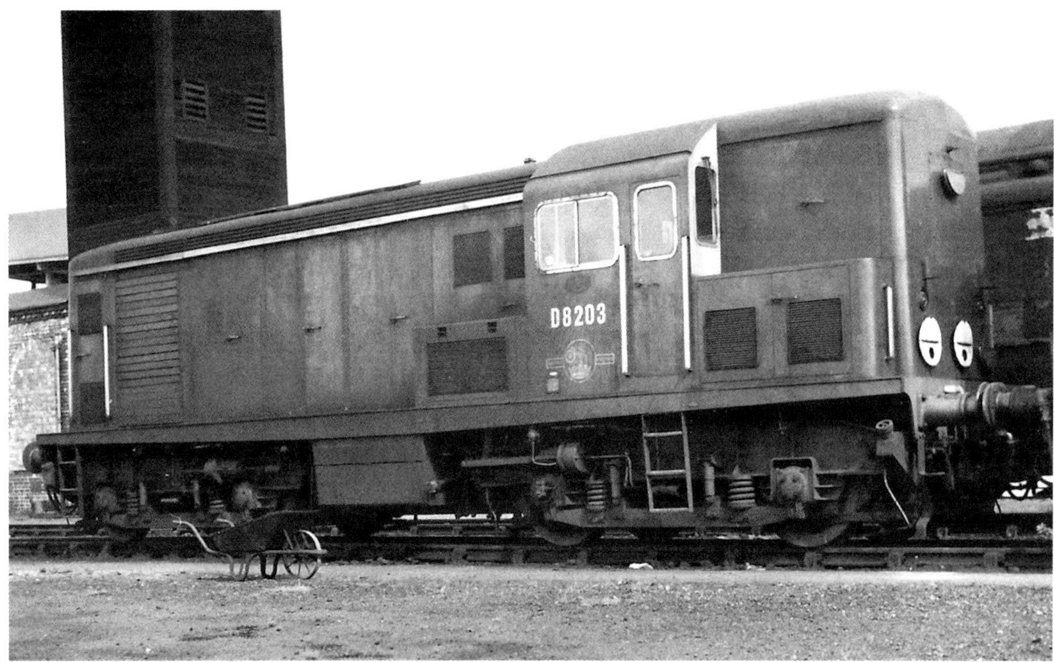

**Type 1** BO-BO No.D8203 at Willesden depot on 21 September 1958. Note the difference in bonnet lengths on the locomotive. *John Scott-Morgan Collection*

BO-BO locomotives built to the lowest power classification used in the scheme, type 1. Both had very long bonnets in front of the cab in one direction and stubby short bonnets in the other.

The class 16s were poor, suffering from frequent reliability issues, especially with engine seizures caused by inadequate ventilation. Fortunately only ten were built by North British. The Class 15s were similar in appearance and although they were better than the 16s they were still unreliable due to issues with their power units. Despite the issues, forty-four were built although like many other pilot scheme engines they had woefully short lives, all being withdrawn in the late 1960s in favour of one of the few pilot scheme classes that was successful.

BR decided to request a new type 1 design in 1962 in response to the perceived vision issues experienced with all the first group of type 1s caused by the long bonnets at one end. The answer, BR believed, was in a centre cab design, with low bonnets at each end, and a large cab with big windows. The result was the utterly woeful class 17 designed by Clayton.

The Class summarised in one type everything that was wrong with the pilot scheme. The locomotives were of a BO-BO configuration, but the low bonnets specified meant that each bogie was powered by a separate diesel power unit, which had been intended for powering railcars. The engines proved to be extremely unreliable. The long bonnets were found to restrict visibility directly in front of the locomotive and they were totally incapable of hauling heavy freight trains. Even after extensive modification the class were still unreliable. Despite all its issues, and with a much better type 1 already available, for reasons only known to BR a total of 117 of the machines were built between 1962 and 1965. The class was withdrawn in the late 1960s.

The sole type 1 which was a success was the class 20. Introduced in 1952 and built by English Electric. A total of 228 were built. The engines are of a BO-BO configuration, with a single large bonnet containing the power unit and other equipment, and a large cab at one end. Whilst the view forward when running bonnet first has limitations, it is no worse than on a steam locomotive. A solution was later found when two engines were coupled together nose to nose effectively mimicking the double ended design of most other modern locomotives in Britain. The 20s were a great success and are still in use on Britain's railway in 2025, although many have been withdrawn.

The next power classification, type 2, ranged from the exceptional to the downright awful. The class 21s were built by North British to a BO-BO configuration, using Diesel-Electric power, where the diesel power unit works as a generator powering electric traction motors on the axles. This configuration would become the standard on BR, ousting the other options of diesel-mechanical (although this worked well on the 08 class shunters) and diesel-hydraulic which was adopted by Western Region. Fifty-eight of the class were built and proved to be horribly unreliable and were withdrawn by 1969, although twenty were rebuilt into the class 29 with new engines. The 29s were much better but as a small non-standard class they soon fell foul of BR and were withdrawn for scrapping.

BR asked North British to build a version of the class 21 with diesel-hydraulic power units for Western Region, which were delivered between 1959 and 1962 as the class 22. Often referred to as Baby Warships due to their similarity in appearance and equipment to the much larger class 41, they were superior to the class 21. A combination of reduced work and the bankruptcy of North British in 1962 meant the class was steadily withdrawn after 1967.

One of the poorer type 2s were the class 23 BO-BO or Baby Deltics which looked like a very small version of the class 55, and used a smaller version of the Napier Deltic engine. Unlike their big cousins, the class 23s were beset with reliability issues and only ten were built. Not all the type 2s were bad.

The classes 24 (151 locomotives), 25 (327), 26 (47), and 27 (69) were all BO-BO designs which gave good service to BR well into the 1980s, some until the mid-1990s. All were diesel-electric and used variations of the same Sulzer 6LDA28 engine which proved to be extremely reliable. The class 30 and 31, type 2s despite having a 30 series class number, were also relatively successful. The two classes were very

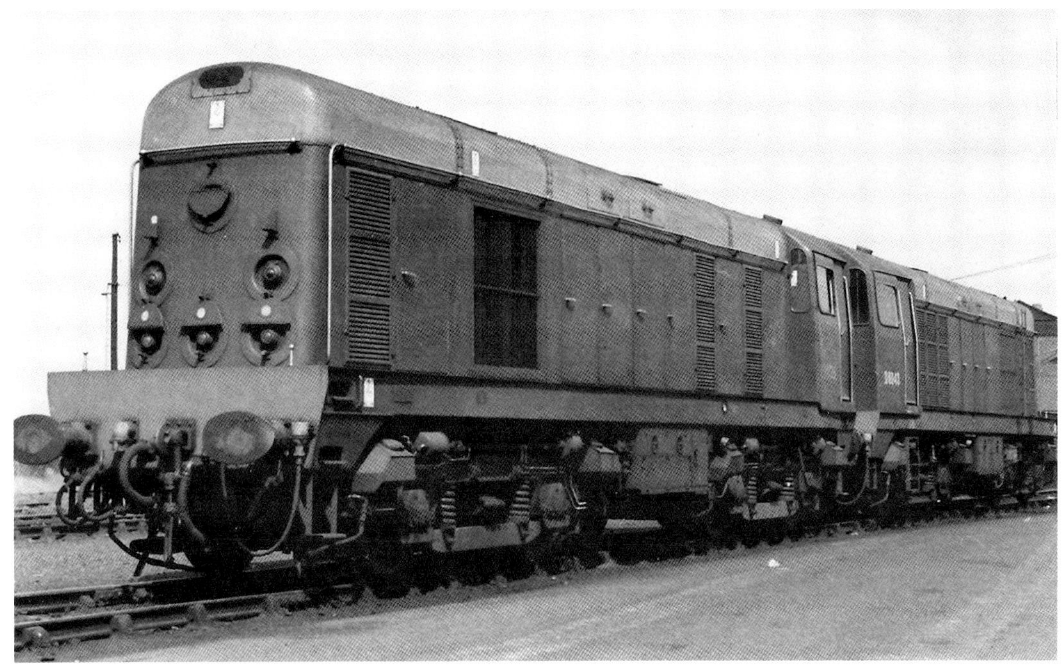

**Class 20** (type 1) BO-Bos Nos. D8015 and D8043 at Willesden depot on 7 May 1960.
*John Scott-Morgan Collection*

similar, the main difference being the power unit. The class 30 had a Mirlees engine, the 31s had English Electric. The Mirlees engines were later replaced with the better English Electric unit, and all class 30s became Class 31s. Both were A1A-A1A designs of which a total of 263 were built between 1967 and 1962. The classes were spread across Britain, although many were used in East Anglia to replace steam.

The last type 2 design is one which divides opinion. The Class 28 CO-BO locomotives were designed by Metropolitan Vickers for high-speed freight services. The design appears to be fundamentally solid, my conversations with members of the design team revealing the reasons for decisions made in the design process. It seems that the locomotive might have been less a poor design and more a case of trying to push the engineering envelope too far. Nevertheless, the class 28s suffered frequent failures with the Crossley engines which were also noisy and emitted overly smoky exhaust fumes, although maybe the accusing finger of history should be pointed more at the power unit than the design of the locomotive. The entire class was sent back to Metropolitan Vickers for modification of the engines, and to solve a problem with cab windows falling out while running. The author's conversation with a member of the design team revealed that the cab window issue was not a design issue but more down to poor quality control on the shop floor. The design of the cab was changed to support easier construction. Whilst the cab and electrical system issues were resolved, Crossley never managed to completely cure the issues with the power unit. Thought was given to replacing the power units with BR going as far as asking English Electric to quote for the work, but the small, non-standard class were all withdrawn and all bar one scrapped.

The type 3s and 4s were generally much more successful. The influence of Swindon can be seen in the type 3 and 4 ranges with a selection of their preferred diesel-hydraulic powered locomotives entering service after 1958. The first were the Class 42 Warship class, all of which were named after notable Royal Navy warships. It had become clear to the management of Western Region that Germany had mastered the use of diesel-hydraulic power units and so, seeking not to fall into the trap of ordering unproven designs, a licence was negotiated with German industry for a scaled down version of the Deutsche Bundesbahn (German State Railway) class V200.

The licence was agreed and new locomotives were created based on proven engineering components and principles. The result was the Class 42, 38 of which were built between 1958 and 1961. The machines were powered by German Maybach engines, manufactured under licence by Bristol Siddeley, apart from two which received Paxman Ventura engines for comparison. Both power packs drove a hydraulic system which was linked to the wheels. The class were all of BB arrangement, where the two axles on each bogie were coupled together mechanically rather than the separate traction motors seen on Diesel-Electric BO-BO classes.

The locomotives were used on Western Region expresses from London to Birmingham and Cornwall and whilst relatively reliable, issues with rough running at speed were reported by the drivers of fast trains working at around 90mph. The problem was eventually found to be in the rigid coupling between bogie and body which had not been seen in Germany where a slightly lower speed limit of 87mph was imposed. The Class 42 were limited to 80mph over concerns about potential derailment at speed which might be caused by the rough riding of the locomotives.

A second series of thirty-three locomotives based on the German V200 were built by North British from 1960, becoming BR class 43. Whereas the Swindon machines had Maybach engines connected to Mekydro hydraulic transmissions, the Glasgow batch were given MAN engines connected to Voith transmissions which were less reliable in traffic. All apart from three, scrapped in 1969, were withdrawn in 1971.

At the same time as the Class 42 was introduced, BR introduced the Class 41 which had been ordered from North British, which was also a diesel-hydraulic but to a A1A-A1A design and the large Class 40 which was built, mainly, by English Electric to a 1-CO-CO-1 arrangement. The 41s were built as comparisons to the 40s, only five being constructed. The 41s were also named after warships, but Western Region didn't want them, preferring their own Class 42 and later class 43 locomotives.

The five diesel hydraulics were really no more than a political play by the British Transport Commission against Western Region and were obsolete before they left the drawing board.

The Class 40s were one of the success stories of the modernisation plan. Large and powerful, they were an instant success on both fast passenger trains and heavy goods, but by the time the last units were entering traffic in 1962 they had been supplanted by more powerful locomotives. They remained in service for a long time on secondary fast passenger services and freight, the last leaving BR service in 1988. A similar story applied to the ten class 44s built in 1959 and 1960, also to a 1-CO-CO-1 arrangement. Inspired by the two LMS 'twins' the class was built at Derby, for express services on the West Coast mainline until it was electrified when they were moved across to the old Midland mainline from St. Pancras.

The Classes 45 and 46, known as Peaks as were the class 44s, due to the names applied to some members of the class, were also 1-CO-CO-1 designs, which used a slow revving marine Sulzer 12LDA28B engine. For a time the Class 45s became the main source of power on the Midland main line out of St. Pancras until they were replaced by High Speed Trains (HST). The class 45s then found a new home on both Trans-Pennine services between Liverpool, Manchester, Leeds, York and Newcastle

**One of** the first batch of British Railways Class 40 (type 4) 1-CO-CO-1 diesels, D262 is seen at Heaton depot on 4 September 1960. The first batch were built with steam age route indicator discs and gangways doors at each end to allow them to be worked in multiple. *John Scott-Morgan Collection*

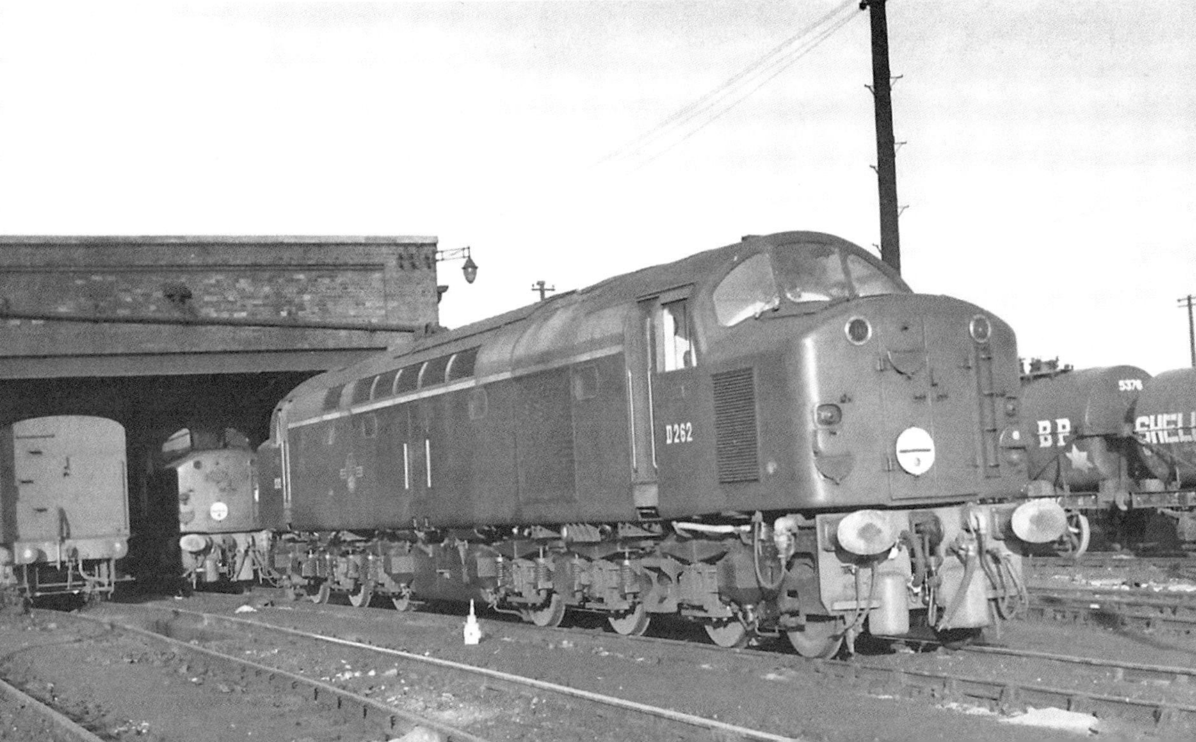

and the Settle and Carlisle line's trains between Leeds and Carlisle. They were all withdrawn by 1989.

The fifty-six machines of the Class 46 had the same bogie arrangement, and the same engines at the Class 45 although they had issues with cracking of the bogie frames for a time. They were used on the same kinds of services although they were spread much further afield, allocations including Plymouth and Gateshead (Newcastle). Long distance freight workings were common, one of the most notable, the china clay trains from Cornwall to Stoke-on-Trent. The class, like the other big 1-CO-CO-1s lost most of the work they were designed for and all had been withdrawn by 1984.

The 1960s saw many new designs of diesel locomotive entering service as steam traction withdrawals accelerated. Western Region received their last two diesel-hydraulics, the type 3 class 35, and the type 5 class 52. The class 35, known as Hymeks due to their hydraulic Mekydro transmissions were a BB design built by Beyer Peacock. They were a medium power machine aimed to fill a gap in Western Region on secondary passenger and freight work. They were very capable and for a time replaced withdrawn King class steam locomotives on Paddington to Cardiff and Swansea expresses, although they were replaced on such trains with the arrival of the more powerful class 47s and 52s.

Britain's last mainline diesel-hydraulics were the class 52 Westerns which arrived in 1961, with seventy-four built when production at Swindon ceased in 1964. The locomotives were powerful CC arrangement machines, with all three axles on each bogie mechanically coupled. The class were introduced for long distance express passenger services, which the other Western Region hydraulics were not powerful enough to handle. Like their predecessors they had two engines, one powering each bogie, although the initial design sited them each directly behind a cab at each end. Driver complaints of excessive noise led to the engines moving to the centre. There was an issue with the transmission which prevented them reaching their design top speed of 90mph, particularly when in need of an overhaul.

All of the diesel-hydraulics were withdrawn as non-standard, the class 52s falling out of favour once more conventional class 50s were made available following electrification of the West Coast mainline. The Class 50s were introduced in 1967, with fifty examples built for express passenger trains. The engines were large and powerful CO-CO designs with a top speed of 100mph, easily capable of handling expresses on the West Coast and later the Western Region. They carried the banner for the western's services until the arrival of HSTs in 1976 when they took over long distance services from Waterloo to Exeter and intermediate distance services on the western, until the latter were also taken over by HSTs.

The last type 5s were the 22 Class 55 Deltics introduced in 1961 all built by English Electric. The large Napier Deltic engines gave the locomotives huge hauling power, enabling them to take the heaviest of expresses from London King's Cross to Leeds, York, Newcastle and Edinburgh with ease. A top speed of 100mph cut journey times to a level that would only be surpassed with the introduction of HSTs on the East Coast mainline in 1978, by which time the CO-CO Deltics were mechanically worn out, the last members in service only being kept running by cannibalising withdrawn machines for parts. At their peak the class were as popular among travellers and enthusiasts as the A4s and A3s they replaced had been.

Three further classes of diesels introduced in the 1960s were excellent designs, and had long service lives. These were the Classes 33, 37 and 47. The 98 class 33s were Diesel-electric BO-BO machines designed for Southern Region and were built by the Birmingham Railway Carriage and Wagon Company (BRCW) with Sulzer engines and Crompton Parkinson electrical equipment, becoming known as Cromptons. They were needed to handle passenger and freight traffic on the non-electrified parts of the region and were BR's most powerful BO-BO design. The BRCW locomotives were superb machines able to meet the needs of Southern Region for over six decades. The class were regulars on the Weymouth Harbour Tramway, taking trains right up to the ferry terminal in Weymouth docks, often having to inch past parked cars on the quayside.

There were two sub classes, the 33/1 were fitted with equipment that enabled them to work with electric multiple units in push-pull mode west of Bournemouth, where it was viewed as uneconomic to extend electrification although this was eventually done making the sub-class surplus to requirements. The 33/2 were a subset of twelve narrow bodied locomotives to work the reduced width of the Tunbridge Wells to Hastings line.

The 390 CO-CO Class 37s were built between 1960 and 1965. Built as freight locomotives, the class could be found everywhere in Britain. During the 1980s they proved extremely valuable to ScotRail, taking over nearly all of the services in the highlands. The class were also very frequently put in charge of passenger trains on secondary routes in East Anglia and many other places. The class is still at work on the railway in 2025, still proving useful in a variety of roles.

British Railways introduced the class 47 in 1962 and created the diesel equivalent of Stanier's Black 5. The 512 class 47s built up until 1968 by Brush Traction (Loughborough) and Crewe works were go anywhere, do anything locomotives. The class could be found in every corner of Britain, apart from branch lines and lighter secondary routes, for many years. The powerful CO-CO design was based upon a single prototype built as a private venture in 1962 by BRCW and Associated Electrical Industries Limited, named *Lion*. The locomotive was trialled by BR and seems to have done well, the resemblance to the Class 47 that followed is remarkable. The engine was withdrawn in 1964 when BR decided to purchase its new type 4 from Brush rather than BRCW. The Class 47, fitted with the Sulzer 12LDA28 engine, was capable of high speeds and hauling everything from freightliner container trains to cross country fast passenger services. Still in service at the privatisation of British Rail, many passed to rolling stock leasing companies and continued in use for many years. Thirty-three were rebuilt with new engines and remain in service as Class 57.

Electrification was an area that the new nationalised railway was keen to expand although this took some time. The Southern Region was already well provided for through a fleet of EMUs, but the newly nationalised railway realised that it would need a dual power locomotive which could run off the third rail but also from a diesel engine where there was no electric power. There was also a need for purely electric locomotives to handle freight and non-electric passenger stock.

The latter problem was dealt with in the form of the class 71 BO-BOs introduced between 1958 and 1960. The twenty-four locomotives were purely electric, collection of current being achieved either through a shoe on the bogies on the mainline third rail, or through a pantograph from overhead lines in yards where it was too dangerous to have live rails at ground level. The machines were fairly simple in appearance, a slab-sided body with a sloped wedge fronted cab sufficing. As for all electric locomotives and EMUs, acceleration was dramatic allowing the class to meet tightly scheduled service timetables but despite their usefulness they only had short working lives. Ten were converted to Class 74 electro-diesels in 1967 and 1968 since there was less work for the class and the diesel powerplant gave them the ability to work off the third rail, making them more useful. Rationalisation of motive power in the late 1970s saw all the remaining fourteen class 71s withdrawn. The Class 74s met the same fate between 1977 and 1981. Both classes were withdrawn in favour of the class 73.

The forty-nine class 73s were designed from the beginning as an electro-diesel, having both shoes to collect power from the third rail and a diesel generator to allow it to work away from it, although with less power. The design aimed to create a mixed traffic machine which would use the third rail whilst working trains, the diesel engine used when the locomotive was working in unpowered yards. The class was not expected to power trains using its diesel engine, although more recent attempts to do so through working a pair in tandem have been successful in certain conditions. The locomotives were fitted with vacuum, air and Electro Pneumatic Braking which was used on EMUs and which was also fitted to the class 33/1s. This meant that the class could, and still do, work with all stock present on the railway.

Electrification of the West Coast mainline was finally completed in 1974. The line had been electrified in short stretches but only in 1974 were there no longer any gaps. The new electric railway needed new locomotives and these arrived in the form of classes 81 (built 1959-64, twenty-five locomotives); 82 (1960-62, ten); 83 (1960-62, fifteen); 84 (1960-61, ten); 85 (1961-64, forty); 86 (1965-66, 100) and 87 (1973-1975, thirty-six). All of the new 'electrics' were equipped to run off of BR's now standard 25kv overhead electric system, and were all BO-BOs. All of the classes 81 to 85 looked very similar, with a slab sided body and sloping ends with large cab windows, whilst the class 86 and 87 bore more of a resemblance to the class 47.

The Class 81s were mainly for use on fast passenger services and had a top speed of 100mph, although two were geared for freight use, sacrificing speed for power they were limited to 80mph. Three were withdrawn early, going before 1972 due to accidental damage. A further pair were withdrawn in 1983, also as a result of accidental damage. The remainder of the fleet survived until the late 1980s and early 1990s when they were replaced.

The Class 82s had a short life, all withdrawn in the early 1980s when replaced by the class 87s. Two were reinstated for empty coaching stock workings around Euston until 1987. The class 83s were similar to the 81s insofar as the class was split for passenger and freight working and geared accordingly, but with little need for them the freight versions were reprofiled to match the passenger engines. The class had issues with the mercury-arc electrical rectifiers used to convert AC current, needed for long distance transmission over the power cables, to the DC current needed to run the traction motors. The issue was shared with the class 84 which also used the same rectifiers. Both classes were rebuilt with more reliable silicon rectifiers after a period in store. The reprieve came about because BR needed more electric locomotives for the increasingly busy West Coast mainline, and refitting them was cheaper than increasing the quantity of class 87s then under construction. The class 83s were withdrawn in 1983 bar three, which were dispensed with in 1989. Two of the class had already been scrapped due to accident damage in 1975 and 1976. The class 84s were not so fortunate. After rebuilding a new issue manifested involving traction motor failures, and BR gave up on the locomotives, withdrawing them for a second and final time in the late 1970s.

The class 85s had issues with rectifiers too. The first thirty used germanium rectifiers which proved as temperamental as the mercury-arc rectifiers fitted to the 83s and 84s. The last ten were, however, built with silicon rectifiers which performed faultlessly, and so the initial batch were retro-fitted with the newer equipment resolving their problems. The class were capable of 100mph although later a number were rebuilt to work as freight locomotives, which were classified class 85/1 and restricted to 80mph. The class served BR until the early 1990s.

The class 86 was also not without fault when introduced. They became known for rough riding at speed especially near their top speed of 100mph. The rough riding was so bad that the locomotives caused damage to the track, which was identified to be caused by the axle hung traction motors instead of the bogie frame mounted ones on earlier designs. The class were refitted with a flexicoil spring to support the motors which solved the problem. Three class 86s were used as test beds for the proposed Class 87, with more powerful electrical equipment, and classified class 86/1 with an uprated maximum speed of 110mph. The trials conducted with the 86/1 helped reduce teething trouble with the class 87. The class 86s were not only used on the West Coast mainline. A number were moved to East Anglia following the extension of electrification of the lines out of Liverpool Street beyond Colchester to Ipswich, Norwich and Harwich in the 1980s. The class 86s then took over inter-city passenger services in East Anglia until replaced with more modern traction. The class had many subdivisions related to modifications which are too numerous to discuss in a work of this size.

The Class 87s were probably the best of the original series of AC electrics. They were able to work both passenger and freight traffic over the West Coast mainline for their entire lives capably handling expresses between Euston and Glasgow as easily as heavy steel and other freight trains until the early 1990s. All thirty-five of the class were passed to rolling stock leasing company Porterbrook and then leased to Virgin Trains at the privatisation of BR in 1997. The new company's drive to provide new, state of the art, trains saw the 87s displaced by the new Pendolino multiple unit trains. Once teething troubles with the new units were resolved the class 87 became redundant, the last working taking place in 2002.

The last of the electrics was introduced in the 1980s. The Classes 90 and 91 for the West and East Coast lines respectively, which like the earlier types were both BO-BOs. The 90s arrived in 1987, the last of the 50 entering service in 1990. Designed as a mixed traffic locomotive they were a modernised version of the class 87, all of which were built by British Rail Engineering Limited (BREL) at Crewe. They differ from the early locomotives in having more aerodynamic wedge shaped cab ends, but like the 87s are capable of 110mph. Used on both passenger and freight on the West Coast and East Anglian lines, the class were eventually displaced by EMUs on passenger services after privatisation, although 25 were retained for freight and occasional charter work.

The Class 91 is a very different machine, one end having a shape not unlike the class 91, the other a flat plane with cab windows. The 'rear' is only intended to be used for coupling to the coaching stock or for movement around depots. The driver operates the train in service either from the leading cab of the class 91, or from a cab in the last coach of the consist, the Driving Van Trailer (DVT). The locomotives are semi-permanently coupled to the train, running in push-pull mode. The class were built by BREL at Crewe as subcontractor to GEC who won the bid for the new locomotives despite British Rail owning BREL, even though at arm's length. The thirty-one locomotives were built between 1988 and 1991, and after rebuilding to modernise them between 2000 and 2003, all bar one remain in service on the East Coast mainline in 2025.

The railway moved away from locomotive hauled passenger trains during the late 1970s and into the 1980s, with HSTs and a series of updated EMU and DMU designs taking over. Freight was, and is, different. The needs of freight operators demand the flexibility of a separate locomotive. British Rail introduced two classes for just that purpose. The class 56 was the first, which were built by BREL between 1976 and 1984, at Doncaster and Crewe. A batch was contracted to Brush, but their workshops were full so they internally subcontracted it to a Romanian subsidiary, although on delivery it was found that the build quality was lacking and most had to be subjected to a remedial rebuild. One hundred and thirty-five of the CO-CO locomotives were built. The class bears a resemblance to the class 47, no doubt a result of the BREL designers using the house style in the design. Powered by Ruston Paxman diesel engines the locomotives are more than capable of meeting the demands put on a type 5 freight engine, although their maintenance demands were relatively high when compared to contemporary locomotives. A large number were withdrawn early in the twenty-first century, although a small number soldier on with private locomotive leasing companies.

In the 1980s, BREL was looking for a design which could form the basis of an export locomotive, whilst at the same time BR was seeking to find a better freight engine than the class 56. The result was the class 58. The new CO-CO was a dramatic departure from traditional British locomotive design, BREL opting to adopt the American practice of modularisation. With the plan to use the locomotive as the foundation for an export locomotive, BREL must be applauded. The modular approach would have allowed elements to be changed easily to meet the requirements of potential customers across the globe but this was not to be. The locomotive proved a disappointment on the export market, not entirely because of shortcomings in the design as others have written, but more because of political issues in the export arena which was never a level playing field for BREL. Fifty were built for BR between 1983 and 1987 all by BREL at Doncaster and they have divided opinion ever since.

One final class was built in Britain, Brush's class 60 of which 100 were built between 1989 and 1993 at Loughborough. Once again designed to be a freight locomotive the new CO-CO design was produced to replace the class 56s in Railfreight's operations. Capable of a modest 60mph, the class were ideal for heavy freight and served BR and the freight operators that followed privatisation well, the entire class ultimately becoming owned by EWS through a series of takeovers and mergers. Although capable, more modern traction has replaced them with the first of the class going for scrap in 2020.

These were the last of the British mainline locomotives, the more recent new machines built for the freight operators on Britain's railways are American, Canadian and Spanish designs which were manufactured outside of the United Kingdom and so fall outside of the scope of this book.

# Chapter 9

# NARROW GAUGE AND LIGHT RAILWAYS

Britain's mainline railways were built to the standard gauge of 4ft 8½in, other than the GWR's broad-gauge. This was fine for the mainline companies, but others had a need for something else in mainland Britain. The need to save money, or difficult terrain made it necessary to adopt a narrower gauge of railway and whilst many of these were initially horse drawn increasing traffic led to the need to adopt the iron horse. In many cases the passing of the Tramway Act (1870) and Light Railways (1896) Acts assisted in the building of increasing numbers of lighter railways as the Acts allowed for much less expensive lines to be built.

It is not possible to provide a complete survey of Britain's narrow-gauge railways; what follows aims to give a flavour of some of the locomotives built for these smaller lines.

Some were built to gauges around 3ft where a more expensive standard gauge line was not viable or where the geography needed sharp curves as the railway worked its way along valleys and hills. The Cambourne and Redruth Tramway, which opened in 1902, was built to 3ft 6in gauge. The company purchased two steam locomotives for the transport of tin ore wagons from East Pool mine. In the far north, the original Ravenglass and Eskdale Railway was built to 3ft gauge to allow it to negotiate the geography of the Lake District. The line was built to link the Furness Railway at Ravenglass with the iron ore mines near the village of Boot. The railway opened as a freight only operation in 1875 but demand from local residents led to the introduction of a passenger service. The line was steam hauled from the earliest days.

On the Isle of Man, a gauge of 3ft was found to be ideal and was adopted as Manx Standard Gauge. The Isle of Man, Manx Northern and Isle of Man Electric Railways all adopted the island's 'standard gauge'. Both the Isle of Man (opened 1873) and Manx Northern (1879) Railways were steam hauled from the outset. The Isle of Man Railway's distinctive steam engines were all purchased from Beyer Peacock of Manchester and are all outside cylinder 2-4-0 tank locomotives. The Manx Northern Railway adopted the same wheel arrangement to begin with but purchased their first two locomotives from Sharp, Stewart & Company, whose engines were both outside cylinder tank locomotives, they then bought in a third 2-4-0 but this time from Beyer Peacock to a similar design to the Isle of Man Railway's fleet. The Manx Northern found that they needed a larger locomotive and approached Dübs and Company who sold them a large 0-6-0 tank engine.

The Southwold Railway was opened in Suffolk during 1879 but closed in 1929. The railway was also built to 3ft gauge and operated by steam. The fleet of locomotives were mainly purchased from Sharp Stewart, with three 2-4-0 tank engines (1879) and one 2-4-2 tank engine (1893) supplied. A final engine, an 0-6-2 tank was supplied by Manning Wardle in 1914.

Even narrower gauges were needed where railways were to be built through mountainous or difficult terrain to access slate mines, or within quarries. The Welshpool and Llanfair Railway was built to link Welshpool and its connection with the Cambrian Railway, to Llanfair Caereinion, 8.5 miles away. The line was intended to develop the economy of the area and was operated from the outset by the Cambrian Railway, becoming part of the GWR at the 1923 Grouping. The route of the line is extremely tough and involves a number of sharp curves as it winds its way to the terminus at Llanfair. The proposers of the railway opted for a gauge of 2ft 6in which suited the terrain and allowed the railway to squeeze through the town to make a connection with the Cambrian Railway station. The line opened in 1903 with steam traction from the outset. Its first locomotives were a pair of very large, for a narrow-gauge railway, 0-6-0 tank engines purchased from Beyer Peacock. The two engines were named *The Earl* and *Countess* in honour of the Earl and Countess of Powys since the Earl had been a great supporter of the project.

The Corris and Talyllyn Railways were both built to 2ft 3in gauge to reach the local slate mines and connect them to local ports and railways. The Ffestiniog Railway was built with same aim but to 1ft 11½in gauge. All three railways were steam powered, with the Corris sourcing their engines from the Hughes Locomotive Company in Loughborough who provided three 0-4-0 tank engines in 1878 which were later rebuilt into more stable 0-4-2 tanks. A fourth locomotive was purchased from Kerr Stuart in 1921, which was sold to the Talyllyn with the third of the Hughes engines after the Corris closed and the Talyllyn had been taken over by preservationists.

The Talyllyn's locomotives originally consisted of just two tank engines built in 1864 and 1866, both by Fletcher Jennings of Whitehaven. The first was an 0-4-0 saddle tank without a cab, although when it was rebuilt into an 0-4-2 it was provided with such a convenience. The other was an 0-4-0 well tank, also supplied without a cab, which was later added.

The Ffestiniog Railway's first three locomotives were a trio of George England and Company (London) 0-4-0 saddle tank and tender engines, referred to as Small Englands built in 1863. The railway seemed to like the design, purchasing another four. The railway was home to other innovative locomotives as well. The Fairlie

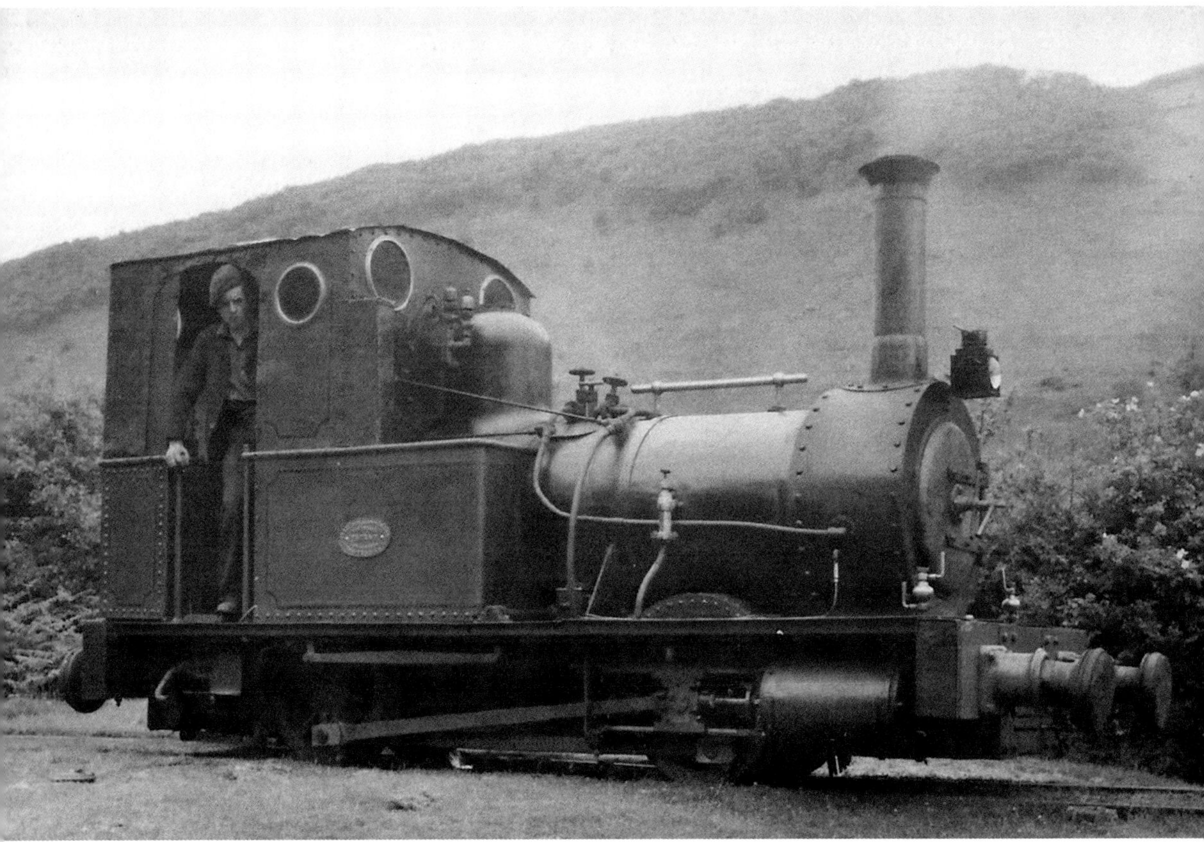

**Talyllyn Railway** Fletcher Jennings & Co. 0-4-0 well tank No. *2 Dolgoch*. *John Scott-Morgan Collection*

Patent locomotives became synonymous with the railway, although a small number were built to the patent for other railways. The patent addressed the need to provide larger more powerful locomotives on a railway with sharp curves, precluding the use of long wheelbase engines. Instead, the patent related to an articulated design, but one very different to that designed by Garratt.

Instead of a single boiler on a bridge connected to two power units, the Fairlie design consisted of two boilers with a central cab which sat on two steam powered bogies, or one boiler with a single powered bogie and an unpowered bogie under the cab. The locomotives on the Ffestiniog consisted of a pair of 0-4-0 bogies, resulting in an 0-4-4-0 tank. The first two were built in 1869 and 1872 for the railway by George England and the Avonside Engine Company (Bristol). The engines were known as Double Fairlies. One single Fairlie was built for the line in 1876. The railway's own workshops built two more in 1879 and 1885.

Elsewhere, larger narrow-gauge engines were in use. The Leek and Manifold Railway (2ft 6in) and Lynton and Barnstaple (1ft 11½in) preferred bigger engines.

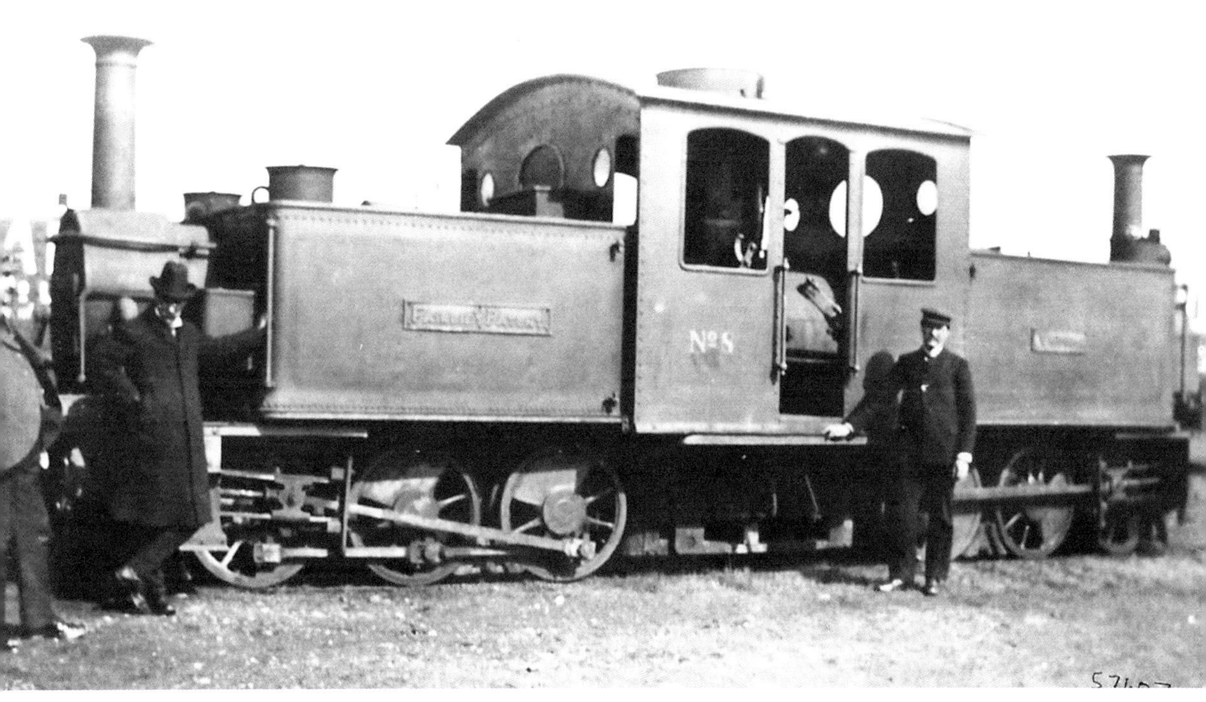

**Standard gauge** Double Fairlie 0-6-6-0 tank No. 8. *John Scott-Morgan Collection*

The Leek and Manifold in Staffordshire used a pair of 2-6-4 tank engines built by Kitson & Co in 1904, the first 2-6-4 tanks in Britain. The Lynton and Barnstaple in Devon, preferred to order three 2-6-2 tank engines from Manning Wardle of Leeds in 1898, followed by a single 2-4-2 tank engine built by Baldwin Locomotive Works of Philadelphia, USA.

A narrow gauge engine type of note is the Quarry Hunslet. The Hunslet Company of Leeds produced a dazzling array of locomotives throughout its existence, but one of the most produced were variations of a sturdy little 0-4-0 tank engine designed for quarry work. The locomotives became known as Quarry Hunslets but could be found working in a broad range of industrial sites.

The manufacturers of narrow-gauge locomotives were also busy supplying standard gauge engines to light railways. Many of these railways had an array of new and second hand locomotives from many manufacturers, and the ability of the engineers to keep such a collection of machines working deserves much respect. The large array of railways which eventually came into the possession of Colonel

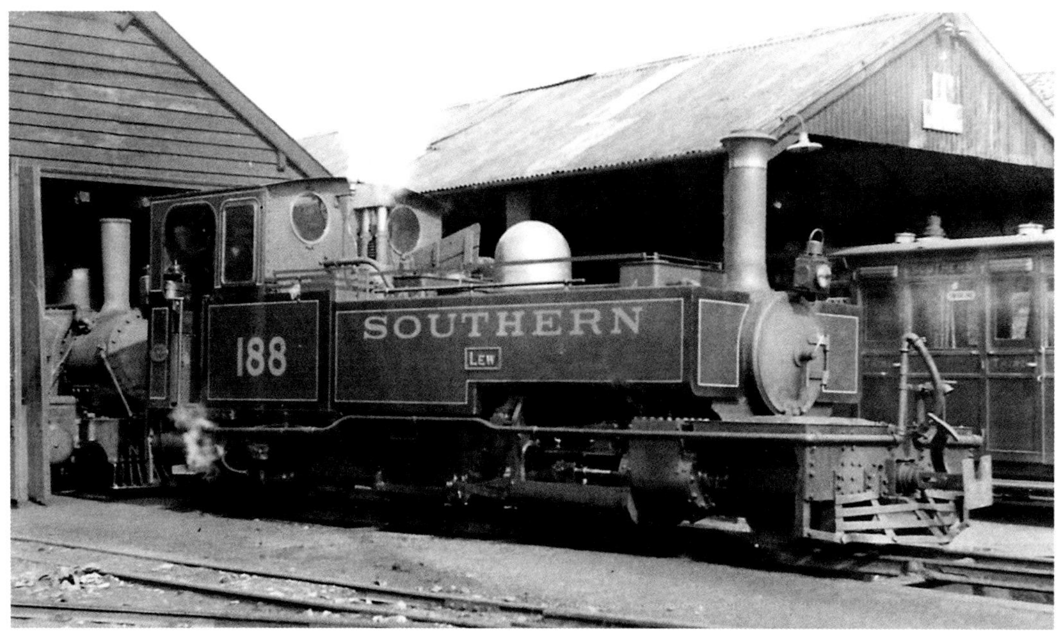


**Lynton and** Barnstaple Railway Manning Wardle 2-6-2 tank *Lew* at Pilton Yard, Barnstaple after 1923 when the railway was absorbed by the Southern Railway. The fate of *Lew* has intrigued researchers for many years. It was exported to Brazil in 1936 after being used to dismantle the railway after it closed in 1935. It seems to have been delivered but all trace of it has since disappeared. *John Scott-Morgan Collection*

Holman Stephens's light railway empire ranged from recycled ex LBSCR Terrier and P classes to Manning Wardles, Hunslets, Pecketts and many other manufacturers engines of all shapes and sizes.

One short railway, the Wantage Tramway, had a selection of tram engines over its existence as well as standard gauge Manning Wardle and George England 0-4-0 tank engines, the latter of which survived into preservation, thanks to the efforts of the GWR. The tram engines are of particular note as they were all the first of their type which went on to be sold to other tramways across the world once proven at Wantage. Two tram locomotives from Merryweather and Sons, the first they had built, were the progenitors of a type which were sold across the world, the tramways of Paris, Barcelona and Wellington, New Zealand being among that number. Classes of tram locomotives by Hughes of Loughborough and James Matthews, trialled at Wantage, were also to be found on other city tramways.

Whilst many of the designs discussed so far in this book proved successful, clearly some were poor designs from the outset. There were times though when the engineer's plans were doomed to failure from the outset.

# Chapter 10
# PUSHING ENGINEERING TOO FAR

Engineers push boundaries, that is the only way to make progress. Forever repeating the same design results in stagnant technology and may cause the engineer's company to become bankrupt if it is overtaken by more innovative designers.

Sometimes though, the engineer pushes too hard and exceeds what is possible with the technology and materials of the day. What follows are just a handful of examples of when too much was tried too early.

In the earliest days of the railways, Britain's engineers were attempting to build machines, the like of which had never been seen before and often failed. One of the more interesting are a pair of locomotives built by R & W Hawthorn to designs of Thomas Harrison. Harrison's two engines, *Thunderer* and *Hurricane* were innovative in the extreme for the time. In order to meet Brunel's specifications, a different approach was taken from other locomotives of the time. On both the boiler was carried on an unpowered 6-wheel frame, with *Thunderer* provided with a separate 0-4-0 powered unit in front creating an odd 0-4-0+6 arrangement. *Hurricane* was even stranger, the boiler still on a 6-wheel chassis but with a leading power unit consisted of a large single driving wheel of ten foot diameter and a supporting pair of wheels fore and aft of it making up a 2-2-2+6 engine. On both, the boiler fed steam to the engine units by flexible pipes. Both were abject failures in 1838 but Fairlie's later design, just thirty years later, solved the problem of articulating power units and boilers. Harrison was pushing too hard too early but his ideas were sound, the materials science and experience in locomotive design just wasn't available at the time.

Many engineers sought ways to make the steam locomotive more efficient, and two involved the attempt to use very high-pressure steam. Henry Fowler and Nigel Gresley both used different approaches to their experimental designs. Fowler's *Fury* of 1929 consisted of a new 3-cylinder Royal Scot frame with the centre cylinder working from high pressure, with the outside using low pressure steam, combined with a complex three stage boiler built by The Superheater Company. The aim was to use superpower steam to drive the engine more efficiently but the boiler was overly complex. The three stages consisted of a sealed high pressure circulating unit filled with distilled water which was used to transfer heat to the main high pressure drum which raised steam at a pressure of 900 lb/sq. in, most boilers at the time working to around 250 lb/sq. in. The third boiler was a conventional fire tube boiler working to a more usual pressure. The locomotive proved to be a failure as it was too complex.

Gresley's solution was to use a high pressure marine water tube boiler, which was a proven technology, in combination with a 4-6-4 four cylinder compound locomotive. The resulting W1 of 1936 was a big machine, its streamlined casing giving it an attractive shape however. It was a failure, steaming poorly and developing leaks, none of which were really resolved. The engine was no better than something with a conventional boiler and so the experiment was abandoned and the locomotive rebuilt in 1936 with an A4 boiler, three cylinders and A4 style streamlining.

Britain's locomotive engineers later became fascinated by the possibilities offered by gas turbines. Steam turbines had been used for some time on ships, the steam being used to rotate the turbine blades to produce power. Two attempts were made to apply turbine engineering to steam locomotives. The first was Stanier's *Turbomotive* of 1935 for the LMS. The chassis was the third of his new Princess Royal class with turbines instead of cylinders to drive the coupled wheels. It was relatively successful when compared to engines like the W1, showing reduced coal consumption in trails, but it suffered from a fundamental flaw inherent in turbines. A turbine works best when running at a constant speed, which was usual in ships. They are not as effective when constantly being throttled up and down as needed for a railway locomotive. A turbine failure in 1949 was deemed beyond economic repair and BR rebuilt the engine as a conventional Princess Royal class.

Two more attempts were made to combine locomotive and turbine. The first saw a pair of gas turbine-electric locomotives, numbers 18000 and 18100 constructed. 18100 was ordered first but delivered after 18000, the order from the GWR placed in the late 1940s with Metropolitan Vickers was delayed by the Second World War. It arrived in 1951 and spent its life working Western Region passenger trains. The turbine-electric combination was an intriguing solution to the need to run a turbine at constant speed. When acting as a generator it could do just that, the voltage supplied from the batteries could be varied as needed without effecting the turbine. The CO-CO locomotive appears to have been relatively successful compared to other early alternative designs, but as a non-standard BR type its days would always have been numbered, especially with BR's workshops not being acquainted with the needs of turbine maintenance.

18000 was a Swiss design ordered from Brown Boveri & Cie in 1949 by Western Region. The A1A-A1A wheel arrangement with electric traction motors powered by the turbine engine which was an industrial type designed to run on cheap fuel oil. The machine was not a success. The heavy fuel oil used created soot which damaged

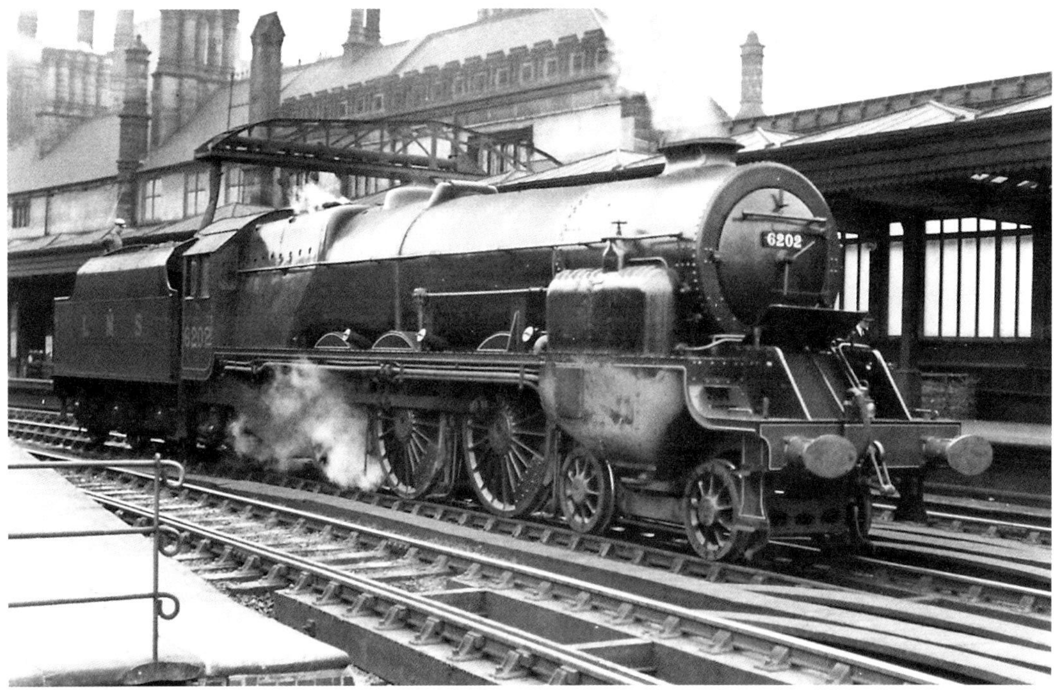

**Stanier's innovative** 'Turbomotive' 4-6-2 No. 6202. *John Scott-Morgan Collection*

the turbine blades and the electrical control system were overly complex. When the locomotive ran well it was very promising, unfortunately those occasions were rare. At the end of 1960, the machine was withdrawn and stored at Swindon until it was returned to Europe. The machinery was removed and the locomotive was used for other trials. Its remains were purchased for preservation in the 1990s and it was returned to the UK.

The last attempt was GT3 in 1958 in which English Electric attempted to use a gas turbine on a 4-6-0 locomotive chassis. It resembled a steam locomotive in outward appearance, but the tender carried kerosene fuel. The locomotive was based around an English Electric jet engine. The turbine powered a drive shaft which operated the centre coupled wheel. The power unit actually consisted of two turbines, a slow speed one which could run at constant speed and a high speed one which could be used to provide more power when needed. The machine seems to have met the designers' expectations, never failing to meet its booked workings whilst being tested, and it received good feedback from its crews. As promising as GT3 might have been, the prototype needed further development for which neither English Electric nor BR were willing to provide funding. The locomotive was withdrawn and scrapped.

# SELECT BIBLIOGRAPHY


British Railways Locomotives 1948 (Ian Allen, 1948)

British Railway Locomotives and Other Motive Power: Combined Volume Summer 1959 (Ian Allen, Repr.2023).

The Great Western Archive (http://www.greatwestern.org.uk/index.htm)

Hillier-Graves, Tim, *The A4 Pacifics after Gresley: The Late LNER and British Railways Periods, 1942- 1966* (Pen & Sword, 2023)

Hillier-Graves, Tim, *The Turbomotive: Stanier's Advanced Pacific* (Pen & Sword, 2017)

Hillier-Graves, Tim, *The Princess Royal Pacifics* (Pen & Sword, 2018)

*The Locomotives of the GWR, Volumes 1 to 14* (RCTS, 1952)

*The Locomotives of the LNER, Volumes 1 to 10B* (RCTS, 1963-1990)

Maidment, David, Midland Railway and LMS 4-4-0 Locomotives: Their Design, Operation and Performance (Pen and Sword, 2021).

Maidment, David, Southern Railway 0-6-0 Tender Goods Locomotive Classes: A Survey and Overview (Pen & Sword, 2021)

Maidment, David & Meanley, Bob, Great Western Castle Class 4-6-0 Locomotives, 1923-1959 (Pen & Sword, 2022)

Marks, Richard, *A History of British Rail Engineering Limited* (Pen & Sword, 2024)

Marks, Richard, *The Wantage Tramway: The Story of a Bucolic Road Side Steam Tramway* (Pen & Sword, 2024)

Nock, O.S., *British Locomotives of the 20th Century Volume 1: 1900 to 1930* (Patrick Stephens, 1983)

Nock, O.S., *British Locomotives of the 20th Century Volume 2: 1930 to 1960* (Patrick Stephens, 1984)

Nock, O.S., *British Locomotives of the 20th Century Volume 3: 1960 to the Present Day* (Patrick Stephens, 1985)

Nock, O.S., *GWR Steam* (David & Charles, 1972)

Nock, O.S., *LMS Steam* (David & Charles, 1971)

Nock, O.S., *Southern Steam* (David & Charles, 1972)

Nock, O.S., *The Age of Steam, 1959-68 (v. 1) (Locomotive Practice and Performance: Highlights from the Celebrated* Railway Magazine *Articles)* (Patrick Stephens, 1990)

Sayer, Anthony P., *The Metropolitan-Vickers Type 2 CO-BO Diesel-Electric Locomotives: From Design to Destruction* (Pen & Sword, 2020)
Waters, Laurence, *Great Western Star Class Locomotives* (Pen & Sword, 2017)
Welsh Railways Research Circle (https://wrrc.org.uk/index.php)

Various files from the National Archives, including RAIL 390, RAIL 399, RAIL 418 and RAIL 422.